The Tota

"Carolyn has done it aga   ..eeps producing treasures. This new book is another one—gold for building a profession that changes lives. And all the while enriching us with the inimitable, irreplaceable, irrepressible voice of knowledge, vision, experience, and humility that are Carolyn. Her focus on creating a coaching business offers us new insights into how she navigates the world, and leaves us with not just her brilliant guidance, but also the means to think for ourselves about it.

"She encourages us to read the book twice, 'once for information and again for transformation.' I'd say and yet again for the sheer pleasure of it."

~ **Nancy Kline,** author of *Time to Think: Listening to Ignite the Human Mind*, *The Promise That Changes Everything: I Won't Interrupt You,* Founding Director of Time to Think, Originator of The Thinking Environment

"Freyer-Jones's book was fantastic for me. It provided a granularity—giving specific examples of behaviors—that in turns showed me what a superstar I am as a coach and business developer and then showed me CLEARLY how I can be of MUCH greater service and be a MUCH *better* business developer. I am forever in her debt. It's quickly become my first reference for what to do and how to do it (and who I aspire to be) as a coach.

"I have been a professional coach for twenty years, following careers in law and education. I direct a coaching school. I read more or less everything on the topic of coaching business development. There is no other book that provides such clear, unescapable, actionable insight into how to show up and make the right moves to thrive as a coach.

"It is required reading for my coaching students."

~ **Joshua Hornick,** Director—Hornick School of Coaching

"If you are wavering at all in your KNOWING that you can create a thriving LIFE as a professional coach, read this book. Immediately, if not sooner. Carolyn is a master coach and has managed to distill her incredible wisdom into these jam-packed, easy-to-read pages. With everything that Carolyn does, she brings a depth of wisdom, humor, love and service. This book is no exception. The way she shares her story and the intricacies of what it takes to build a thriving coaching business are captivating, engaging and simple to understand. I can't wait to share this book with every single client of mine who is also a coach, as I know it will exponentially increase their knowledge of how to do what it is they most want to do: make a meaningful difference doing work that truly matters.

"This is not just a book about creating a robust and prosperous coaching practice, it's a book that will help you transform and evolve into a happier, more peaceful, more inspired, optimistic and loving human. It's a book that lives up to its name and more.

"Before you read any other book, or take any other course, dive in here, and let it transform you, your life and your coaching practice."

~ **Aila Coats, M.A.,** author of *Coaching Teens Well: A Way of Being with Teens and Their Parents*

"*The Total Coaching Success Book* is the most complete of its kind in the coaching industry, and it's shared by one of the best coaches in the world. Through her masterfully crafted stories, insights and specific strategies, Carolyn has given every coach the opportunity to step into being a master coach with a prosperous business. If you're a new coach or have been around for a while, there is no doubt this book is for you. It will make you a better, more skilled coach while giving you the opportunity to create a thriving coaching business."

~ **Devon Bandison,** Go To Mind Coach, NBA, author of *Fatherhood is Leadership*

"This has to be a strong contender for the best book ever written for coaches wanting to ethically create a thriving business. I knew within a few pages of reading this that it would be on the curriculum of my next coaching school."

~ **Ankush Jain,** Founder of the AJC Coaching Career School

THE TOTAL COACHING SUCCESS Book

THE TOTAL COACHING SUCCESS *Book*

Everything You Need Internally and Externally
to Create a Financially Successful Coaching Business

CAROLYN FREYER-JONES, M.A.

The Total Coaching Success Book: Everything You Need Internally and Externally a Create a Financially Successful Coaching Business.

Copyright © 2024 by Carolyn Freyer-Jones

All rights reserved. No part of this book may be reproduced or copied in any form without written permission from the publisher.

Contact the author: carolynfreyerjones.com

Editing: Chris Nelson, www.prose-alchemy.com

Cover design: Carrie Brito, www.carriebrito.com

Los Angeles, California

ISBN: 978-1-7379475-2-3

Library of Congress Control Number: 2024901887

First edition

Disclaimer: Names and identifying details of clients referenced in this book have been altered and in some cases are composites. Any resemblances to individuals alive or dead are coincidental and unintentional.

Dedication

This book is dedicated to professional coaches everywhere across the globe—the beginners, those who are wondering if they can do it, and those who are already making a difference every day. When one of us wins, we all win, and when one of us gets a client, we all get a client.

This book is also dedicated to the two people who sit with me every night and make my world immensely more magical and joy filled: my beloved husband, John, and my glorious daughter, Lucinda. Thank you for loving me, for supporting me, and for being who you are. I love you. If we could be together every night for a million more years, I'd take it.

Lastly, this book is dedicated to Michelle Bauman, my best friend and business partner, who I'm pretty sure would have co-written this with me if she hadn't died (no judgment). I love you. Thank you for making me a real writer . . . because you were the writer, and then you left, and then I wrote more, and it's another gift you gave me.

Table of Contents

DEDICATION	9
FOREWORD: SPARKS FLY WHEN YOU READ THIS BOOK	15
INTRODUCTION: THE ANATOMY OF ENROLLMENT	21

BUSINESS BUILDING AS A PROFESSIONAL COACH — 27

1. Service Context	29
2. My Crooked and Flawed Journey to Business Ownership	33
3. Building a Bridge to Professional Coaching Starting Right Now	37
4. Pick a Number, any Number! What to Charge as a Professional Coach	45
5. Agonizing Over Your Fees Is Not Helpful	53
6. The Dark Side of the Coaching Profession	58
7. Purposeful Work	69
8. Being "Agreeable" Is Hurting Your Business	75
9. Kitchen Renovations and the Wild, Wild West	81
10. Pivoting in Crisis: A Client Story	86
11. Converting Envy into Inspiration	91
12. Entering the Coaching Profession from Other Professions	94
13. Are You Certifiable?	99

CLIENT CREATION AND ENROLLMENT AS A PROFESSIONAL COACH — 107

14. Where Do I Start?	109
15. Filling Your Practice Is Not Like Ordering from Amazon	113
16. "Enrollment Is the Hard Part!"	118
17. The Layer Cake of Commitment	122

18. How Many Followers Do You Need?	131
19. Renewals	136
20. Because You Never Ask	142
21. Groups Creating, Filling, Delivering and More	147
22. The Burrito Guideline Converting Social Relationships into Professional Ones	157
23. Well-Paid Babysitter or Professional Coach?	162
24. Situationships	167
25. We Are Never Ever Getting Back Together Clients Who Disappear	171

SERVING CLIENTS AS A PROFESSIONAL COACH — 177

26. Loneliness Is the New Pandemic	179
27. Outrageous Acts of Service	185
28. Do You Let Your Client Think?	192
29. Learnings from a CEO's Email	197
30. Your Client's Calendar	202
31. Coaching the Uncoachable	205
32. Sacred Real Estate	212
33. Build a Library	216
34. Judgment	220
35. The Art of Heartfelt Curiosity	226
36. Stories Matter	230
37. Be Gold	234

COMMUNICATION AS A PROFESSIONAL COACH — 237

38. Letting Communications Die on the Vine	239
39. How to Use Social Media	244
40. What Will People Think?	250

41. The Crime of Slime Cleaning Up Your Emails	254
42. A Coach Who Dared to Stop Being so Agreeable, "Nice" and "Friendly"	262
43. Who's Answering Your Email?	266

UTTER COACHING NONSENSE TO AVOID AT ALL COSTS — 271

44. Thought Leaders and "Coaches of Influence"	273
45. AI Is a GREAT Coach (you should hire them/it)?!	277
46. Hell No to the Hell Yes	282
47. Six Figures in Six Weeks	288
48. Hiring Other People to Get You Business	291

SERVING YOURSELF: PERSONAL GROWTH AS A PROFESSIONAL COACH — 297

49. Coaches Adrift Without Coaching	299
50. My Barbie Dream Camper	304
51. Grow Yourself	308
52. I Can Build Anything	311
53. Coaching, Loneliness and Community	316
54. The Universe Has My Back	321

CONCLUSION — 325

HANDOUTS & SAMPLE COACHING AGREEMENT — 327

Handout 1: Anatomy of An Enrollment Conversation	329
Handout 2: Coaches and Money	337
Handout 3: Professional Coaching and Your Professional Self	347
Handout 4: Your Calendar Is Everything	355

HANDOUT 5: CONNECTING	365
HANDOUT 6: INVITATIONS	377
HANDOUT 7: ENROLLMENT QUESTIONS	397
HANDOUT 8: COMPASSIONATE SELF-FORGIVENESS	403
HANDOUT 9: BEING A GREAT PROFESSIONAL COACH VS. WANTING TO BE LIKED	411
SAMPLE COACHING AGREEMENT	421
RECOMMENDED RESOURCES	427
ACKNOWLEDGMENTS	431
ABOUT THE AUTHOR	435

Foreword

Foreword
Sparks Fly When You Read this Book

When I met Carolyn Freyer-Jones, more than a decade ago, she had already acquired the two most important basic skills for success in coaching (without yet having become a coach)!

The first and foremost skill was the ability to sit with someone and, through the process of a deep and powerful conversation, help them change their life for the better.

This skill was acquired from her years of attendance at the University of Santa Monica, where she immersed herself in and changed her own life through USM's rigorously experiential programs in spiritual psychology. It's a school that (I later found out) keeps its promise to support its students "in awakening more fully into the awareness of who they truly are—a Divine Being having and using a human experience for the purpose of awakening—while living more fully into their life purpose and making a meaningful contribution in their world."

And fortunately for her future remarkable success as a professional coach, Carolyn later took over the University's leadership in marketing and enrolling students into USM's classes. This is the second most important skill for a coach:

gracefully and effectively enrolling someone into a life-changing experience they have no way of fully trusting ahead of time.

Carolyn excelled at that skill through creativity, compassionate listening and a consistently wide-open, learning mindset. Through that approach, she got better and better every year at enrollment.

When she decided to leave the employ of USM and venture out on her own to be a full-time professional coach, she had every new coach's worries and butterflies about whether it would work out.

I had the honor of being her coach at the time, and given what I knew about the profession—and what I knew about Carolyn—I had to hide my amusement. Her worries were unfounded. I knew she would make it big time.

In the years following Carolyn's departure from her position at USM she flourished as a coach. She and her best friend, the late and truly great Michelle Bauman (also a USM grad and coach) did a number of joint ventures as group facilitators for women. And Carolyn's solo practice featured one-to-one coaching successes with men and women from all walks of life.

After a number of great and prosperous years on her own, Carolyn joined Michelle and me to create and facilitate a University program to teach USM graduates how to create professional coaching practices. Given the success of that venture, and after the sad and devastating passing of Michelle from cancer, Carolyn decided to create a school of her own: The CFJ Coaching Success School.

That school keeps growing year by year, and it has given

Foreword

hundreds of coaches the tools and systems to master the skills of client acquisition and financial security in this profession known as "life coaching," "leadership coaching," and "business coaching"—a profession that is relatively new (and which was previously unstable as a reliable means to thrive and flourish financially).

This book you're about to read is a surprisingly lively and accessible version of the work she put into making that school function as effectively as it has for coaches who attend.

There's an old cliché in spiritual and self-help circles that says, "You can't get it from a book." Once you read (and eagerly apply) this book, you'll disagree with that skeptical opinion. You *can* get it from this book.

What can you get?

All the tools, ideas, communication systems, and inspiration needed for enrolling clients into your own coaching practice.

It's all here. And the good news is that it's not in some kind of tiresome academic prose. No. Because it's Carolyn. And those of us who receive her weekly emails know that when she writes, it's always full of spark, spunk and badass pizazz.

Her short, punchy chapters knock me around. I laugh and learn with some . . . and wince with temporary shame with others as she makes mock of my missteps and egoic self-centeredness that get in the way of making it easy and compelling for people to hire me as their coach. But in the end I am transformed. Even before the end of this book, I know exactly how to get clients.

The rest is up to me.

This isn't to say, however, that the book will always be a total replacement for attending her school—although it comes as close as any book could. In fact, in a perfect world, this book will be the book that has you able to afford her school! And make you want to go there, too, because the in-person version of this book can add the element of creating a group of coaching colleagues for life and enjoying the dynamism of a live experience.

In our modern world of high-tech, pandemics, political upheaval and anger, it is no wonder that we are experiencing what sociologists are calling "an epidemic of loneliness." But what professions right now are actively countering that trend?

I say coaching is one of them. A profession that was once mocked and taken lightly by the academic and media elite has risen by the force of its own workability into a new era of respect. And there are few coaches (if any) who have done more for this movement than Carolyn Freyer-Jones.

This lively and vibrant book you're about to read and enjoy is another major contribution to that movement.

Steve Chandler
Birmingham, MI
December 2023

The Total Coaching Success Book

Introduction
The Anatomy of Enrollment

You are taking the time to read this book and for that I acknowledge you. It means you are sincere about your work as a professional coach, and you are clear about creating financial success for yourself in this profession. Right out of the gate I want you to know that my intention is to serve you outrageously, so let's start right now.

In 2013 I co-developed and facilitated the Soul-Centered Professional Coaching Program at the University of Santa Monica, alongside my business partner Michelle Bauman and our coach Steve Chandler. As part of that program, we ran a segment called "Anatomy of Enrollment: The Gap Conversation."

The "gap" is the space between where a client is now and where they want to be. If everything in the client's life stays status quo, they will head into a "default" future. Our job as their coach is to support them in teasing out and creating their vision of what they really desire their life to be.

Michelle led this section, and she shared about it this way:

> The purpose of a gap conversation is to assist both you and the person sitting across from you—the prospective client in SEEING where the gaps are in their inner and

outer life. Work, relationships, health . . . everything. Then you can assist the person in determining if shifting in these areas—crossing the gaps—is important enough to them to invest in themselves with a coach and dedicate time and attention to the process. The gap conversation generally takes place within the first longer coaching conversation. It provides a kind of roadmap that allows the coach to create context and assist someone in getting an overview of their current life along with their unlived life. We as coaches are the boat that the client steps into to move across the gap. We are the safe container—aka the boat that keeps them steady on rocky waters, that shines a light ahead into the future when possibility grows dim. A strong enrollment conversation demonstrates an experience of how coaching works as a process for partnering together to close the gap.[1]

As you open this book, my invitation to you, coach, is to remember: YOU are the boat.

You are the container that will get people from Island A to Island B, from their current life to the life that is calling to them.

---

[1] At the back of this book I've included a handout from our original program, which goes into greater detail about the gap conversation and how to facilitate one. (Handout 1: Anatomy of an Enrollment Conversation). Additional handouts cover other aspects of business building and client acquisition. These handouts are, in effect, bonus chapters containing valuable enrollment and coaching tools, so take advantage of them!

Introduction

You can help them see life the way they always wished it would be.

Hearing that you might think, "Oy, Carolyn—I can barely row my own banged-up dinghy! How can I be a boat that carries someone else towards transformation in their lives?"

At the beginning of my professional coaching journey, I barely had the equivalent of a paper boat that I could put in a pond at the park. My boat required significant expansion with newer, more durable materials, and a much stronger captain (a much stronger me) before I could invite others to step into it. You, too, must build your own boat before you help others cross the sea of their lives and reach greater fulfillment, success, joy, and well-being.

Steve Chandler was my boat for more than eighteen years. Steve had to fix and strengthen his own leaky rowboat to become the boat he is now, still my magnificent coach and friend. Michelle was also my boat, in a different way; she was the friendship and partner boat that helped get me from my Island A of "I don't think I can actually become a full-time boat" to Island B: "I'm a boat that can transform lives, do it full-time and make my own life great." I loved Michelle very much, and I still do; her spirit breathes throughout this book. Much of what I share here we learned together. Her boat was gorgeous, and she put in the time to make it so. And when I first met her, she never thought she'd ever have or be a boat; she was a successful lawyer and thought she'd stay one . . . until she changed her mind and crossed that gap.

And now, coach, remember: *You* are the boat.

And you, like me, like all coaches I know, will always be building a stronger, more beautiful boat to carry people. That's one of the many amazing things about this business—we never stop growing, learning, becoming. It's like Steve Chandler says, "This is the only highly paid profession I know of where ongoing spiritual and psychological growth are a job requirement if you want to really succeed. And it's exactly why I love the profession so much."

That's the purpose of this book: to help you build that beautiful boat *and* learn new boating skills along the way. It's for any professional coach, at any stage of their journey. Whether you're brand new or have been in the profession for three, six, ten or more years, I think you'll find something of value here. It's for coaches seeking to strengthen their business and their coaching—specifically in ways grounded in serving, connecting, and slowing down. It's filled with tools and insights gained through years of practical experience—my own and that of others. I've broken it into loose sections on topics like business building, personal development, client creation, communication and more, yet in a way all these topics weave together. In this profession *everything* that's going on internally and externally impacts your business and your life.

There's no "right" way to read this book. You can read it cover to cover or dip into chapters or sections that feel relevant to you right now in your business. You can study the handouts at the back of the book for even more detail and practical application. The only thing I'd suggest is that you read the whole book at least twice: once for information, twice for transformation. It takes intention and awareness and repetition (at least it does for me and the other coaches I know) for new ideas to sink in. It's even better when they're grounded in the practical

Introduction

experience I encourage you to pursue throughout this book.

My success as a professional coach is the result of several factors:

- Immersing myself in ongoing personal growth through inner exploration, seminars, work with other coaches, and a growth mindset.
- Being coached deeply by Steve Chandler for over eighteen years.
- The ongoing love and thrill of being an entrepreneur.
- Hours and hours of hard work, dedication, uncertainty in knowing whether or not it would work and recurring financial investment in myself.

I never thought I'd own my own business and be an entrepreneur, let alone love it. Learning how to serve and consistently turn up (or down) the flame in my business continues to be the most fun, difficult, engaging, growth-filled and creatively challenging professional opportunity I have ever experienced. In other words, I really like it.

That's an important point: I discovered I really, really liked being an entrepreneur . . . and I hope this book assists you in discovering the joy and possibility of being a strong entrepreneur and coach yourself.

Carrying people across the waters of life and work is a privilege. We can take people to new places inside and out—ones they have previously only imagined—towards heartfelt dreams, improved relationships, greater professional fulfillment and success, deeper peace and joy, and more.

First though, let's get your boat stronger. Let's take your business to the next level, shall we?

Business Building as a Professional Coach

1

Service Context

As you read this book it's important to know that the growth of my entire business, and all the different ways I coach professional coaches on the growth of *their* businesses, takes place within a service context.

Not a selling context.

Not a marketing context.

Not a "scale-your-business-in-thirty-days and make-six-figures-in-two-days-a-week" context.

A service context.

I was initially introduced to what a service context is at the University of Santa Monica (USM), where I earned my Master's in Spiritual Psychology. USM offers a distinction: we can have a service-centered life or an issue-driven life. Until I arrived at USM I definitely had an issue-driven life. My life was not focused on serving others. To be honest, I'm not even sure I was thinking much about others. I was a kind person, a caring person, simultaneously frustrated by my parents (especially my mom), my bosses, my husband, my brothers and the world. I was not particularly anchored in, "How can I be of service here?" My USM education changed all of this for me, and being of service became my center.

Then I met Steve Chandler, and he became my coach. I was the Marketing Director at USM, doing a little bit of coaching on the side for fun. Steve introduced me to the world of professional coaching. He showed me what truly giving generously, no-holding-back looks like. Specifically, he taught and coached me into service-based enrollment.

Through slowed-down, meaningful conversations that have real impact and depth, through nurturing relationships and sharing useful resources, we give an experience, and we provide a high level of value. We build relationships over time and ultimately, through our serving, people decide to work with us. There's no selling. There's no "get" energy. Michelle would say to coaches, "I'm of service all day long. Some people become my clients and some don't, and I'm serving all day long."

An example: a year ago I was coaching a company, one that has a mission by which I have been personally impacted in profound ways. Because I had been served so beautifully by the organization, I was inspired, and I offered to the owner that I'd be willing to have a conversation with the CEO. The owner said, "Yes, that would be great." So I had a few long conversations with the CEO, and then offered three months of individual coaching (a total of six coaching sessions), waiving the fee.

The CEO immediately said yes. In those six sessions, I coached no differently than I would have done in a paid coaching relationship. At first glance, this may seem like a really stupid business model. Giving six sessions of "free" coaching? You

Service Context

might be thinking, "I thought you were a successful coach, Carolyn? Was I dumb to buy this book?"

But wait—there's more . . . Over the course of those six sessions we began exploring the CEO's leadership skills and their ability to inspire their teams and create clear agreements. We also began to work with teams on their communications with clients, looking at how they were sharing about the organization's work and how they could be slowing down in conversations, among other things. There were immediate, positive results, including the owner of the company moving into greater willingness to raise fees, create different programs that serve people at higher levels, and in general to look at the level of value they are providing.

At the end of the six sessions the CEO said, "How do we do more with you?" I offered a one-year, robust coaching program that included individual coaching for the CEO, coaching for the teams to teach them service-based enrollment, and a series of leadership workshops. I received a strong yes.

You might be saying to yourself, "Carolyn, you did three months for FREE. That's so much time!" As it turns out, I spent approximately six to eight hours serving to create a great, year-long client at high fees (over $100k). For me, that was time very well spent. I demonstrated what was possible through giving them a real experience. In six sessions I showed them the significant shifts we could start to make in ways I wouldn't really be able to help them with in one to two conversations. And here's a key: they were *so* grateful for the complimentary coaching. They were shocked that I was giving it to them, and it became the foundation for a fantastic working relationship where they felt served, and they also were clear I was not "looking" for anything by serving for free.

And I wasn't. If they'd said nothing other than "Thank you" at the end of the six sessions, it would have been totally okay. My business model has this built into it. There's no grabby, needy energy where I'm doing a "loaded give."

Like Michelle, I serve all day long. Through this, some people enroll and become clients, and some don't.

Having a service context for your business is both simple and not simple, because it requires you as a coach to drop attachment and learn what it means to serve with no agenda. For some coaches this comes more easily than others. For some coaches, they give away too much, over and over, and don't convert people into paying clients (this usually has to do with professional self-esteem, no leadership or direction, and possibly not strong coaching skills—more on all of these later).

To serve with no agenda is freeing, *and* it takes learning and practice to undo all the unconscious selling we have bought into and do—often without even knowing it. As Steve Chandler says, "If selling worked, I'd do it." It doesn't work . . . especially in the coaching business, which requires trust, relationship-building, and a clear demonstration of value.

Asking the question, "How can I serve?" makes everything simple and beautiful. Throughout this book I invite you to lean into expanding into this way of being, which can result in a professional life beyond anything you could ever imagine, and a personal life filled with joy and peace.

2

My Crooked and Flawed Journey to Business Ownership

My personal plan didn't ever include being a business owner, let alone a successful one who thrived, made decent money and was overjoyed to co-create my own work by honoring my calling.

For starters, I was math-challenged in elementary school. My third grade teacher wrote of me that I was "a good worker but has trouble with math." In high school, my father forced my older brother Paul to tutor me to get me through the tenth grade geometry Regents exam. I passed . . . barely.

Bad at math = bad at business = doomed to disaster.

Right?

Up until 2011, I earned a solid paycheck doing work I loved and was called to do. In addition to my day job, I had a tiny professional coaching practice, maybe two clients at a time. I did this work by phone, at night mostly, in the only private spaces I had at the time: either sitting in my car in the parking lot of the apartment building where I lived, or on the bathroom floor. I wasn't thinking about coaching full-time. I couldn't imagine that I could "make it work." It seemed scary and difficult to not have the safety of a job where someone else was responsible for making sure I got paid.

(Newsflash: even at a "safe" job like that we are still the ones responsible for making sure we get paid; it's just harder to see it that way sometimes. And, of course, you can always be let go from a "safe" job too.)

Then my beloved friend (and soon-to-be business partner) Michelle came along—a successful lawyer, super-smart, loving, and very drawn to the field of professional coaching. Everything changed. Somehow we began a conversation around the idea that we could *do* this—together and separately, because we each wanted our own practice along with doing collaborative work. So we were scared together, which was far more fun and entertaining than being scared alone.

And we had a few things going for us. We had our coach, Steve Chandler, who believed in us. We had our distinctive skillsets. And importantly we also had the hunger and willingness to mess up badly—and to learn from it. To make huge mistakes, try again, then do better the next day. We were committed to learning how to sell from our hearts, not from pushiness or attachment, and not because we thought we "knew what someone needed."

We learned how to be curious and connect deeply. How to lead, how to close, and how to agree with objections (I used to argue with them a *lot*). We learned how to share our fees without apology or trepidation. We learned to accept "no" for an answer and not let it derail us. And we learned that there's nothing greater than the power of willingness and practice, of continuing on regardless of how many no's we received or how quickly others were speeding past us, leaving us in the dust with their income and their rates. We learned to be strong, to dare not to follow marketing gurus or spend money on lists or high-end websites or social media. We learned how to only do what would be fun for us, what mattered to us.

Within her first year of being a professional coach, Michelle left her work as a full-time lawyer of eighteen years and replaced her income without a dip (she was very committed to doing this). I left my job as a VP of Admissions and Marketing and tripled my income in my first year.

How was this possible for us? Four keys made a big difference.

1. We had a coach.
2. We had each other (community).
3. We didn't let perfection get in the way of good enough. We sent out the emails, did the things, and were good with good enough
4. We were willing (and eager) to work our a@!% off.

I'm NOT saying that the same will occur for you. I have no idea if it will . . . and I can say that there's a much higher likelihood if you use these four keys. Michelle and I had strong professional backgrounds prior to launching our own businesses, which helped a great deal. We had powerful financial motivation as well—for example, Michelle's kids' private school tuition and my husband's and my desire to buy our first home.

You can learn the same things we did and co-create your own success. For some people it happens more quickly, and for others it's slower. The only thing that gets in the way of this is stopping. And as my coach, Steve Chandler, says, "Stop stopping."

3

Building a Bridge to Professional Coaching Starting Right Now

Michelle and I built part-time practices on the side. I coached on the floor of my bathroom in my one-bedroom apartment, or in my car parked under the carport. I coached during my lunch hour. For me, there was the uncertainty of being a business owner: "Can I really do this full-time and make enough to assist my family, create the life I want, pay my bills and more?" I wasn't familiar with the entrepreneurial life, I didn't really know any entrepreneurs (except my coach, and I didn't really think of him as an entrepreneur). For Michelle it was much the same.

However, as I look back on it all, something else was afoot too. We were letting go of what appeared to be a world we could control, one we knew, one we could "count on." Many of us (myself included back then) find it easy to get into the habit of relying on a day job and other areas of our lives being "permanent fixtures" that we don't want to risk letting go of. Of course, that perception of permanence isn't accurate; it only appears that way sometimes. The reality is we can't control anything, ever, nor do we know what will occur. Things can change instantly (like your best friend and business partner dying).

When we transition into coaching from another career, whether it's corporate or something else, we are letting go of a particular set of rhythms . . . a boss, colleagues and so on. Other people are often setting the priorities and determining the direction of the organization and our work. Charting your own path forward as a professional coach is a very different experience. As I look back, I see that for me this was all a process of letting go of being in what felt like a safe yet constricting box, and exchanging it for the wild freedom, creativity, and extraordinary ability to create my own work without requiring any permission or input. As professional coaches we have to adjust to the responsibility that comes with that.

At the time, our coach said to us, "Let your coaching work drown out your day job."

So we slowly, messily, and often fearfully grew our coaching work, individually and together. Some things went by the wayside, as they must when you're working full-time and building a new business on the side. For example, our houses were often not sparklingly clean. (Michelle would say to me, "Keep the lights off, less dust will show.")

We scrambled. We prepared. We wrote mediocre emails, and we wrote really good ones. And, of course, we continued to get coached and work on ourselves and our business in other ways. We read, took seminars, and practiced, practiced, practiced. I scheduled enrollment conversation after enrollment conversation, and even when I questioned whether I was ready for something, I dove in anyway if I'd vetted the idea with myself and my coach.

I continued to panic about leaving my day job. I stayed probably two to four years longer than necessary because I just didn't know if I was ready. Michelle was the same. She worried about money a lot. Our coach talked to both of us about our limiting money stories.

Fundamentally, we realized that building a coaching business is not a fairy tale—it's a real possibility. And at the same time it's easy to get caught up in the glow of the idea of the business right at the beginning, when enthusiasm and excitement are high. It's also easy to keep yourself in check, until you are "truly ready."

The Land of "Someday I Will Be Ready"

There is a land of "Someday I Will Be Ready"—otherwise known as "The Land of Rainbows and Unicorns and Perfectly Fluffy Coffee Drinks." This is a magical place where all the successful coaches live, everything is possible, unicorns run free, rainbows are everywhere and all your coffee drinks taste perfect. In this beautiful land, there are more books to read, more programs to take, more certification opportunities, more workshops, more gurus to listen to, and so much more to learn before you need to get into action.

This land is sparkly and filled with new possibilities. It's also filled with lies. Not mean, angry lies—fluffy and gentle ones, just like coffee drinks. One of them is that if you stay in this land long enough, success will come like magic. All you need are more strategies, more confidence, more self-belief. Then you'll be ready, and magical glitter will flutter down from the sky.

This elusive "readiness" is always just a little further ahead, like a will o' the wisp you think is leading the way to real success and financial prosperity, but which is really leading you further astray. And when the illusion slips you are thrust into darkness, the haunted streets of your mind, the demons of doubt, fear, low self-confidence . . . No one is cheering . . . No one is calling . . . And the coffee is bad and has cream blobs in it that won't dissolve.

It's possible to stay in the coziness of sparkly unicorn land for a very long time without actually getting into the real world—namely, into action. Yet the truth is that there's no perfect number of programs, groups, schools, or workshops that will prepare you enough, that will have you ready—the kind of ready where you have loads of clients, are always in your comfort zone, and have forever left behind worry and self-doubt.

But that's the biggest lie: that you need to be ready, that there's a day when "ready" will be stamped on your forehead and the Universe will sing and money and hundreds of clients will rain down from the sky. The programs, schools, groups, and certification programs with tons of encouragement and no calls to real action are not acknowledging the truth that you need to *start where you are right now.*

What you want is to be pushed out the door, into the world where people are waiting for you. This is what Michelle and I needed, and this is what our coach helped us with, and what we helped each other with.

Building a Bridge to Professional Coaching

We were needy. We watched other coaches and compared ourselves to them. But we got into action anyway. We were painfully regular and methodical in

Don't avoid learning the building of your business. It will serve you for the rest of your life.

our trajectory even when we would've preferred unicorns and rainbows. There were no magic carpet rides. No glitter pouring down from the sky. It was a far cry from being at the Taylor Swift Eras tour, where everything is beautiful and perfect and people are handing you friendship bracelets . . .

When I seemed to be delaying longer than I needed to be, Michelle was the impetus for me moving. She DECIDED. She got out of the magical land of "waiting to be ready" and said, "I'm done being a lawyer. I'm not returning from my sabbatical. I'm doing this full-time."

The truth is FOMO (Fear of Missing Out) was a big factor in me finally giving my notice and getting out of "waiting to be ready." Not the most evolved, right?

And it worked. If Michelle was doing it, I wasn't going to *not* do it. Obviously I'd been preparing for this for a considerable amount of time, and this was what gave me the final push.

And now? Now I look back at this time as one of the best in my life. We were doing something new for which we had no road map and no five-year plan. It was scary but it was also fun. We were learning, growing, making mistakes, and having our coach reflect those mistakes to us with enormous humor. He would show us different ways to strengthen ourselves and our businesses.

Allow me to ask the same of you. Michelle would often ask

people, "What if THIS is the Fun part?" What if this thing called growing your business, learning how to enroll, connecting, falling down and getting back up again is the fun part? Maybe you're transitioning into your own coaching business. Maybe you're already up and running, or at least up and stumbling. What if THIS is the fun part?

Don't miss this part. Don't avoid learning the building of your business. It will serve you for the rest of your life. Don't fall into the trap of thinking, "The coaching part is fun—the business building is not." Make this one of the best parts of your life. Michelle and I were not "special." We just didn't get bogged down (too much) in getting it "right" or trying to be "the best." We learned to be pretty happy with "good enough"—and to keep reaching. We were very happy serving people and laughing together.

So I invite you to stop waiting to be:

- good enough
- prepared enough

Stop waiting to have:

- enough credentials
- enough "content"
- your book written
- a website
- a podcast
- the one, right, PERFECT idea

Building a Bridge to Professional Coaching

And stop waiting for it to be fun. What if it can be even more fun *without* the unicorns and the rainbows. Coaching is one of the best professions on the planet, because we get to engage with the magic of real life. Dive in. Don't let the world wait another day for you.

Practical Questions

One last thing for your consideration. Here are a few practical questions to ask yourself if you're building a bridge from a day job to full-time coaching.

- Have you successfully enrolled 3-6 clients in your part-time practice?
- Have you had people renew with you?
- Have you replaced the clients who did not renew (relatively consistently)?

The above questions are *data* for you. Meaning, if you answered yes to them, you have data that demonstrates you can do this full-time. If your answer is "no" to these, it doesn't mean "don't proceed," *and* it does indicate that you want to explore what's contributed to your no's. Was it simply that you haven't put in the time and effort required? Or is it that you have opportunities to dial in your enrollment skills more?

Some other practical considerations:

- Do you have any financial buffer? That is, say, three, six or nine months of financial resources to fall back on as you go full-time and get into the rhythm of enrolling over and over again?

- Do you have a coach, a group, or a school to be your scaffolding as you do this? Someone who is going to guide you into what it takes to be successful full-time, and a community to hold your hand and cheer you on when it gets bumpy or when you have wins?

People sometimes jump into professional coaching with no net—financial or otherwise—and they succeed. And some don't. For some of us, building a bridge works better, perhaps because of family responsibilities or our ability to tolerate the discomfort of the unknown. It's okay to recognize you'll do better with a bridge versus leaping out of an airplane.

4

Pick a Number, any Number!
What to Charge as a Professional Coach

When newer coaches ask me, "What should I charge?" my answer is typically: "I don't know. What's your sense of what you should charge?"

I'm not being coy. I'm pointing to the fact that it's important to navigate this question yourself and determine your own answer. My answer won't be yours, and if we attempt to outsource this responsibility we miss the growth involved in the process. There are many factors to consider—and we'll do so below and in the next chapter—all of which involve taking stock of where you're at, what you want to achieve, what you're afraid of, and more. Probably the most important thing to consider early on is that your fee is a *starting point*. It's not set in stone, and it need not become a stumbling block before you even set foot on the coaching path. This is where "pick a number" comes in.

Our fees start where WE are. If we have little experience coaching and are really at the beginning of our professional journey, there's no "wrong" answer: $50/hour, $100/hour . . . Whatever works for you. In the beginning your primary job is to *get practice coaching and enroll paying clients.*

You might be surrounded by coaches making more than you. You might read books or see Facebook advertisements telling you that you can make six figures in six months in this profession. All of that is noise. Your first step is to become a paid, practicing coach.

And . . . because newer coaches like being given answers about this (and who can blame them?) . . . here are some more things to consider:

1. **Pick a number that you can say without gagging or sweating profusely.** Nobody hires a nervous, sweaty, trembling coach. Nobody. Pick a number, any number—and relax! This is a beginning. As you work with a few clients and start to gain some experience and confidence, you'll start to think about raising your fees. It will happen—I swear! Raising fees is a process, not an event. It can happen naturally as your practice fills up.

2. **Practice saying your fee anytime you raise it.** As Steve Chandler says, "You want to say your fee like you say your phone number." Do you cringe when you say your phone number? Is your phone number too high? Do you keep it a secret? Of course not; it rolls off your tongue without a thought. You want to be able to say your fee the

same way. So say it in the mirror, practice it with a colleague or friend. Make saying it second nature.

3. **Remember that your fees aren't a reflection of your value as a person or as a coach.** Lower fees, higher fees, it's all part of the process in this profession. My fees started in the neighborhood of $1500 for three months. At the time that seemed like a lot of money. My fees went up from there. I remember when my fees were $12k for six months and $25k for a year, and I thought, "This is IT. This is amazing." I felt confident in my fee. The level of value people received when they worked with me was significant.

At the time of writing this book (over ten years later) my fees are $40k for six months and $85k for a year. These may get higher in the coming years. Coaching fees are not about what the market will "bear"—that thinking doesn't apply in the world of professional coaching. There's no "going rate." Some people and various certification programs will say there is, and that's simply not accurate. We are markets of one. Nobody can do exactly what I do. Nobody has my coaching skills, my professional background or my wide range and depth of personal life experiences, all of which I bring to bear with every person I coach. *The same is true for you, and for any other coach.* We are unique. All we have to offer someone is our consciousness. (And to reiterate a frequent theme of this book, this is one of the reasons I continue to do my own growth work—in service to myself and to bring more to my coaching.)

BUSINESS BUILDING

You may feel a twinge of outrage at seeing my fees. Some people's point of view is that "high-fee" coaches are "wrong," and that being one makes coaching inaccessible to too many people. It's insensitive in many socio-economic situations. Yet everyone gets to charge what is right for them, based on their life circumstances, their financial responsibilities, what their earning goals are, and so on. I don't ever think anyone's fees are "wrong." I might invite someone to consider increasing their rates—for example, when they are clearly bringing more value to the table than they realize. Or I might invite someone to consider lower fees—for example, if they're just starting out and don't have any clients.

Do people get extraordinary value when they coach with me, such that profound and priceless things occur for them inside and out? Yes. People who choose to work with a coach who has what are considered high fees are willing to make a significant investment because they want significant outcomes. It might be something deeply personal, like dealing with a broken relationship. It might be a significant professional dream that it's time to take action on. It might be a leadership crisis in their corporate role, or it might be inner challenges and questions that are impacting their quality of life—all of which require time to uncover and transform.

I also have ways for people to work with me who cannot pay $85k. That is important to me, and one of the reasons I have some flexibility here is because I am comfortable and successful charging what I charge.

Pick a Number, any Number!

If you are a female coach reading this, take note. One of the reasons my fees are high is that I'm not willing to take a back seat to male coaches who are charging similar fees . . . and I encourage you not to either. Female professional coaches want to be aware of their own biases, where we are potentially playing small and buying into unconscious gender norms. Women tend to earn less in almost every profession for a number of reasons . . . and one of them is because we continue to allow it.

Been Coaching for More Than Three Years?

What if you're not a "newer" coach? Maybe you've been doing this for a few years or consider yourself a seasoned coach. Are you wondering, "Should I raise my fees?"

I have a (disliked) answer for this question too:

I don't know. There is no "should" in this business.

Then I continue in greater detail:

It depends on different things. Are you consistently getting clients at your current fee? Is it your experience that your clients are having transformational experiences and feel they are receiving great value from their work with you? Are many of them renewing?

A general guideline here is that if all of your clients are saying "yes" to starting or continuing their work with you, it's time to raise your fees. If you are instead hearing "no" a lot, it might not be time yet (and there may be things happening—or not happening—in your enrollment conversations that you need to work on).

BUSINESS BUILDING

Another question to consider is this: are you earning an income as a coach that works for you and your life? Are you living life the way you want, paying your bills easily, saving appropriately, and so on? I'm not talking about buying mansions or living in Tahiti (not that there's anything wrong with that). I'm simply suggesting you assess the basics of where you are and go from there. Creating significant earnings as a professional coach requires effort and willingness. And an important question to consider when you're deciding what to charge is this: "What fees will help me create a sustainable practice that meets my needs?"

Fee Guidelines for Seasoned Coaches

What can more practiced coaches helpfully do when raising their fees? The same guidelines above apply here.

1. Don't jump your rates so much that you are gagging or sweating profusely when you say them.

2. Practice saying your new fee in the car, in the mirror, as you open your refrigerator, to your dog . . . See above regarding your phone number. Get to where you can say it without thinking. And this means stripping it of any secret power you've given it. It's just a number to say, take it or leave it, no special meaning to it.

3. Remember: your fees aren't a reflection of your worth as a person or coach. They're simply what you can and do charge. Coaches are notorious for comparing themselves to other coaches. As a good friend of mine says, "To

compare is to despair." Coaches despair over what other coaches charge, are outraged over what other coaches charge, and use what other coaches charge as evidence of their own unworthiness to be in this profession. Let your fee come from within you, from your own considerations around what you need in order to create the practice you want to create. Comparison is not helpful.

Money Stories

Growth around the "money component" in creating your business is usually a tremendous area of opportunity for coaches. It's an area that can psych coaches out because we make it mean so much. The issue of fees pits us face to face with our own money stories and limiting beliefs. Ideas we grew up with can wreak havoc with who we are today, even if we think we abandoned them long ago.

For example, we might stumble saying a fee, not because it's particularly high to us (it's all relative), but rather because growing up we were told that people who make a lot of money are greedy. Others of us received a direct or not-so-direct message as a child that, "Poor is pure." Or perhaps you had very little growing up, in terms of food or other basic needs, and this might have created survival issues that greatly impact your relationship with money.

These can all be worked with and transformed, and it's important to take on this work as a professional coach. You can change your relationship with money, and this translates into your ability to serve people around *their* relationship with money. When we do this work with ourselves, we are literally changing our ability to earn a strong living, and we are forever untangling the spaghetti-like thinking around money and self-worth. Spoiler alert: they are 100 percent separate.

Allow your relationship with money to be transformed. I live a life where I am able to share my resources—giving to people, organizations, and projects that speak to my heart. It's one of the most joyful, amazing things to be able to do. And it never would have occurred without having done the work on my own money story.

When a coach drops—or even loosens the hold of—their own money story it benefits the entire profession. More importantly, it's a game-changer for us personally, as well as for our clients and families. As Steve Chandler says, "Money is not oxygen." Yet all too often we see it as exactly that. So when in doubt, don't let your fee be what stands in the way of hitting the ground running.

Pick a number, any number, and get into conversation.

Changing your relationship with money can translate into an ability to serve your clients around *their* relationship with money.

5

Agonizing Over Your Fees Is Not Helpful

The question "What do I charge?" can derail us. At a minimum it can slow us down as we go back and forth in our minds and postpone actually coaching while we figure out what to charge for it.

"Fee, oh, fee, wherefore art thou my fee?" We might wonder plaintively. Or we might go deep and spiritual and say, "I have not received guidance from my angels as to the fee that resonates with my chakras . . ." Or, to cut to the chase: "Can someone just TELL ME what to charge so someone will say 'yes' and I don't have to think about how uncomfortable I am?"

In many ways this profession is like the wild, wild west—and this is one of the things I love about it. There are so many variables involved in what your fees will be. There's no "limit" and there's no governing body saying, "You can only charge X."

BUSINESS BUILDING

This requires us to put a stake in the ground and make a choice—any choice!—that we can get behind, even for just a short period of time. Doing so helps us remember: this is a profession, and we get paid for it.

What you don't want is to be questioning yourself over and over (as so many coaches do). Your fee is not a referendum on who you are as a human being. At the end of our lives none of us will be asking, "Should I have charged more?" We will be asking if we have served well.

Your fees can and will evolve. It's better to start with a lower fee that feels easy for you to say. Your fees will go up as you gain experience and as your professional self-esteem grows. If saying your fee makes you want to pull the covers over your head and hide, people will almost certainly sense that, even if you manage to say it without stumbling over your words or cringing as you say it.

Remember, there's no "going rate" in coaching. That's not a thing. There's only what the right fee is for you based on where you are currently. You might know some coaches who charge fees that you see as a pipe dream, or you wonder if they are living in an alternate universe where the streets are paved with diamonds . . . That's not the "going rate." That's *their* rate. Some have arrived at their rate through lots of time in the profession and thoughtful consideration, and others have simply declared, "I'm charging X." It's not a science, and it's very personal. Fees can equate to excellence in coaching, and they can also equate to ego and reaching. Don't get caught up in the fees of someone who's further down the road than you are—other than perhaps to simply make a mental note: "Okay, that could be possible for me.

Agonizing Over Your Fees Is not Helpful

We'll see."

In truth, you can charge whatever you want if you can enroll someone at that fee. In other words, enrollment is the proof in the pudding. If you've been trying with a certain fee for a while and failing to enroll at it, that's your cue to consider revisiting the fee. It doesn't mean you'll never charge that fee, or that no one else is charging that fee. It just means that if you're getting all "no's" then lowering your fee for a period of time might prove very useful. After all, we can't create a strong coaching practice if we're not coaching. Similarly, if everyone is saying "yes" to enrolling with you, it's a good time to consider raising your fee. "Yes's" and "No's" are simply information; they can give us feedback on where to set our fee.

Your fee is not about you personally. To you, your fee is your ability to pay your bills and cover rent. To your client, your fee is their rent, vacation, future investments, and so on. Your fee has less to do with you than you could ever realize, and way more to do with how open your client is to what's possible for them. As we mentioned in the previous chapter, your fee has nothing to do with who you are as a human being. A high fee is not "better" than a low fee. Learning to separate your fee from who you are is important for you as well as for your clients—it allows you to serve them powerfully regardless of your rate.

In a way, fees are more related to a client's level of

> **Enrollment is the proof in the pudding. You can charge whatever you want if you can enroll someone at that fee.**

commitment than they are to a particular level of value attached to them. Michelle Bauman used to say, "Look at someone's calendar and you'll know what's important to them." We tend to think that we'll pay more for something that is more valuable, and that value is related to what matters most to us in our lives. If our prospective clients feel they'll get that value by working with us, they are more likely to see the fee as part of their commitment to their own success.

What this means is that a higher fee generally requires more enrollment time, more time in conversation with someone. Nobody I know ever hired a coach whose fees are above $1500 with one twenty-minute conversation. Coaching is a relationship business. We start out serving and create a relationship that the client wants to continue. Through those initial conversations we're not "selling" them but helping them create a vision of what's possible for them. This takes time.

What's more, in my experience there are no slam dunks in terms of getting clients, no special groups of people out there for whom saying yes to coaching is tremendously "easier." Magical communities of people who run to throw money at coaches do not exist. There *are* people whose context of affordability, personal experience investing in coaching, and funding sources are different. And even in these instances, creating a real yes—where someone is clear about moving forward in their professional and personal lives—still requires effort for both the coach and the client. This is good news, because an easy yes could mean a client who might not stick with the uncomfortable work that coaching can require.

With all these guidelines, practice is key. If you're willing

Agonizing Over Your Fees Is not Helpful

to practice being truly unattached to the outcome, to work on who you are being, and to learn to make your enrollment conversations as deep and impactful as possible, any agonizing about fees will slip by the wayside, and you'll truly move the needle for your client and your business.

BUSINESS BUILDING

6

The Dark Side of the Coaching Profession

Eight Reasons Why You Might Be Making Less Than Minimum Wage

A lot of coaches I know, or know of, live the "coaching life." That is, they:

- Have one or more certifications.
- Frequently attend workshops and trainings.
- Read tons of books on coaching and related subjects.
- Are members of coaching communities online.

And yet many of them are barely making enough money to survive as professional coaches. Many are making minimum wage. Sometimes they make a bit more, but almost always they are stumped as to why they haven't cracked the code to six figures, or even $60-75k a year. Here are eight things that can be in play in these situations.

1. Not a Good Enough Reason

People go into this business with a lot of heart. Usually it's because they've been positively impacted by a coach or done personal growth work themselves, so they have experienced firsthand what it can do for people. These are solid reasons to enter the coaching profession, but they are not good enough by themselves to keep you there. For that you need a really good reason beyond these. What are some possibilities?

- "This is a profession where I can use my skills, gifts and prior experience as a corporate leader in more personal ways."

- "I am going to facilitate and lead women into greater self-acceptance because I walked through that when I healed my eating disorder."

- "I loved being coached as an athlete in high school/college. It changed my life. I became more confident, more at ease with my physical strength and my inner strength. I want to help people in their lives the way I was helped in sports."

- "I get to express myself in fun ways *and* help people. I also get to choose my own schedule, plus there's no limit as to what I can make financially. I love the freedom in that."

- "I was a teacher and I realized the part of the work I loved best was actually coaching the students in how to find their own voice. Coaching allows me to do this even more directly."

Having a clear sense of *why* helps sustain people longer, especially—but not only—when they're in the early days of growing their business. A powerful *why* helps them tolerate the rough patches when things are uncomfortable and they begin to see that everything requires more effort or time than they originally imagined. It helps them stay in it without collapsing entirely. They get back up again faster, they gain traction, and they start making good money.

2. No—or barely any—connections or community

Coaches require people. We can't coach goats. The successful coaches I know have communities and networks they can tap into. These relationships are often from prior careers, although not exclusively. I know moms who have participated in their children's communities and who have translated this into coaching clients. I know a new coach who tapped into the community at her beloved gym. So it's not like you have to have had a big job prior to entering the coaching business. Yet it's helpful to have pre-existing communities or to learn how to cultivate new ones. This is where learning to slow down and connect comes in—and anyone can learn to do this.

What if you don't think you have a community to connect with? You aren't alone. Lots of new coaches don't have a community. AND—just like money—community can be created.

The Dark Side of the Coaching Profession

Steve Chandler used to give free, weekly talks at his local library. Guess how many people showed up initially? Four. Four people. He didn't walk out and say to himself, "Screw that—I'm not doing a talk with *four* people." Instead he served those four people in the same way he would've served an audience of four hundred people. He kept doing this, and that number grew from four to eight to twelve to twenty . . . and the rest is history.

Some of the coaches who have gone through the CFJ Coaching Success School have done events via Eventbrite. People came to those events, and then kept coming to subsequent ones. The coaches nurtured these people and eventually created clients from that audience.

Tarita Preston, a fantastic coach on the school faculty attends all sorts of events in her local community. Women-in-business events, leadership events, you name it. She goes with an intention to serve and connect, and she almost always leaves the event with someone who asks for an email from her and a resource.

Communities get created, one person at a time. I know a fantastic book editor who's also a coach. I'm waiting for him to do a complimentary event on, "You Have a Book in You that You Haven't Written Yet? Write It Before You Die."

People are waiting for you and the community you can create. Build it and they will come.

3. Living in people-pleasing / "I don't wanna be a professional; it's HARD!"

Building a coaching practice requires us to stop living in the land of "social self" and wanting to be liked. We must commit to leading people in professional conversations where we support them through meaningful, transformative conversations. If you don't learn how to do this, you'll keep having conversations in which people think you're simply being generous and friendly—and they won't know how powerful coaching can serve them. You will struggle to get clients.

So how do you behave like a leader? Practice it—literally. Look around your life and identify where you embody heart-centered leadership. Is it with your kid? Your kid's teacher? The receptionist who makes your dental appointments? Your dad's doctor? Look for the place where you are clear, calm and guiding the conversation, where nothing is deterring you from the desired direction you want to go. Everyone has a minimum of one place where they do this.

Next, put this into a coaching context and practice it. Of course, as a coach your main job isn't to direct the client where to go, but to keep the discussion focused, to create the container where you

Coaches require people. Successful coaches have communities and networks they can tap into.

can truly support them. There's no room here for you to people-please or be concerned about getting a client. So take out the more wobbly, tentative language. You can practice in front of the mirror, imagining a client in front of you and saying to them, "Let's slow down and look more closely at what you just said . . ." Or you can practice the beginning of an enrollment conversation with a friend; ask them to stop you every time you sound nervous, tentative, or unsure.

When I first moved to Los Angeles I got a job as a tour guide at Universal Studios. I was bored being a temp in different offices, stuffing envelopes or making copies, so I went and auditioned. I made the cut, only to then spend two weeks on the studio lot, learning the different history and stories I needed to memorize so I could share them at the drop of a hat. That way, if the tram ever got stuck somewhere, I'd be able to fill the time in a relaxed, easy way.

I was nervous when I took the final test—really, really nervous. And guess what? I faked being relaxed. I faked sounding at ease. I pretended to be confident and not at all concerned that I didn't know the material. And I got the job. And after the first twenty or so tours, I finally relaxed for real. *Then* I was a confident pro. In other words, at first you can fake feeling comfortable as the leader of the conversation—because before long you'll see how comfortable it can be to drop your own people-pleasing tendencies and anxieties and instead focus on the person in front of you.

People want to be led. They want to feel like the person calling themselves a coach not only knows where the conversation is going, but that you can help take them where they need to go. So practice, practice, practice. Fake it, fake it, fake it—and then confidence grows.

4. You Are Not Accurate With Your Time

Most of us think we do not have enough time. This generally isn't really true, yet it's what most of us feel like. We're almost programmed in our society to talk about how busy we are. Yet if I could share with you how many conversations I've had with coaches who have way more time than they need to build a coaching practice, you'd be surprised. I'm talking lots of time, like full days and evenings. And somehow they are not "finding the time" to focus on their business, send out invitations, connect, and more.

I've also had many conversations with coaches who have far less time than is necessary to build a practice. They have kids, full-time jobs, and other responsibilities . . . and yet build a practice they do. They build it twenty minutes at a time, even when it seems like there's no way.

What does this tell us?

If you are not accurate with your time you are going to struggle to build a coaching business. In the Chapter "Purposeful Work," I share about the calendar game we play at the CFJ coaching school, and how it helps coaches get an actionable understanding of their time and how to manage it. The key lies in not giving in to the default belief that "there's not enough time" and instead acting with intention. Ask and answer the questions: what actions are most important for nurturing your business and where will you create the time to do them?

5. Your Relationship with Money (or Lack Thereof) Is Getting in Your Way

Many of the coaches who show up at the CFJ Coaching Success School have never really looked at their money up close and personal. They don't deal with it—it's an avoidant relationship, as in, "I won't bother you if you don't bother me." I used to barely open my eyes to look at my money. "I hope it's all okay over there!" was my approach, all the while living in terror that an email with the header "insufficient funds" was coming my way.

Yet we are in a business where dealing with money intentionally is important—for ourselves and often for clients. When I learned how to handle money, to be in a relationship with it, to know what was happening with it in my personal and professional lives—everything changed.

The first change from simply covering my eyes and ears and hoping it all worked out for the best was taking a financial freedom course at the University of Santa Monica. Here was where I learned I didn't need to be afraid of money—I could learn how to take care of it. Money was simply a tool—not a force out to make me feel bad about myself. I stopped projecting negative human qualities onto money, and I started treating money as something that could be a huge help to myself and others.

If you are not accurate with your time, you are going to struggle to build a coaching business.

It's really hard to be a successful success coach who is not successfully handling their own relationship with money. And to the degree you transform your relationship with money, you will be able to assist your clients in doing the same.

(For further consideration, check out Handout 2: Coaches and Money, at the back of this book.)

BUSINESS BUILDING

6. Personal Integrity

I lied a lot as a teenager. I changed my report cards to show better grades, I lied about where I was, I lied about my schoolwork, and I lied about who I was with. This was not a great phase of my life; in fact, I almost tanked in high school. When I quietly realized that college could be my only ticket out and the only way my parents would stop being angry at me, I somehow managed to change things. Just barely.

So I mean it when I say I understand what it means to have a loose relationship with one's word. Again and again it stops coaches who want to grow their business. The thing is, if you can't count on yourself to show up when you say you will, it will be almost impossible to make things happen. You're the boss here—*you* are growing *your* coaching business. So it's up to you to show up when no one else can see you.

You can learn what it means to keep your word. You can become someone who can be counted on by others as well as yourself. The funny thing is, it's sometimes easier to show up for others—there's an outside reckoning there. But if you're "just" showing up for yourself, who will notice if you don't?

Many people I grew up with are VERY surprised at my success and the fact that I coach for a living. I hear things like "It's *hilarious* that you coach people, Carolyn. We cut school all the time and were drunk at 11:00 a.m., vomiting into a couch. And you make good money now too?!"

In other words, if I can learn how to keep my word and become a responsible adult who gets stuff done, you can too.

Here are a few baby steps to start with:

With yourself, keep the promises you make. If you set aside Monday morning from 9:00 to 11:00 for enrollment calls, show up by your phone or computer *on time* and ready to go. Don't wake up at 9:00, make coffee and sit down at 9:20. This is your show. Being your own boss means making sure you show up to do the work.

With others, if you honestly *can't* for some unavoidable reason do what you said you would do, tell the person(s) involved as quickly as possible. Don't wait. If you are going to be late, let the person know asap, with a clear, new timeframe for when you will arrive or when X will get delivered. Also, when you know you don't want to do something, or can't go someplace, say no, and say it fast. Get used to clarity and direct communication—with yourself and others.

7. You Haven't Been Trained Well

Many coaching certification programs are not serving this profession well. They do not even begin to open the conversation around what building a coaching business requires in a real, depth-filled way, nor do they actually cover anything about what it means to truly, deeply connect with someone, and the impact that this has on enrollment. There's little about leadership and more about social media, niches, and websites.

But even if you do go through a stellar certification program, you can *always* add to your training. Don't stop at getting certified. Keep going. One of the themes of this book—and one of the keys to success in growing as a coach—is to continue your own self-education. The impact of this may be even more noticeable as you're just starting out and trying to crack that minimum-wage barrier, because there's so much to learn (not that this matters much if you don't also *practice*!).

The most successful coaches I know are constantly adding to their growth and development. They continue to receive coaching and challenge themselves in new modalities.

8. You Don't Want To

I remember a conversation with Steve Chandler many years ago about a coach I was coaching. I asked him for coaching on this person in one of my own sessions, and I shared what I was seeing—namely not a lot of activity, no progress, and few or no enrollment conversations.

Me: "What do you think?"
Steve: "She doesn't want to do this as a profession."
Me: "WHY? What's making you say that?"
Steve: "Because she's not doing it."
Me: "Huh. You're right. She's not doing it."
Sometimes you just don't want to—and that's okay.

This doesn't have to be an instant decision. It involves paying attention to why and what you're doing, and when. You can start doing the things that are required to grow a coaching practice—and get messy and make mistakes and move forward—or you can decide it's not for you. And you may reach a point where you acknowledge, "I don't want to do this. If I did, I'd be doing the things that are required." It's an honorable, truthful statement. No judgment. People will come and go in this profession, and being truthful about where you are will always be helpful.

7

Purposeful Work

In 2023 I took the CFJ Coaching School solo. Up until then I'd taught every session with the amazing Amber Krzys. She would read and comment on coaches' reports with me and provide masterful coaching as well. It was a gift having her there, not just to share in the labor, but because of who she is and her way of being.

The change in 2023 came about because Amber was called to shift into a visiting faculty role in the school instead of being there every session. Simultaneously, I was being nudged inside to do something different, and hence, a new version of the school came to be.

That first solo year my heart expanded in new ways. The coaches were a fun, wildly courageous group, and I had more time alone with them than in any previous year—a full day and a half without my outstanding guest faculty members. I was also the only one reading their monthly reports. The experience deepened me. Being with the class on my own created greater intimacy between us. Reading every coach's monthly report allowed me to get to know them better, and I got to see their thinking and progress each month.

One could look at all of my new duties and say, "Carolyn, that's so much MORE work!" And they'd be accurate. In fact, there was a part of me, at the start of the year, that had a momentary, quiet, internal, "Ugghhh, really? This is going to be a lot."

Almost immediately I heard my inner response: "It's going to make it better. I'm going to be able to go deeper with each coach every month, and it'll give me new insights into how to serve them."

And I was right. Not only was it a different experience, it was one well worth the extra effort.

I'm sharing this story because I often experience coaches running—or slowly, cautiously backing away—from more work. The kind that comes with planning, enrolling for and implementing events, groups, and workshops. Or the work of nurturing and serving prospective clients by emailing and messaging them. Or that of tracking billings and invoicing. Whatever it is, there's this subtle, whispered (or actually spoken aloud), "Ugghhh, really?"

And the answer is: "Yes, really."

I am super clear that more work, in and of itself, is not something to back away from. Depending on the situation, more work is an opportunity for growing one's professional self. It's an opportunity to stretch, to run experiments, and to serve in more profound ways. I'm not an advocate for overworking, grinding, or hustling. I'm for breathing in life. For having space to be inspired, for having fun and strong self-care. It's a requirement as far as I'm concerned, because I can't serve and be a source of inspiration if I'm depleted. I also can't do my best work.

When we play the top-secret Calendar Game in the CFJ School (okay, I'll give you a hint—it's about what's on or *not* on your professional calendar) it's often revelatory for coaches. Some realize they're drowning in work. They have clients back to back without breaks, and their self-care and well-being are nowhere to be found. They are prioritizing everything but themselves—a surefire recipe for burnout and, ultimately, a less successful business. For them, the opportunity is to use this insight to make a powerful shift inside and out and start nurturing the self that nurtures others.

Alternatively, we have coaches in the school who quickly discover that their calendars don't even remotely reflect a full day's work. They find they are doing a whole lot of *not* working. When they see the actual hours they're putting in, they get to face the reality of their days (and handle the shame or judgment around that). Together we home in on what they were actually doing between noon and five last Wednesday and Friday . . . Why don't they have a single enrollment call on the books for the coming month? For these coaches, the Calendar Game provides a powerful wake-up call. They can move forward from it to make new, more empowering choices and direct their efforts. (For more about calendars, please see Handout 4: Your Calendar Is Everything.)

This is all part of entrepreneurship. We are co-creating our own days, our mornings and afternoons. If we have a coach, they

BUSINESS BUILDING

can help us see all of this, which has tremendous value. And, of course, they can't "make us" do anything differently; that's up to us. We are our own bosses now.

Successful coaches value purposeful work. We realize that if we don't do the work, it won't get done. Also, if I avoid "more work" that I believe will support my practice, I'm not the only one who loses. Everyone I could have served loses as well. My business won't grow, I won't grow, and any new clients I might have served won't grow either.

I've heard coaches talk about things they yearn to do, whether it's creating more clients and making more money, launching a new group, writing a book, holding an event, taking their practice in a new direction—and so on. All of that takes purposeful *work*.

Yet for many coaches it stops at talk.

As I write this chapter I'm in the middle of completing my second book—the one you're now holding in your hands. I didn't have a co-writer for this one like I did with my first: *What if This Is the Fun Part? A book about friendship, coaching, dying, living and using everything for your learning, growth and upliftment*. That one I had the privilege of completing after my business partner and best friend, Michelle Bauman, passed away. She had started the book, but because of her illness she was unable to complete it. So, strictly in terms of book writing, I lucked out. She had bequeathed me the solid beginnings of an excellent book!

My second book is all me. And yes, consequently, when I was planning and working on it, the thought occurred to me several times: *Ugghhh! More work!* And yet it's purposeful

Purposeful Work

work. Not busy work. It's fulfilling. It's the kind of work we cannot avoid if we are going to create the things we are called to create. Believe me, editing my own work is not my favorite thing to do in the world (though it helps to have the outstanding editor and fantastic coach Chris Nelson involved). And . . . I remind myself that this book has a real chance to serve people, to help them open new doors in their lives and businesses, creating what they want to see in the world. So I want to finish it and give it that chance in the world. And it's not going to write itself.

What I share next won't be "nice." It won't be something that earns me popularity points in the profession. But it's true. I've seen enough coaches who don't want to work hard to create the things they say they want. It's not a good look when professional coaches get whiny, complain-y or frustrated when another conversation would serve a prospective client, or when nurturing a client means sending them something and emailing them regularly, or when filling a group requires *lots* of conversations and emails. As professionals, we get to choose every day who we are going to be and what we are going to create or not create. There's no requirement to put on a happy face and love it all the time. It's okay to think or say, "Ugghhh! More work!" And then to put in the effort, attention and work.

Creating more clients, launching a group, writing a book . . . all require purposeful work. Yet for many coaches it stops at talk.

It might help to know that you matter to this profession. You have something to contribute that only you can contribute—and it's going to require you to bring it forward through your own effort and attention . . . through your own purposeful work. This is how businesses are grown and lives are created.

My good friend and world-class coach, Devon Bandison, says something that's simple and valuable. (Devon served on the school faculty for five years; the coaches who were privileged to experience him saw what it means to be a coach with a huge heart, one who is willing to say the truth as he sees it, in service, caring so much for the person he's coaching that it doesn't matter to him whether they like him or not). The simple thing he says is: "Let's GOOO!!"

That's it! Let's go with *purposeful work*. Let's go with creating what you are being called to create. Choose it and do it, in service to yourself and the people who will benefit.

> "One lesson I've learned is that if the job I do were easy, I wouldn't derive so much satisfaction from it. The thrill of winning is in direct proportion to the effort I put in before. I also know, from long experience, that if you make an effort in training when you don't especially feel like making it, the payoff is that you will win games when you are not feeling your best. That is how you win championships, that is what separates the great player from the merely good player. The difference lies in how well you've prepared." ~ **Rafael Nadal**

8

Being "Agreeable" Is Hurting Your Business

What if coaches and other professionals who allow people to walk all over them make less money than those who have strong boundaries and policies (especially women)?

A study led by professors from the University of Notre Dame, Cornell University, and the University of Western Ontario,[2] found that, on average, less agreeable people make significantly more per year than agreeable people. For men the mean was $10,326 more, and for women $3,213. (This isn't the place to dive into the different ways our culture views the roles of men and women. Suffice it to say that being "disagreeable" in the ways I'll talk about below is often more acceptable from men than from women.)

---

[2] Judge, Timothy & Livingston, Beth & Hurst, Charlice. (2011). Do Nice Guys-and Gals-Really Finish Last? The Joint Effects of Sex and Agreeableness on Income. Journal of personality and social psychology. 102. 390-407. 10.1037/a0026021.

BUSINESS BUILDING

For clarity, "disagreeable" doesn't necessarily mean being disrespectful or unfriendly. Rather, it can refer to a practice of being unwilling to compromise boundaries or sticking to your guns when fighting for something you believe in, rather than "going with the flow" to keep the peace. And it can mean being unwilling to say yes just to be liked.

People everywhere have a hard time setting boundaries and an even harder time enforcing them. And if you own a business (your coaching practice, for example), you might find it challenging to communicate your personal policies for fear of "seeming harsh or unlikable."

Let's look at some ways this desire to be agreeable plays out in our personal and professional lives—and the price we pay for it.

1. A prospective client asks you to discount your services because they can't afford your rates. You don't want to, but you agree anyway for fear that standing firm on your fee will make you appear unsympathetic and mean. The end result: they sign with you, but you feel taken advantage of and underpaid for your work. Not the best way to start a coaching relationship.

2. Your fifth grader, whom you fed just twenty minutes ago, interrupts you to say they're hungry *again*. You drop everything you're in the middle of to whip up more food for them, rather than asking them to make a bowl of cereal or to wait for you to finish. Good parents respond to their kids' needs right away, don't they? So you lose your train of thought in the process of making a grilled cheese

Being "Agreeable" Is Hurting Your Business

sandwich . . . and don't find it until an hour later when you finally get back in the flow.

3. A client is late paying you. They come to their session and you don't address it. That would be uncomfortable. You're a coach, not a bill collector. You start to feel resentful and miss an opportunity to serve them around their commitment.

4. You do the bulk of the household chores with a full week of clients while your spouse or significant other hasn't lifted a finger in weeks because they're "tired." You don't communicate around it, and neither do they. Instead you let your frustration build up around the issue and carry it with you throughout the week.

5. Your new client writes requesting to move their first coaching session. You agree. A week later they ask to change it again. You reschedule without any conversation around it—either time. Agreeable people are accommodating. It doesn't matter that you have to adjust your own schedule accordingly; in fact, you were going to work on group enrollment at the only time your client's available next week, so you'll have to find another time for yourself. Once again, you miss an opportunity to serve your client around ideas of commitment, prioritizing and scheduling.

6. Your client tells you they can't meet for a full hour for the next three sessions because they now have a meeting with one of their colleagues. They share how "busy" they

BUSINESS BUILDING

are. You say, "I understand! It's fine to do thirty minutes." Yet you know that the full session time would serve them far more. Furthermore, since your sessions were already scheduled, it could help your client to sort out why they are prioritizing their work meetings over time they dedicated to themselves.

7. Your sister calls you on a Monday, upset. "Can you come over?" She's in the middle of a divorce and there's a lot going on. "I need help with paperwork and the kids are melting down!" You have a number of emails you need to respond to, both from current and potential clients. You were going to draft a plan for enrolling for your new group. There's laundry in the washing machine that has to get into the dryer. But you drop everything and rush to help your sister. No emails go out that day, the laundry stays soggy, and your group remains unenrolled.

Do any of these sound familiar?

Obviously there are times when life will get in the way of your business. And there may be times when it really is important for you to help your sister or your brother or your kid, or when a client reschedules for a fantastic, totally legitimate reason. But even these times will be easier to accommodate when you learn to be less agreeable in service to yourself, your family and your clients.

Let's say you really do need to unexpectedly help your sister or brother or kid or client. It will be a lot easier to do this if you've been "disagreeable" elsewhere: your partner can put the laundry in the dryer because you've already talked with them

Being "Agreeable" Is Hurting Your Business

about household chores. You've already started enrolling for your group because you didn't permit your client to reschedule on a whim and take up the time you'd planned for enrollment. And the emails—well, they're important, but maybe you can send at least one and then go help your sister in her time of need. You can take a quick look at your calendar and find a time tomorrow to send out the rest.

It is 100 percent doable to:

- Establish policies and boundaries in your personal life and your business and STILL have close relationships, great friends and wonderful clients.

- Practice the language of leadership in service to your business, your clients, and prospective clients who are learning from you. Practice looks like taking new language into your next client session and saying, "Let's handle some housekeeping: I didn't address the late payment, and that's on me. I apologize. We'll slow it down now: tell me what occurred that created the breaking of the payment agreement."

- Catch yourself in social/friendship-lite mode and really see what it's costing you in dollars and how you're being perceived. An example of this is allowing a prospective client to "chat" with you at the beginning of your second conversation for twenty minutes about a new show on Hulu or their recent bathroom renovation. You don't pause them; you just listen and nod your head. Instead you can hold sacred the container in which they will create transformation.

- Discover how many client opportunities you are leaving on the table because of low professional self-esteem.

When it comes to leadership and running your own business (and life), there's the requirement to have policies and boundaries—and there is also the absolute requirement to communicate those policies and boundaries with finesse and leadership. *This* kind of so-called "disagreeableness" is actually a willingness to serve yourself and others with integrity and grace. A coach who communicates this way inspires their clients to learn to do the same in their own work and lives.

(Please also see Handout 3: Professional Coaching and Your Professional Self at the end of this book).

9

Kitchen Renovations and the Wild, Wild West

My coach Steve Chandler once said to me that being an entrepreneur is like being a gunslinger in the Wild, Wild West. Many people with "regular" jobs don't understand the wild, wild west in this context—namely, the ability to co-create, more or less, whatever the circumstances.

A turning point for me getting this was when I became fully committed to turning up the flame and co-creating $100,000 over and above my usual income in about six weeks. The situation was this: my husband, John, and I had just bought our first home. The house was sorely in need of a new kitchen, as well as an office for me. Our initial, more modest plans quickly snowballed into a full-blown home renovation that included all-new flooring, a new master bath and kitchen, a garage renovation and more. That might sound like a nightmare scenario financially—the kind that could make a homeowner look wistfully at their child's college savings account, or at least wonder how bad it would really be to have your office in the kitchen next to the twenty-year old stove.

I was clear that I wanted to do it all. Steve said to me, "Great, let's go."

My coach did NOT say:

"That's not wise Carolyn."

"I don't think it can be done."

"Too risky. I don't recommend it."

"Are you nuts?"

My dad, a relatively conservative businessman and former banker, was shocked to hear me say that I simply intended to make the extra money to handle the renovation. He said, doubtfully, "Well, okay, if you think you can do it . . ." He did not understand the Wild, Wild West. He loved me, he supported me, and he could not relate to a professional world where if you wanted to do something, you could decide to create the resources to do it.

Fast-forward seven months and the renovation was completed. At the time, Steve said to me, "You know, you could have earned that much or more at any time. You just haven't wanted something enough." I paused when he said that to me.

Hmmm. "Really?"

"Absolutely. Look at what you just did. You wanted it and you decided to make it happen. You can do that about anything."

He was 100 percent accurate. In fact, it was fun to create the money. I realized this was duplicatable.

Nowadays I don't think about it a lot—I simply do it. If I want to create a big trip for my family, I create the money. I'm aware this can sound a little ridiculous. I'm not a wizard making money out of thin air. Yet I do understand now, through experience, that anything is creatable. If that's true for me, it's true for you too.

Now, a few things: I was already a number of years into my business. I had a lot of prior work and experience with client creation and enrollment under my belt. I had already made a significant number of mistakes and learned a great deal. I also had my business partner and best friend, Michelle Abend Bauman, rooting me on (despite being sick with cancer at the time).

And I was also *on fire*, as in, fully engaged—ready, eager and willing to *create*. Who knew a house renovation could inspire me in this way? What's *your* inspiration?

One of the key realizations that led to my creating the additional income was this: *there are always creative, inspiring ways to serve people more, to create more value, to GIVE.*

This meant, for example, slowing down and seeing how I could serve my current clients in greater ways. And it also meant asking what new offerings I could add to my existing "repertoire." Let me share some of both with you here.

Offerings to Current Clients

- Created new packages that included unique, full-day intensives. I allowed them to enroll early (as they were still in their current package) and to receive a cost reduction. That is, "If you enroll and pay in full by next week, it will be $X less. If you wait until our current agreement is complete, you will pay the standard fee to continue.

BUSINESS BUILDING

- Offered current clients the opportunity to re-enroll for another six months or a year—regardless of where we were within their current agreement. If they did so within a certain timeframe, I added on two extra months of coaching at no additional fee.

Offerings to Prospective Clients

- Unique, one-day intensives that had not been previously available.
- Smaller packages (3 months).
- Longer packages with two months additional coaching added if paid for within a certain timeframe.

The other key was keeping my eyes on the prize. This was a matter of focusing—every day—on co-creating the money for the renovation project. I did not allow myself to lose sight of this goal or let it slip into the rear-view mirror. Consequently, outside of serving my current clients, every email and conversation I engaged in was about this. There were no conversations about future projects, only projects that could occur *now*. Only people I could serve now. No distractions.

You might be a newer coach reading this and thinking, "That's all well and good for YOU, Carolyn, but it won't work for me." Or maybe you're a more seasoned coach thinking, "I like this idea, and I'm also pretty sure it's not really doable for me, at least not in my current situation."

Whatever the case, I hear you. And I offer you a challenge. Consider something you want right now. Maybe not a kitchen

Kitchen Renovations and the Wild, Wild West

renovation. If you like, start smaller. Perhaps a business-class flight to visit your parents or your kid in college. Or maybe a new couch or desk, or attending a personal growth seminar that's been on your list. Ask yourself: if I knew I *could* create this, what would I do? How would I serve?

Then make it a game. Get committed to what you want. Make it your priority, day and night. Things *will* happen. Will you co-create what you want? Of course, we can't say for certain. Was I 100 percent sure I would make the money? No. Not at all. What I was, however, was *committed*. I was all-in, no holding back, and this was a critical key. Simply *playing the game* provided me with key learnings, and the same will happen for you too, if you pay attention.

Remember: as an entrepreneur you're in the Wild, Wild West. Yes, that brings with it a certain degree of challenge—but also the ability to powerfully create what you want.

BUSINESS BUILDING

10

Pivoting in Crisis: A Client Story

Allie Wik and Sandy Sullivan are highly coachable, smart, and hungry to learn and grow. They own The Alchemy Group, a company dedicated to growing leaders across the globe. At the time this story begins, I had been coaching them for more than three years. In addition to being coached privately by me, one of them was in the 2020 CFJ Coaching Success School, and the other joined in 2021. Up until the COVID pandemic arrived, the majority of their work consisted of *live* events inside major corporations.

Then the pandemic hit.

Every single event on their calendar went poof. POOF! Ninety-eight percent of their business for 2020 was gone within a matter of days. After all, even before the lockdowns went into effect, who would want to attend a packed corporate training event and risk getting COVID, no matter *how* good the information was?

Naturally, Allie and Sandy were freaked out. As they said

Pivoting in Crisis: A Client Story

to me, "Carolyn, we've flatlined. Clients have disappeared in droves. *WTF are we going to do?*"

Allie was on the plane to attend a CFJ School session (which turned out to be the last one we did for over a year) when she next emailed me: "Oh my god, another one bites the dust…" One of their few remaining clients had just pulled out of their contract. Allie shared with me that she was about to jump off the plane over Kansas.

When her flight landed, she, Sandy and I got on a spot call—well, a longer-than-usual "spot" call.

Sandy had major dread and doom in her voice. There was *no* place inside of her that had any sense of possibility. Allie was a panicking close second.

As I listened to them I thought, *Nobody was prepared for this. Certainly not me.* (Believe it or not, I do not have a coaching certificate in pandemic coaching.) Then I said to them, "This is going to be the best thing that ever happened to you."

This was met with a long silence, until Sandy said, "Uh, what?"

I said again, "This is going to be the best thing that's ever happened to you and the business."

Both of them said—with tangible doubt in their voices—something to the effect of, "Tell us more."

"This is going to change everything," I said. "I don't know how—and it's going to require you to consider different things. Weren't you going to start working on your new, smaller Advanced Group, the one with a higher fee? Now could be the best time—and maybe you make it so it is virtual to start, and then have a live component you can do later, one that's not held inside a corporation. I don't know..." My voice trailed off as I caught glimpses of other possibilities.

They started to slow down and talk. I offered to them that this was actually a time to serve their clients *more*, not less. Even if corporate clients were canceling events, Allie and Sandy didn't have to cancel. I said, "Do not let those people go unserved. *Do not go dark.* Call your clients and tell them that you will gift their teams ninety-minute group coaching sessions, where you're with those twenty-five leaders and you slow them down and assist them *right now*. Do it complimentary; keep serving those organizations, because that's what people are going to remember when we look back on this. Who was there for us? Who helped us, and who was rock solid for us at a time when things were falling apart?"

And that's what they did.

Allie and Sandy got back into action. They called their clients and offered monthly group coaching calls to leaders. Neither of them were Zoom or tech-savvy—in fact, both Allie and Sandy had, no exaggeration, a very strong, entrenched assumption that in-person sessions were the best and only way to do what they did.

They soon learned that they were wrong.

They simultaneously started actively getting into their new product (their advanced group for leaders), handpicking the people they wanted to offer it to, and getting conversations on their calendar. They wrote a short piece about the group, they identified the dates and how it would work, and they determined the fee. Within ten days, their advanced group was taking shape and conversations were on their calendar. Within twenty days,

Pivoting in Crisis: A Client Story

they had their first two enrollments. Within thirty days, six of the fourteen spaces were full, with down payments in the bank and more conversations on the calendar.

Not long after initiating this brand-new offer they had filled up their slots. They had also led over thirty complimentary, ninety-minute video calls and coached more than three hundred people in over twelve organizations. Before long they had their first paid virtual event—with the *same fee* they charged for live events—and with a NEW client. And business kept coming in.

In a coaching session we had at the time, we talked about how none of this would have occurred if it were not for the pandemic forcing them into new action. Their advanced group would not have happened as quickly, and they would not be in a new reality of seeing that their business does not require live events to thrive. And the icing on the cake was that they got to serve people at a time when the world felt like it was in turmoil. They were needed more than ever.

The Moral of the Story

What's the moral of this story? Well, for one, Allie and Sandy will never again be residing in an assumption—lived as if true—that they cannot weather an unforeseen storm in their business. They are now, in a word made famous by Nassim Nicholas Taleb, *antifragile*. They have not only benefited from shock but blossomed because of it.

So the real moral is that *this story is possible for you.* If you're reading this and thinking, "This is all great for them, but not for me because ." STOP!

BUSINESS BUILDING

The odds seemed stacked high against Allie and Sandy. And it's easy for us to think that when we're in a slump or worse, things are never going to improve. But instead of listening to that naysaying voice in your mind, consider the possibility that this is true for all of us, *all the time, no matter what.*

No matter if there's a global pandemic, political strife, natural disasters, or something else.

And it's not just true for *you*. As a coach, you want to be modeling this for your clients too. In fact, I offer that you *must* be modeling this for your clients. If you're not, it might be time to consider a new line of work. Choose growth now. Choose action now. Choose to remember that we all can pivot and experience new growth in the face of significant challenges.

Now let me highlight one more important detail of this story: Allie and Sandy had help. They had a coach. It just so happened to be *me*, but that's not the important bit. The important part is that they had someone objective to support them as they engaged everything that they already had within themselves and created a new business model from the ashes of the old. So what's the moral of *this* part of the story?

A familiar one, if you've read this book so far: Get coaching—from someone or someplace that can assist you in creating the business *you* want. You don't even have to wait for a worldwide crisis! Getting coached throughout your career *as* a coach, on your business and yourself, is what makes *the* difference between mediocre coaches who don't earn what they want and truly great coaches who *do* earn what they want—and more.

11

Converting Envy into Inspiration

Have you ever noticed that the coaching profession is ripe with the potential for comparison and envy?

I wonder if other professions experience this phenomenon. Do dentists compare themselves to other dentists? Do they post pictures on Facebook of the latest root canals they've been doing? Selfies next to the car they bought on the proceeds? Do airline pilots post stories on Instagram showing themselves flying during turbulence with one hand on the controls? Do other pilots secretly grit their teeth thinking how obnoxious this is?

Of course, the possibility for envy and comparison is everywhere, in every profession. But it seems to be particularly ripe when it comes to coaching. So many coaches. So many Facebook and Instagram posts of coaches doing amazing things. You might look at these and think, *Meanwhile, here I sit in my house... dog hair lighting up the corners of every room, laundry on the floor by my bed, and my daughter's room strewn with make-up containers and various pieces of clothing.*

BUSINESS BUILDING

Michelle Abend Bauman and I used to laugh when one of us got into the comparison mindset state. When she was there, she'd say things like:

"We need to do a blog."

"We need a plan."

"We need a better website!!"

When I was in this place, I was not as constructive. I generally devolved into commenting about what OTHERS were doing, and making it "less than"—as a way to make myself feel better. (For example, "That coach's wife has lots of wealthy people in their community; *that's* why they're getting high-fee clients.") Of course, this was at best a temporary "fix," until I felt the "yuck" of my own judgment.

Comparison is the "easy" way out. It keeps us out of the courageous, diligent, conscious work of growth. It takes us out of who we are and has us focusing on other people and their work. It keeps us out of our own lane, out of our own game, and out of our own generative abilities.

When Michelle and I were in a small coaches group run by Steve Chandler, there was a coach in the group who was in the big leagues already, insofar as earnings went. She was already at 200k+ a year and was in Steve's group to take it further.

We knew this because in this small group of nine coaches, we shared our billings in a report we sent to Steve. Seeing each other's reports and receiving Steve's coaching around them was one of the most transformative events in my early career. Michelle and I decided that if this other coach could do it, so could we. We "chased" her, as a game. We watched everything she did. We listened closely to the coaching she received from

Converting Envy into Inspiration

Steve. Instead of envying her, we saw her as someone who *created possibilities for us*.

Is there someone you can "chase" and make it a game? Someone who is running the kinds of groups you long to run? A coach who is writing blogs and posts that speak to you because of their clarity and depth? Maybe it's someone who seems relaxed in their work?

If so, slow down and ask yourself: what is it about this person that you admire? I don't mean just looking at their vacation pictures (though you can if it motivates you), but *how* do they serve? What are they creating? Your answers may tell you more about what you'd like to cultivate. Courage? Boldness? Compassion? Humor? Do you see that they demonstrate some kind of expertise that you'd like to develop mastery in? If so, how can you do that? What action would be required to bring forward your own authentic expression of what you admire?

Chasing people in the spirit of growing ourselves serves. It's WAY more productive than hanging out in comparison and jealousy. It's not about having the perfect car or vacation getaway. It's about growing who you are through service and your own growth. That's how successful businesses are built.

A fantastic coach I know made an entire project out of chasing someone. They actually posted about it on social media, tagging the person and naming the game, calling it, "Chasing XX."

It was productive, it was uplifting, and it was *helpful* to the coach. It converted envy into inspiration, and everyone following the coach was uplifted in the process.

12

Entering the Coaching Profession from Other Professions

I was recently asked to speak to a group of coaches who had just completed a well-regarded coaching certification program at an enormously respected, prestigious university. These coaches already had significant educations and successful professional backgrounds, ranging from high-level corporate positions to heading up companies in the startup space, and more. They had asked me to speak about growing a coaching business.

I love it when people join the coaching profession after having had success in other professional backgrounds. Highly accomplished people are valuable to this profession. They bring that experience to the table for their clients. What's interesting, though, is that the very thing that allows them to add value to their coaching relationship is often the very same thing that gets in the way of growing their business.

Especially at the beginning, growing a professional

Entering the Coaching Profession from Other Professions

coaching business can be uncomfortable. We often feel clunky, green, awkward, and very inept. Highly accomplished people are often used to things happening easily for them—or at least they are used to being able to *make* things happen quickly. So there can be an extra layer of challenge for them in the early stages of growing a coaching business. More than in their past careers they are met with insecure thoughts and feelings of discomfort. There's a lot of, "I don't know WTH I'm doing."

Cultivate a bias for action over contemplation. Get good at being *good enough* and not bound to perfectionism. Stay in the game, get coached and be coachable.

Either they don't remember these feelings from the start of their previous career, or they never had the joy and pleasure of experiencing them in the first place.

Professional coaching requires building muscles that often aren't necessary inside large organizations—at least, they aren't required of everyone in the organization. You can rise through the ranks without ever taking on a customer-facing role. You can connect to people in broad, general ways—say in the boardroom—and not in the kind of intimate, one-on-one situations that are the bread and butter of professional coaching.

What's more, when we have developed self-confidence, poise, and credibility in another career, we are often unprepared for the experience of being an entrepreneur. We're not used to getting "no's" and we are unprepared for the sheer capacity required to stay on the court, serving and connecting without looking for an "end game."

And ROI? Ha! When we come from other professions, we are often accustomed to business plans, timelines, and being able to forecast a return on investment. There is no forecasting in the professional coaching business. I cannot, nor can anyone else, guarantee an outcome or predict how you will do as a professional coach—anyone who tells you they can is not being truthful with you.

I can't predict how you will perform as a new coach because I can't predict your ability to tolerate the unknown. I can't predict your ability to tolerate the discomfort of feeling green and clunky. I can't predict your ability to tolerate rejection or your willingness to keep going and not make it mean anything about *you*.

I don't know your capacity to press on without knowing what will occur. I don't know if you can learn to have fun being an entrepreneur. I'm not sure about your level of willingness to use this process to uncover your own blind spots, your neediness or your desire to unconsciously push or manipulate. We all have these places inside—I had a TON myself at the beginning of my professional coaching career.

One of the phrases that came up a lot in the group I was speaking to—the coaches who had just finished the certification program and were exploring how to grow their business—was this: "I need to contemplate that."

These people had well-developed, sharp minds. They were used to using them to think of new ideas, new strategies, new processes. And having a well-developed mind and thinking of new ideas and strategies is often rewarded. It certainly was in their former careers.

Entering the Coaching Profession from Other Professions

And . . . in the business of growing a coaching business, contemplation equals *broke*.

Okay, I'm exaggerating, but only slightly.

Far more than contemplation we need *action* to grow a coaching business. We need to be willing to be in conversation, to be connecting and serving, over and over and over and over. This is another thing I cannot predict: your willingness to be in action as opposed to contemplation. And what comes with action is messiness and imperfection. Where are you with those? Are you willing to make mistakes, be messy, fall in the mud and get back up and do it all over again? That's part of the process.

If you are willing to build your coaching and business-building muscles, if you can actually see the potential for joy, for possibility, for growth, you won't need me to predict anything.

As I mention above, my business partner Michelle and I were both accomplished professionals in other fields before we became coaches. We were really strong in a number of areas—and we were not great in a *lot* of others. Fortunately, we were really good at being in action. We had a bias for action over contemplation. We were also really good at being *good enough*. We were not bound to perfectionism—at least not in the growth of our coaching businesses. We had plenty of other blind spots, and perfectionism was not one of them. (And we also had our own coach to help us see them.)

So what I explored with these recently accredited coaches is what you can explore with yourself: Can you accept you're in a new professional world? Can you build your new coaching muscles, overcome perfectionism and create a fantastic coaching business where you serve in amazing ways?

I'm biased. As I've said, I can't predict it in your case, and yet I think that the answer is probably *yes*. If you are willing to stay in the game, stay on the court, get coached and be coachable, and use all of what comes forward for your growth and learning, you will get there. I don't know how long it will take, because I never do. Some people get to over $100k in one year. For some it takes five years.

I know that if your previous career was accomplished and successful, it's very likely you can help people. In fact, *especially* if you "failed"—if you crashed and burned and got back in along the way—you can help people.

This profession wants you. You have much to give, and much to gain.

13

Are You Certifiable?

Coaching certification programs can be valuable and helpful, depending on who you are. They give structure and offer a framework and a "how-to-coach" process. If you are someone who does better learning while using a structured approach and having clear "directions" at the beginning, such programs can be invaluable. I've known many wonderful coaches who've participated in them.

At the same time, they aren't necessary. Self-made, highly successful coaches are out there in spades: Steve Chandler, Devon Bandison, Amber Krzys, Sandy Sullivan, Tarita Preston, myself . . . The coaching school I've run for years hosts these and other coaches as faculty. To date, none has been formally certified, but they are—hands down—among the most successful coaches I know.

A lot of coaches coming through the school are certified, and many are not. The coaches who aren't certified have no reference point. They haven't been "told" to use social media and determine who their client avatar is. From my perspective, this can be helpful; there's less "clean up" to do. And on the other hand, sometimes coaches who haven't done certification or training are more insecure in the coaching itself; they don't have a "protocol" they learned in a program to use as a starting point. So there's learning to be done all around, which is par for the course in the world of the professional coach.

I love that this is an unregulated profession. I am not interested in seeing it change. Regulating the industry will not produce more effective coaches. Therapy is regulated and in my experience there is no relationship between being licensed and being a good therapist. And in terms of self-work, my experience is that a good number of licensed therapists have only completed the minimum requirement for their own therapy as part of their training—sometimes as low as forty hours. This is in some ways comparable to coaches who have never been coached themselves. Yet the best therapists and coaches I know have done enormous amounts of their own growth work. This speaks to what Drs. Ron and Mary Hulnick, Co-Directors of the University of Santa Monica, say: "We can only assist others to the degree we have assisted ourselves. We cannot take people where we ourselves have not gone."

That said, certification programs have become a huge business. But most of these programs are missing an essential element, without which many new coaches fall by the wayside within a year or so of completing their certification. Anecdotally, I can share that the certified coaches who come through my school are sometimes more frustrated at the start. They have been attempting to grow their business in limited ways that don't work very well, and in their certification program they never received any real, honest talk about what it takes to grow a business. So they often start the school with a lower sense of possibility, already feeling somewhat defeated. It takes work to shift out of this mindset, work that we do together in the school.

New coaches leave certification programs armed with marketing and networking ideas and not a lot else in terms of business development. Many of them think you can't earn a strong income as a professional coach, that the best you can hope for is making twenty to thirty thousand dollars a year.

This is a lie. In fact, it's one of many prevalent lies in our industry. Here are a few more:

- You need a social media presence and strategy and intensive marketing; you need to go to networking events.
- You need a niche.
- You need to have written a book.
- You need to charge by the hour, and there's a "going rate" that you should base your fees on.
- It's not a good time to become a coach and there are too many coaches already.
- You can make six figures in six weeks as a brand-new coach.
- Brand-new coaches are already earning twice as much as you.
- This is a really hard profession in which to earn a living.
- This is a really easy profession in which to earn a living.

BUSINESS BUILDING

The truth is far more balanced. This is a profession where if you want to have a financially successful business you can, earning an annual $80k, $90k, $100k, $150k and more. But in my experience, and in that of the coaches I've worked with, you don't leap out of the gate this way. Like almost any other endeavor in life, you have to put in the effort.

You need to learn how to connect with people. Nobody is going to hire you because of your website, your Instagram feed or your certification—in fact it's unlikely you will ever be asked about certification. You *will* be hired by someone for whom something profound has occurred during your enrollment conversation with them . . . when their conversation with you inspires them to become hopeful and see new possibilities in their lives.

Beyond Certification

It will likely take more effort than you think to create a strong coaching business. But there are ways to measure your progress. For example, your calendar is an indicator of whether your business is growing. If you do not have conversations with live people on your calendar regularly, your business will not grow. Beyond this, and beyond certification, some of the things that will support you, your business and your clients include learning:

- How to lead enrollment conversations and invite people into conversations with grace and warmth, without seeming needy or creepy.

- How to communicate effectively with clarity and strength.

- How to slow down and let go of attachment to "getting a client." This is how you are being with people, not what you are doing.

- How to share your fees and how you work in a way that's relaxed and clear.

- How to practice coaching, lead the close, and how *not* to rush when someone seems interested.

- How to grow your business one person at a time, and to fill groups in the same way.

And at the risk of repeating the message that runs throughout this book—you need to be coached into growing your business by someone who has what you want. Your training as a professional coach isn't done until you can say that you have a consistent track record of generating strong clients and not panicking when your income takes a dip—when your business consistently earns you the level of income you want to live the life you want, and you can turn the flame up or down depending on what you want. And in truth your training doesn't really stop there. We must always be willing to grow

This is the greatest profession on the planet. Don't become the coach who thinks, "This is too hard. It's not possible. Nobody can make a living at this." It's not true. If you haven't put yourself in the hands of someone who can teach you and show you the ropes, who has a track record of helping coaches become strong business builders, you are cutting yourself off at the knees at not

BUSINESS BUILDING

Nobody is going to hire you because of your website, Instagram or certification. You *will* be hired by someone when their conversation with you inspires them to see new possibilities in their lives.

giving yourself a fair shot. Don't believe the hype about this profession, and don't buy into the narrative that it's impossible and there are too many of us. As the great Steve Chandler says, "There are eight billion people on the planet—there are infinite clients."

Coaching as a profession has a low bar to entry—anyone can call themselves a coach. There's almost no overhead, it's not federally regulated, and there are no "tests" to pass. But to do the work as a Professional Coach—to commit to this work as a calling and as an answer to a deep desire to serve, to make a difference, to make a living while making a meaningful contribution—requires us as coaches to be willing to grow.

Not because we "need" to—but because we realize that through our own continued transformation we become better coaches, which means we have more to offer others.

Ultimately the way to be a prosperous coach is to be a great coach—not from the ego level, but from the heart level. To be a great coach means you are willing to continue to grow in your skills, in your consciousness, and in your leadership as a business owner.

A coach who wants to be truly great doesn't shy away from learning how to grow their business more effectively. They look at what's happening in their business and they ask themselves, "What can I do to get better?"

Then they get coaching.

Client Creation and Enrollment as a Professional Coach

14

Where Do I Start?

This a question newer coaches are often plagued with. And yet it's not really, "Where do I start?" but more like, "With whom do I start?"

When we're just beginning, where do we find potential clients? My answer is always, "Start with who you already know." This might seem odd for some. To believe the advertisements that pop up in your Instagram or Facebook feeds (for example), as a coach you should run your own ads, build up a following on social media, network online and so on. Yet that's not where I started, nor is it where Steve Chandler or Sandy Sullivan or Devon Bandison or all the other successful coaches I know started. They began with people they already knew.

This meant people from former jobs, people in their kids' school communities, people at their gyms, churches, book clubs, synagogues, mosques, pickleball clubs . . . all the communities they had been in or were still in. You can do the same—first look to the people and communities you are already familiar with.

CLIENT CREATION

Why not start with people you *don't* know? That approach feels much safer, more anonymous and less vulnerable, *right*?

Your job, first and foremost is to be with the person, be curious, and build the relationship without any agenda beyond simply connecting.

Yet the people who know you already have a sense of who you are. There's already some trust there. Remember that coaching is intimate. People don't tend to jump into allowing themselves to share with just anyone. So the people who already know you see you as someone who has some credibility—at a minimum as a fellow human being who has walked alongside them in similar ways.

For those of you with little to no community, your job has an extra step: you need to *create* community. This means going out, maybe to meetings of your local rotary club or women in business groups. You could take the salsa lessons or art classes you've always wanted to take and meet people that way. You could give a complimentary talk at the local library. It makes sense that, because coaching is about connection, you *start* with building connections.

A coach who was in the CFJ Coaching Success School had multiple communities she spent time in, some of which I was familiar with. In all of them, she was seen as someone who could be relied on for assistance, open discussion, and thoughtfulness. When she wanted to create a group, I pointed out that she had quite a significant community that was hungry for what she had to share. She just needed to start talking to them and inviting them into deeper connection and conversation. She was

Where Do I Start?

uncomfortable, yet she still decided to do a live, complimentary event at her house. She invited twenty women, created a theme, and did a full, complimentary workshop. I coached her each step of the way in creating, sharing and inviting around the event.

Three months later she had twenty women in her home, all of whom were thrilled to be there and discover more about who this coach was. She knew every single one of them from other areas in her life. They already bought into her as a person—now they were buying into her as a professional coach. She invited women from this complimentary session into deeper conversation, and one by one she started to enroll people into her group.

The same is possible for you. Of course, it's not a requirement to do a group early in your trajectory as a coach; this coach happened to want to create groups. You could simply start to connect and invite people you already know into one-on-one conversations, especially if you know they're dealing with something challenging, like a divorce or creating a new business, or they just landed a new job or want to create more collaboration on their leadership team. These are things that come out in everyday conversations; you can teach yourself to start listening for them.

Your first goal is always service and connecting. These conversations *may* lead to professional coaching arrangements or paid group enrollments, and they may not. Your job, first and foremost, is to be with the person, be curious, and build the relationship without any agenda beyond simply connecting . . . which is easier said than done. Many of us think we don't seem salesy, and yet we ARE. It's like the QVC network is coming out of our pores—unintentionally. The coaches who make every attempt not to be salesy are often the ones who ooze it in their language without knowing (you may be thinking, "Not me, Carolyn." Consider the possibility that we have so much salesy stuff thrown at us so much of the time that it's something we aren't even aware of consciously).

You don't want any "get" energy in your way of being or your communications. Knowing this you can drop any "salesy" vibes, any feelings that you need to "get" this person from your community into a professional coaching relationship. You are then freed up to do what you do best, and at the very least you'll build your coaching and enrollment muscles while you do it.

Who we know is the start of everything. Something I often suggest new coaches do is make a list of five to ten people they already know, people they think they could help or whom they'd love to coach. Then reach out to them. Connect, see what's happening in their world, be more curious, and gently ask questions beyond, "How are you?" Practice introducing yourself as a professional coach. Get comfortable inviting them into deeper conversations with no strings attached. The most important thing is to be real, build relationships and start serving as a professional coach.

(For more languaging around this, you can look at the Handout 5: Connecting and Handout 6: Invitations at the back of this book.)

15

Filling Your Practice Is Not Like Ordering from Amazon

Lights, camera, action!

> Coach [to Carolyn]: But where can I get clients? I've looked. I went to a few events, online and local. They didn't lead to anything. So I'm serious . . . LIKE WHERE ARE ALL THE CLIENTS? Everyone else seems to get them. And don't tell me they're "everywhere" again or I'll come through the Zoom screen and punch you in the face.

End scene. *Recurring* scene. My face still intact.

I love this question because it often has the feel of, "How can I order clients to arrive the next day, like on Amazon and Target?" As if clients are an item to check off on your shopping list, next to Chia Pets (remember those?), makeup, protein shake mix and coffee filters. Something to pick up on your way home from work.

Obviously I wasn't immune to asking this question myself. Neither was my business partner, Michelle. And there's tremendous value in having a decisive mindset around client acquisition when you're building a business. Steve Chandler has been known to ask, "Are you showing up for work?" Meaning—are you taking the steps to serve people and expand your business?

But something happens when we default into the language and mindset of simply "getting a client."

First of all, do *you* like to be "gotten"? Probably not. Things can start to feel pushy, salesy, and difficult. And it may sound extreme, but in a way we're forgetting our humanity when we think this way. Because in truth there's no such thing as "getting a client." It's more about *building a relationship*. As you've no doubt heard it said before, this is a relationship-building business. It's about deciding that you're going to outrageously serve someone in a slow, thoughtful and conscious way, creating connection and trust. Then deciding at some point whether there's going to be a financial exchange for that service.

Enrollment isn't always a quick process. It's not going to the store, picking up what you need and heading home again. It's the gradual development of a connection between two people: coach and client. There's no hard and fast rule here, but in my overall experience, for myself and other coaches, is that a quick "yes" from a prospect often turns into a "not ready yet" later. Why? Because the yes hasn't been slowed down and tested against all the other variables in their life. It can be easy for a person to get fired up in a session; it may be the first time they see all the possibilities available to them. They walk into their first meeting thinking all their doors are closed and leave thinking they're all open. But when the session's over they return to their routines and their relationships and their habits, and that initial enthusiasm takes a backseat to the day-to-day. It needs more kindling to grow and brighten. And it also takes more time for a person to experience coaching in a slowed down way, where they begin to see what happens through time with you.

Going slow is a big part of this business. You may be able to earn money quickly in the big picture of building your business, but connecting with someone and building a relationship such that you become what Michelle called "a trusted source of transformation"—*that* takes time.

That's our intention: to become trusted sources of transformation. This trust is built on meaningful conversations. Unless they already know you well, people don't often share their inner thoughts and anxieties right out of the gate. If I meet you on an airplane or you're referred to me, it takes time to build a sense of connection and trust. For example, I have a relationship with a company I served a few years ago. I went in and facilitated a two-day meeting of nine men and one woman. It was a fun meeting to facilitate because they were a tough crowd who wanted to achieve certain things by the end of the meeting. I was really committed to having that happen for them. Two years later someone from that company reached out to me and explained they really wanted a coach. We're now entering into our third conversation—it may go to four—and I don't want to rush it. Especially when your fees are high, that's not a small thing to enter into on either side. And when we're new, it also takes time. So we want to go slow. We want to be willing to really spend

CLIENT CREATION

time with someone. Rushing things doesn't make sense for you or the client.

When our bank account is screaming at us and our rent has to be paid, we're more likely to feel desperate to "get a client." But this state of urgency is more likely to result in nothing; people will probably sense our need and be repelled by it. More to the point, the mindset of "MUST GET CLIENT" tends to result in us not seeing a human being in front of us. We're looking at people and seeing dollar signs instead of someone who needs time to share with us and see us as someone who can help them.

What's more, quick conversations, even when they lead to a yes from prospects, don't always lead to meaningful work getting done. True transformation is usually not a quick game. The best coaching relationships I've had have been with people who are hungry and willing to work hard. These clients aren't as interested in surface, goal-line activities so much as they are with making changes on the inside. These relationships are about supporting the client in experiencing more fulfillment and peace, and less suffering and upset. This doesn't happen overnight.

Our goal is to become trusted sources of transformation.

Coaches who have worked with me know that I'm not a fan of the thirty-minute discovery call. I don't think it's possible to "discover" much in thirty minutes, let alone have someone then hand over money, unless it's in the neighborhood of a few hundred dollars. If you have fees that are over $1k, consider your own decision-making process. Do you hand over $5k easily? $10k? More than this? I know I don't buy products on Amazon for large sums of money that I haven't seen or tested in some way.

Building a coaching business is a process. The paradox here is that sometimes when you slow down and take the time to create relationships, the overall impact on your business is greater—and even quicker than when you try to rush things.

So the next time you're thinking, "I need to get a client," ask yourself: is this like going to H&M or Old Navy to get a new pair of shorts, or is it that I want to build a partnership, a relationship with someone whom I can serve in a deep way, so much so that they pay me to create transformation in their lives?

CLIENT CREATION

16

"Enrollment Is the Hard Part!"

Many coaches say things like this to me:
"Filling my practice is the hard part. If I could just be given clients, I'd be great. I *love* coaching! I'm so good at it! It's the practice-building process that's so—"

You can fill in the blank with your own favorite word here: "distasteful," "uncomfortable," "confronting," "scary," "hard."

These coaches fantasize about working for a coaching company that hands them clients so that the scary/hard/distasteful part of client acquisition is banished, and they can shine in the ways they know they are meant to shine in their coaching work.

I can appreciate this in a certain way. It *seems* like it would be so wonderful! No more connecting through enrollment conversations. No more doing the part where we demonstrate value and slowly build trust. All of that is magically handled by someone else, and the pre-enrolled client shows up at our door. All we need to do is coach.

And yet . . . pining for this type of situation reflects that fact

Filling My Practice Is the "Hard Part"

that we are not enjoying the business building. We're indulging in a fantasy, and if we're not careful—if we linger too long in this fantasy world—we're subject to:

- Procrastination (even more than average).
- Fewer conversations (perhaps none, or one every two weeks).
- Fewer clients.
- Slower financial growth.
- Frustration and low thinking, like: "This profession is a hoax!"
- Fantasies of winning the Powerball lottery and going on various game shows.
- Thoughts of finding someone to "take me away from all this."

But what if filling your practice isn't the hard part? What if it's a mindset issue? What if coaching and filling your practice are *exactly the same activity?* Steve Chandler talks about the two halves of coaching (coaching and getting clients) and posits: if we can integrate the two halves, everything can change. At a minimum, we might find both parts equally fulfilling and rewarding.

What if you ran an experiment? What if, just temporarily you played with acting as if filling your practice was as meaningful and as fulfilling as coaching? What would that look like?

For one, enrollment conversations would simply become coaching conversations. There's no "getting a client" because

CLIENT CREATION

you already have one: the person sitting right in front of you. No convincing someone to work with you, no concern about whether they'll run away when they hear your fees. The only thing you've got to do is coach them.

For me this approach was revolutionary. Filling my practice taught me to be a better coach. It's where I learned to listen better. It's where I discovered new insights about people and the kinds of issues they're working with. Filling my practice became a discipline in and of itself, a joyful one where I slowed down and remembered that the next person was precious. They were not a prospect or a client, but a fellow human being on this journey who had heartfelt dreams and behaviors and beliefs they wanted to shift—and I got to support them in doing so.

There's SO much to learn in the consistent filling of one's practice. I learn every time I "need" to refill my own. Filling my practice has become a kind of joyful discipline.

It can be the same for you. If you were to act as though filling your practice were the same thing as *coaching*, what would you do differently? What if you didn't need or want a client, and every conversation was simply an opportunity to slow down with another human being, to use your gifts and skills to listen to them deeply and assist them in uncovering what's working in their lives and what's not?

At the very least, you would:

- Improve your coaching skills—in particular your ability to listen and to ask effective questions. Some questions open people's hearts and minds; some close them. These early conversations where someone isn't paying you are

Filling My Practice Is the "Hard Part"

opportunities to practice differently from when they are paying you.

- Become more adept at connecting and slowing down without an agenda. Coaches often rush to "make something happen," and this can be felt. We want to be with people without an agenda.

- PLAY. Early on, your fees can be low! You can make it easy for someone to say yes with low stakes. Along the way you get better and better at coaching and serving. Playing creates more ease, relaxation and fun.

- Discover that the early conversations are where *gold* is. Something happens when we assist another person in discovering what's happening in their lives. Along the way you realize there's a choice involved—the person is *choosing* to work specifically with you, the coach. You wouldn't get this if someone just handed you clients. There's a unique alchemical reaction that occurs in the crucible you create together, and it's sparked by the *choice* to work with one another.

Of course, you're free, after your period of experimentation, to slip back into the mindset of "Filling my practice is the hard part!" But I'll bet that if you throw yourself into this, you won't want to. This is definitely a case where the fantasy of having clients handed to you simply can't compete with the rewards offered by the reality of creating them yourself.

(Please see Handout 7: Enrollment Questions at the end of this book for additional support.)

CLIENT CREATION

17

The Layer Cake of Commitment

Coaching Beyond Yes or No in Enrollment

When we are newer to the profession of coaching (and sometimes not so new) and someone says yes to coaching in an enrollment conversation, we tend to get excited and think, "I did it! I'm going to get money! This is so awesome! we are a GOOOOO!!" Excitement is understandable—and there are still some important issues to consider.

Namely, does someone really mean their yes?

Is the yes they just uttered in the conversation with us going to stick when they leave the room? Are there others in their personal or professional lives that will (and should) influence or shift their yes?

As professional coaches, one of our jobs is to understand that "yes" does not always mean yes. There are many layers of commitment that are being created, transcended, and completed during the enrollment and coaching process. We need to be

The Layer Cake of Commitment

prepared for different kinds of yes's and different kinds of no's. We want to learn how to pivot and be flexible in our conversations in service to the person in front of us, and in service to being strong coaches who do not get flustered by no's or yes's, or what comes after.

Think of it like a layer cake. Your job is to be able to navigate the layers of commitment with ease, neutrality, and realness, and not to get stuck in frosting or cake along the way. (If you don't do sugar or dairy, think of it as a vegetable medley—your job is to move through the vegetables, not getting stuck in broccoli or cauliflower or the brussels sprouts).

How do you do this? A good rule of thumb is this: after you propose (and even if the prospect says yes to your proposal) *step back into coaching*. Whatever their response, your job is to discern what's occurring around their commitment and serve their possibility through it.

If the Answer is No

If the person says no, you can:

- Take coaching off the table.
- Consider asking them: "What's in the way of your being a yes, if anything?"

Depending on their answer, you can gain insight into how to coach them. At this juncture, step-by-step processes aren't generally applicable; this isn't a one-size-fits-all situation. What matters is your inner guidance/instincts as a coach. Most of the time I encourage coaches to stop at no, because for most coaches the potential to slip into subtle *convincing* or *selling* is pretty high. Coaching around a no can result in slimy feelings and behavior. It's a very appropriate thing to simply say, "Okay, I hear you," and then acknowledge that they don't want to set up a coaching agreement at that time.

That said, here is one *possible* way to move forward after someone says no. You can ask them:

- Would you like to be a yes to coaching?
- If they say yes, ask them if they'd like coaching around the yes—letting them know it's fine to say no.
- If they say no, ask if they are complete, and then acknowledge them again.

Taking on just this practice alone will improve your enrollment skills. People occasionally go from no to yes. What's most important, though, is that you will learn a lot about where you might have missed something, or perhaps assumed something that isn't accurate.

If the Answer is Yes

Consider that yes and no are doors, and we can coach beyond them. There are usually several post-proposal commitments that each person will pass through either before or after committing to coaching. These three commitments are also points of high impact or "red flags" that occur during the coaching relationship. Each of them can alter that original yes, possibly changing it to a no. They are:

The Layer Cake of Commitment

1. Commitment beyond coaching
2. Commitment beyond the client
3. Commitment beyond survival mode
4. Commitment beyond completion

Let's look at each in turn.

Commitment Beyond Coaching

When someone says yes, it's important to get them in touch with their larger commitment. Why do they want coaching, what do they want to create in their life, and how committed are they to it? In order to discern this, we can "Test the Yes."

One reason we do this is because the person is usually the most enrolled in possibility inside the container at the very moment of the first yes. They've spent an hour or more coaching with you. Their vision of new possibilities and their power to engage with them is fresh in their minds, and saying yes feels very natural.

As soon as the client leaves, their commitment will start to deteriorate. Let's not be surprised by this. It's normal that most people start to question their yes on their own or with others. They share about their experience with a partner or friend. They are one step removed from the experience now, and what felt very real and possible in the coaching container might start to seem less so.

What might happen next with your prospective client who initially said yes?

CLIENT CREATION

- They ghost you.
- They miss or request changes to payment dates.
- They pay you, yet are always looking for a way out.
- Their spouse/boss weighs in ("My spouse/boss said no. Sorry!")
- They send you an email that says they've changed their mind.

Again, let's not be surprised by any of these responses. They happen, and they are generally (although not always) an indicator that we didn't test the yes fully. While there are many ways to do this, here are three questions that work well:

1. "If you were to go from being a yes in this conversation to a no after our conversation, before you pay and show up on our first session, what might make that occur?"
2. "I appreciate your yes. I'm curious what could get in the way of your yes that's beyond your control?"
3. "You sound like a very clear yes, and I'm going to ask you something that might seem strange. If you were to say yes and then regret it later—either before you pay or afterwards at any point during our coaching—what do you see now that might make that happen?"

In testing the yes, we prevent these challenges by doing two things at once. We prepare the client for the natural ebb of saying yes and testing to see if the client's yes is solid enough to survive on its own.

The Layer Cake of Commitment

Commitment Beyond the Client

Sometimes when the prospect says yes, that's all that's required. They have consciously or unconsciously designed their lives in such a way that they can commit without consulting anyone. Often, though, when we commit to something, we also commit to enrolling others around us in the work we want to do. These people might include spouses, partners, bosses, etc. Sometimes a prospective client will make this commitment explicit by telling us they need to speak with their partner or boss, but sometimes this process is implicit for them and easy to forget. Ideally, you'll find out if this is the case before you propose, but if you're not sure, you can discover it simply by saying something like: "I'm curious, is there anyone you need to connect with to support you in being a full yes on moving forward?" If enrolling others is a key part for the prospect in making a commitment beyond themselves, then one of our jobs is to prepare them for this practice by:

- Finding out how the person is going to frame the possibility of coaching.

- Discovering what the person or people to be enrolled care about and will use to decide whether to support or resist the prospective client's yes.

- Reviewing the structural elements of the coaching with the above information in mind.

If the prospective client returns from this process with a new no, we want to *agree* with their no, even if everything inside of us is wanting to fight it! Don't get into, "Wow—what's changed?" They will tell you what's changed, and we want to agree, because not agreeing is not cooperating with their new reality, which is now no. We can start to seem like we are arguing for our reality, which was yes. It's not a good look.

Sometimes a client's relationships won't impact their commitment until after they've already begun coaching. One of the most powerful resistances to transformation is the feeling of belonging we share with the people in our lives. As clients change, they often subtly (or not so subtly) become different with the people they love, including spouses, partners in business and life, and family members.

In this context, the coach keeps the commitment beyond the client present. They discern when the client needs to enroll others into a new stage of work. They support the client in creating new kinds of boundaries or sitting with the discomfort of the transformation and the possibility that it's making others close to them uncomfortable too. Remember, when one person transforms, the status quo can shift for everyone in your client's life.

Commitment Beyond Survival Mode

Most often "survival mode" issues will not arise until after the client has been in coaching for a while. At a certain point, their way of being in the world and themselves will start to be challenged as new ways become more real and present for them. This is great news—it means your coaching is making a difference! And it can lead to a client experiencing a significant

The Layer Cake of Commitment

point of discomfort that they can either tolerate or not. It's an exciting time in the coaching, and it can be a tricky one. This might be where people back away from the coaching, ask for a "pause," maybe stop doing assignments. Maybe they ask to move sessions or even say they want to stop coaching. It's like they are in "survival mode." They don't know what lies on the other side of releasing the old way of being, although they can sense it . . . and it feels *really* uncomfortable and sometimes scary.

A strong coach understands this can happen and doesn't get freaked out. They understand that "survival mode" can kick in. They are prepared to be with the sudden emotions and reactions that can arise when a client's "survival mode" shows up, and they can acknowledge their client and support them through the process. Even truly great coaches are faced with this. Sometimes we can assist the client in working through it, and sometimes people disappear. As we get better at coaching, this kind of backing away happens less—though it still does happen.

At times it may be important for the coach to create or renew a client's commitment to moving beyond survival mode—and into a new way of being.

Completion

Completion is the final phase of any commitment process. The original context for the coaching is done. This is a good thing. At the same time, this is where the context of the commitment set at the beginning of the coaching can become the barrier to the next level of possibility. It's time to either create a new coaching context . . . or simply honor the completion. As always, honor the client and your own intuition.

Everything in this chapter (and this book!) is a guide. With each person who sits with us, there are nuances and subtleties. Some people in your world won't have any of the layers of commitment and the coaching relationship will feel simple and easy. Others will have the largest layer cake you have ever seen. And if you have higher fees, the layers of commitment may take significantly longer to move through.

Strong coaches are okay with the different steps of the commitment process. They don't get scared (most of the time) and they don't get frustrated when things slow down or change entirely.

Commitment is a process, not an event. We as coaches are walking people through the steps of commitment, one layer at a time. The more we make all of the steps okay, the more we don't rush or push someone and instead respect the process of building connection and trust, the more skilled we become at partnering with our clients.

18

How Many Followers Do You Need?

Some coaches are seduced by the number of followers they have. They think followers equals clients, a good income and, ultimately, good coaching. They make assumptions about what's happening for other coaches who have a good-sized following, and they attempt to recreate it in their own world with followers and funnels and streams. This kind of mimicry can lead to images of the coach in beautiful locations, hair gently blowing in the wind, and so on.

A lot of this is fake news, or magical thinking, or wish fulfillment. I'm not saying there aren't coaches with enormous followings who make excellent money. I *am* suggesting they are rare—as in, animals-you-only-see-in-certain-remote-rain-forests kind of rare. And the many coaches who chase this vision via social media and growing their followers often have less than two thousand dollars in their business bank account. I personally haven't known *any* coaches who make a strong income this way, although a lot try. And they often go into significant debt in the process.

The appeal, I think, is that of the glamourous life made easy, and the idea is that this can be measured in the size of your following.

Now, my life is beautiful. It's meaningful. It has depth, joy, texture and some big bumps. It has Spirit and good humor and service and many fun things. I love my work and I'm thriving at it. But it doesn't have a lot of glamour. I (and my house) often look like all of us can when we're working, living, growing, cleaning up after our kids or our pets. I'm not bothered by this. I clean up well, and when I'm working, these things are almost always not my focus.

And although I post on social media regularly—about the things I love: coaching, travel, taking my daughter to see Taylor Swift—I don't have a sizeable following by "influencer" standards.

The good news is that there *is* an approach for coaches to grow their practice without Instagram, Facebook, or TikTok even if they don't live glamorously and don't have a lot of followers. If you don't like social media, or if you want to utilize social media differently, there's a different way.

How does it work? One person at a time. Connect and engage with and serve one person at a time. Slow down with one person.

This is an art, and you can develop your skill and learn ever deeper ways of practicing it. I know many coaches who have built thriving coaching practices this way. I am one of them; Michelle, Steve Chandler, Devon Bandison and Amber Krzys, are just a few of the many others.

Now you may be thinking, "One person at a time? That's ridiculous, Carolyn. That's so slow . . . how can anyone do that?" It's easy to think that somehow if you have more followers you'll sign up clients in droves. In some magical way those followers *are* clients.

But, of course, they're not. Some of them *might* someday become clients, but if they do, it'll be like with everyone else: one connected and engaged conversation at a time. In reality this is the only way. The process I'm talking about is one of meaningful conversation, where the person you are speaking with begins to experience you and your coaching. It's not fast, because most people are not going to spend more than a few hundred dollars without some slowed-down conversation that shows them how additional conversations will serve them (and if they do sign up too quickly, they often regret it).

To clarify even more, I'm not talking about "thirty-minute discovery conversations." People don't generally spend $5k, $8k, $10k or more with you after only a thirty-minute conversation—unless you are Brené Brown or someone like her.

Michelle used to say to people that she had conversations all day long—because what else was there to do? What could she possibly want to be doing other than serving and connecting all day long? Some people became clients and some didn't, and that's all part of the business. We are in a relationship-building business, and relationships aren't built quickly. Trust and depth don't come in thirty minutes. Coaching isn't a microwave dinner.

I've had coaches come through my school who already have big social media followings and who are close to being broke.

But when they start to learn the art of slowing down and connecting one person at a time, they are often shocked at what occurs: they start to see that they *can* help, and that it starts with the one person who's right in front of them. Then they start to use social media as a way to connect with individuals who are commenting on their posts. They direct message them and ask what made them comment. They go slow, no rushing.

This process is revelatory for them because they've been so focused on making posts and getting lots of likes (I understand this; I'm not immune!) that they haven't been *focused on an actual person*. Yet coaching actual people is what this business is all about.

We can't grow a coaching business through posts alone without already being established and credible. And even then there's still the requirement to connect with individuals. Even if you want to work with groups—especially where you're asking people to pay significant money to participate—you're still going to enroll one conversation at time. Slowed down conversation, where you connect and start to serve people not in the virtual world, but in *their* real, messy, vibrant world.

You can be messy yourself. You can have a messy house and hide it from view (I usually position the camera *just* right

The good news is that you can grow your practice without Instagram, Facebook, or TikTok—even if you don't like social media. How does it work? Connect with, engage and serve one person at a time.

when I coach via Zoom). What I don't hide is my willingness to connect, to be curious and get into the world of the person in front of me—with no agenda on my part other than serving.

CLIENT CREATION

19

Renewals

Clients complete. It's part of the territory. Every coach faces a point in a coaching relationship when the question of renewing that relationship arises. This can strike fear and anxiety in the heart, but it doesn't have to. We can get tied up in knots about renewals to the point where we somehow forget about serving and turn things into a referendum on *us*. Does this person still like me? Do they think I did a good job? The answer to these questions, we convince ourselves, is whether or not they renew.

Let's get out of the land of feelings and drama—of "will they or won't they renew?"—and venture into a process of *systematizing* how we view renewals. You can use the following to help take the angst out of renewals.

Renewal System Steps

1. Track when it's time to bring up the opportunity to renew. Generally, this can be two or perhaps three sessions

Renewals

before your final session.

2. Consider what's in service to your client. It's valuable to reflect on questions like these: What do you see as possible for this client if you continue coaching them? What would be different in this next round? People want things to be different, to feel that they are moving forward in their lives and towards their goals. Supporting them in this is why they entered into a coaching agreement in the first place. Moving forward, then, what would you challenge them with? How would you raise the bar?

   Be honest with yourself. Don't attempt renewing just for the sake of making additional money if you truly don't see anything more that you can help your client create through coaching. Your client may have accomplished a lot. Maybe you've already worked together for several years. Realize that it's 100 percent fine (and sometimes *better*) to complete with someone.

   If you see more significant growth opportunities, great. Make sure they aren't *your* agenda for the person, versus what you've heard them share as something they want for themselves in the course of the work together. Finally, be open to the possibility that even if you decide not to offer renewal, your client might say, "There's something else I want to work on . . ." Of course, that's great too.

3. Consider offering your client the option of scheduling a separate, long conversation about whether or not renewing is in service to them. This might look like an

CLIENT CREATION

email or a conversation when it's two sessions before the final session where you say/write something like:

Dear __:

We are coming up on the final X sessions in your program. First and foremost I want to acknowledge you for the courageous work you are doing and the level of inner and outer shifts you are experiencing. It's a joy to partner with you and witness the transformation.

I have been reflecting on you and what's next. I want you to know that I see significant possibilities for taking the work to another level if we were to continue partnering together.

Is setting aside ninety minutes to take a look at this, and also to slow down and see what you see as possible, something you'd like to do?

You may be complete with the coaching, and that's totally fine—let me know either way. And no matter what, let's make your final sessions rich, and the most powerful yet.

Sincerely,

4. Remember, you want *real* possibilities to show the client, things you honestly see for them, whether inner or outer. This is where it can get "sticky" for coaches; we can fall into the trap of being attached to having a client renew and unconsciously slip into selling or convincing mode. It's like quicksand. You can be in it before you know it,

Renewals

and then you can't get out. Be vigilant! Like everything else you do in your practice, this is *service*—not selling. Practice high involvement, low attachment!

5. I have sometimes started renewal conversations with a question I got from a great coach named Ron Wilder:

If we were going to work together, what would need to occur to make investing in coaching again the best money you have *ever* spent, personally or professionally? What would need to occur inside? What would occur outside?

This can be a great starter. Your client can start looking at this, and then they might ask what you see. It's great to share *and* be willing to defer to them, to what they see, what their inner guidance is showing them. See this as a coaching conversation like any other, and remember: high involvement, low attachment.

6. Sometimes renewals are as simple as the client receiving this email or being in this conversation with you and saying, "I know I want to renew. I'm clear." We don't want to be shocked or surprised, and we don't have to make a big deal out of this—and we can still have the conversation where we look at what's possible. This can be as simple as saying, "Okay, let's do this. You can send me the fee for the next round of coaching by [date]. Let's put your launch session for this new round on the calendar. *And* let's slow down and look at what you want to create. I acknowledge you for being clear about this."

CLIENT CREATION

Don't make it harder than it has to be!

7. Your client might say no. No to a conversation, no to further coaching. Do not, whatever you do, attempt to dissuade them from this. This is where it's particularly easy to collapse into selling and persuading. All of a sudden, for some reason, we don't trust the client's newfound inner guidance. We think they should trust ours instead! Thoughts like, "How can they not see how dumb it will be for them not to continue?" and "Do they have *any idea* how much we accomplished?"

   This is ego talking. Don't let it run amok! I have seen coaching relationships end with a bad taste in the client's mouth after beautiful, deep work was accomplished because a coach got hooked into ego-centered thinking and became salesy and pushy (I have done this myself; it's not pretty).

8. If your client says no, make this good news—no matter how you feel. End with an acknowledgment of them and their work, and do not let any of your own thoughts and feelings of dismay (if you have any) leak into the final sessions, no matter how much they are present. End like a pro. Keep reminding yourself that clients complete, that this is GOOD, and you now get to create a new client! It's natural to have a variety of feelings when a client completes, especially if you've been working with them for a while. Coaching is intimate work, and we often love our clients. At the very least we usually really *like* them. Take your feelings to your own coach or colleagues—

Renewals

anywhere except to your client.

9. Yes! If they want to renew, fantastic. It's a great feeling when someone decides to renew—and it's great feedback. Renewals generally mean you're doing good work. Bravo!

Some final thoughts: If you don't generally have clients renewing, consider the possibility that your coaching needs deepening. This isn't "bad" news; let it serve as a reminder that's true for all coaches, all the time: there are always ways a coach can grow and become more effective. A client's no to renewing can mean they are complete and deeply satisfied with the coaching they received. It can mean they want time to integrate what they've learned or created. The bottom line is that we want to agree with their decision.

20

Because You Never Ask

Steve Chandler once sent out an email via his online Coaching Prosperity School[3] that touches on an idea so important I'm going to quote it here.

> Dear Coaches,
>
> One of the keys to prosperity is to make sure you are inviting enough people into conversations . . . In Thomas Hardy's *Far from the Madding Crowd*, Gabriel is a victim. (So, he avoids *creative communication*.)
>
> "Gabriel looked her long in the face, but the firelight being faint there was not much to be seen.
>
> 'Bathsheba,' he said, tenderly and in surprise, and coming closer, 'If only I knew one thing—whether you would allow me to win you and love you, and marry you after all—if only I knew that!'

---

[3] Which is truly fantastic, and which you can find out more about here: https://www.coachingprosperityschool.info

'But you will never know'" she murmured.

'Why?'

'Because you never ask.'"

Let's take a closer look at these two sentences in particular:
"One of the keys to prosperity is to make sure you are inviting enough people into conversations . . ."

And,

"Because you never ask."

These two sentences are everything. Everything!

Coaches don't ask enough. Often (but not only) at the beginning of learning the profession, it's not clear how important it is to invite people into conversation. When we are new, we tend to avoid it . . . or are simply shocked that it's even necessary. "You mean *me* reach out to others? I had no idea this was part of it."

This is often compounded by many coaching certification programs that teach social media as the way to create clients, so coaches think creating posts will have people firing off DMs and they won't need to connect personally. Then we'll have a thirty-minute conversation and they'll happily pay us $2K for three, six, nine months of coaching.

In my experience, and in that of the hundreds of coaches I've coached, this is far from accurate. New coaches almost always don't think about their own initiative to create conversations, to reach out, to ask. Seasoned coaches, too, often forget that they can ask more than they may already be doing.

I'm currently coaching two fantastic business partners who are seasoned coaches. They're down to filling the last two spaces in a special group they're offering. What they're discovering is that here, at the final push, they're required to spend even more time inviting and being on the court. Earlier in the process they filled up spaces with current clients and people who knew them or who had taken programs with them before (this is a great way to enroll for a group, but it's unlikely you'll always fill it up this way). To fill these final spaces they are reaching out to people they know and whom they haven't cultivated fully. They're slowing down and thinking of people who could be a great fit for their group. Conversations, cultivating and *asking* are all required.

New coaches are sometimes appalled at the level of inviting required to fill their calendar with conversations. One conversation a week is not going to cut it. Nor will two conversations. That won't lead to a decent income or a full practice (or even a solid part-time one). Seasoned coaches sometimes fall asleep to what it takes to grow another level of their business.

The thing is, if you have a full practice now, it will get quiet again. That's simply what happens. Our business has ebbs and flows. We

Having clients is wonderful. Creating clients is everything. And you do it by inviting people into conversation and serving them.

sign people, work with them for six months, a year or two or three (sometimes longer)—and then they complete. We find a space in our calendar, and we need to invite again.

This isn't "bad news"; it's just news. It is news you need to pay attention to. It's part of our job or, if you prefer, it's the art of enrollment. It's the fascinating, important work of connecting, of slowing down, of nurturing relationships, one by one.

And it can be the best part. The initial connection, the discovery of who the person is, starting to make a difference in their world, serving them. The opportunity is there to do this again and again, with new people, building your community one person at a time. It's thrilling—if you let it be thrilling. It's not an overnight process. Communities are not built in a day, with one email or post. They are built one relationship at a time, one intimate connection at a time, serving, creating value, assisting people.

Having clients is wonderful.

Creating clients is everything. And how do you do it?

By inviting them into conversation. By serving.

But you've got to ask first.

The truth is that you aren't a great coach until you can create clients. And I mean create from scratch, not from a referral.

You might argue with me about this.

"But Carolyn, I'm a really good coach! I'm a USM graduate. I've taken Landmark, Byron Katie, Three Principles workshops and more. I'm CERTIFIED!"

I once had a person coming out of a highly successful corporate career who was moving into professional coaching and starting to invite. I walked her through the process, assisting her in looking at her world and who she'd love to serve. She connected with and invited three people, two of whom didn't respond and the other who did.

She emailed me, "I didn't think it would be like this, people not responding, and it would take this, me reaching out."

I wrote back, "What did you think it would be like?"

"I thought people would come to me—that they'd want me."

This was a huge wake-up call. Many coaches are sorely underprepared/underinformed for the realities of growing a coaching business. It requires us to ask.

I repeat: you are a successful coach when you're able to consistently create clients from nothing. Until you can do this you won't experience your depth and greatness as a coach. Why? Because there are unique muscles built in the process of creating clients from nothing. There's a muscle that's strengthened by patience and learning how to relate to and connect with people wherever they are. There's one muscle built up through creativity, through knowing that what might serve one person might not serve another. There's another muscle formed by generosity, by giving with no "get" attached.

Start building these muscles consistently. And most importantly: *ask!*

Great coaches know how to get into conversation and build a connection from the tiniest of sparks. Learning to do this is the path to greatness, mastery, and deeper coaching.

21

Groups
Creating, Filling, Delivering and More

One of the most wonderful things about this profession is you can do it so many different ways and you can offer so many different things. Here are just a few:

- Individual coaching
- Groups, large and small
- Weekend workshops
- One-day intensives for individuals or groups
- Retreats for individuals or groups

Many coaches I know want to incorporate group work into their practice but are not sure how to go about it. It's a very different experience—working with a group versus an individual—and it requires a different skillset as a coach, one that addresses the dynamics of creating a container where multiple people can experience transformation. You do not *need* to do groups to be a successful coach. And at the same time it can be fun and exciting to expand into this kind of work. It also offers a different financial structure from one-on-one sessions and can lead to growth in both these areas of your business.

Enrollment of Groups—What's My Cred?

My first experience in group enrollment was in my position as Admissions Director at the University of Santa Monica. My job was to enroll 255 highly qualified students into the graduate program in Spiritual Psychology every year. That's a *really* big group to fill, and at first I was new to enrollment and all the nuances it involved. Of course, this wasn't my program in the same way it is when we as coaches create and fill our own groups. However, I was a graduate of the Master's in Spiritual Psychology program. I had deep, personal experience of its tremendous value, and I was deeply committed to the University's work. And it was my job to fill it with the right people. To say I was enthusiastic is an understatement, given how much it had changed my life.

The secret weapon that changed everything for me in learning how to enroll that large group was Steve Chandler, whom the university hired to coach the admissions team—me, the Assistant Director and the Marketing Director.

Under the tutelage and coaching of Steve in my position at USM, I learned an immense amount of what there is to know about enrollment (and specifically large-group enrollment) and what it means to truly serve people. One result is that I am the only Admissions Director at the University to ever fill the class with 255 students *and* create a waiting list.

After I left the University to move into full-time professional coaching, the first groups I created, facilitated and filled were with my business partner and best friend, Michelle Bauman. We started with a four-month group called, "Self-Mastery for Women: Creating an Inspiring Life." We learned in real time the art of filling coaching groups. We created this group and then developed others.

Did we know what we were doing?

No. And yes, sort of.

We were both graduates of USM. We'd watched some of the best facilitators create an environment of safety, openness and learning. So we had a reference point, and at the same time this didn't mean we knew what we were doing. What we *did* know was that we wanted to do a group for women and that we had something to offer. We spent five years creating and filling different groups together before Michelle became too ill to keep going.

What to Do—and Not

That was a formative time, and since then I've created many groups, as well as the CFJ Coaching Success School. Here's some of what I've learned along the way.

1. **You don't need to work out the content / curriculum of the group first.**

   You read that correctly. If you take nothing else from this

chapter, remember this: you do *not* need to figure out/develop/map out/draft/create your curriculum/content as the first step. Michelle and I didn't develop the content for the first day of our group until the group was full. This is actually what made the difference between us filling the group versus having great content with no one to experience it.

Instead, the first things you want to determine are:

- What is the promise of the group? What will occur for people through their participation?
- What is the theme of the group?
- What's the length of the group (three months, eight weeks, six months, or . . .)?
- How many people do you want in the group?
- What do you want to charge?
- What does the group include? How many live meetings, group calls, individual coaching calls (if any)? Will you be available to the group by email? Are participants required to submit reports during the group? Will you partner people up for calls when the group isn't in session? Will you have a private Facebook page?

These are the kinds of things you want to spend time determining. Now, you don't want to spend *six months* thinking about this, agonizing about creating the "right" group. Nobody gets served when we stay in our head! My groups with Michelle were really, really good—and we didn't wait for them to be perfect to start creating them.

After you've taken these initial steps, write a one-page document on the group that can become a landing page or something you can send out as a PDF. This could be a paragraph on the theme and what people can aim to take away from the group. It can contain the fee, the dates and any other pertinent information. You want it all to be well-written and clear. If you were a possible enrollee, would reading it make you want to know more?

2.   Who do you want in your group?

Make a list of the top ten, twenty or thirty people you'd love to have in your group. (If you know fewer than ten people, it's probably too early to do a group. Consider building up your community more first.) Then invite these people into conversation.

3.   How long should you give yourself to fill the group?

You want to give yourself a minimum of three months to fill the group. As a reference, we spent eleven months filling USM's graduate program with 255 people. This was a university with a track record. Some of the interest in our program was generated by referrals. Nonetheless, we took eleven months, and we were a team of two people working steadily. Michelle and I spent a full three months filling our coaching groups for women, and we limited these to only ten participants. These days I spend between six to nine months filling the CFJ Coaching Success School with fifty coaches.

What this means is that you want to give yourself time and

space to enroll. And not just for yourself. Your potential enrollees are going to need some time to consider if your group is for them in terms of interest, cost, scheduling and so on. Just as with enrolling one-on-one clients, this isn't a process to rush.

We coaches can be notorious under-estimators of how much time it will take to fill our groups. Even if your group fee is low—as in less than $1k—it will likely still take more time and more conversations than you can possibly imagine. The fee for my first group with Michelle was $500. We wanted it to be easy for people to say yes, and it still took three months.

A good rule of thumb for filling the group is to take the number of participants you're limiting the group to and triple or quadruple this. That's right: if you are limiting the group to ten participants, assume you'll be sending out thirty to forty invitations and having that many conversations in order to fill the group. (P.S., I suggest advertising the group as "limited to ten participants," and not to a looser "ten to twelve participants" or something even more vague. This is because limitation creates value—events and such don't fill as readily when it's "up to 100 people." Be more specific, so people understand that registering *now* matters.)

4. **What should the enrollment conversations be like?**

Just like your one-on-one enrollment conversations, you want group enrollment conversations to provide tons of value—so much so that the person says to themselves, "Wow—that was amazing. I want to talk to them again." Be in that space where you're serving the person across from you no matter what. With that in mind:

Groups

- Be centered on the person, not the group. This call is about the person and what's going on in their lives. You'll slowly weave in details about the group, but first and foremost, this conversation is about *them*. Get into their world and start serving them with whatever's going on.

- Ideally these calls will be sixty to ninety minutes long—lean on the longer side. If your group's fee is above $3k or if you are new to filling groups, plan on having two conversations. No rushing! You want to be able to articulate the promise of the group in the context of their lives. If I'm talking to someone and they're sharing about a leadership issue in their work, I'm going to say something like, "We're going to be doing a deep dive about this leadership opportunity. You'd get a lot of time to work on that in the group." Now—I'm in integrity here; I fully intend for the group to deliver on this. (If the group isn't going to be a good fit for this, I'll say so.) And I'm still serving them right now; I'm not waiting for them to say yes to the group.

- Don't get into logistics until the person starts to ask. And if they ask at the beginning, say something like, "Let's do this: we can talk about the logistics towards the end of our call if it seems like the group makes sense for you. Because it might not." The reason I approach it this way is because I don't want someone deciding based on logistics: "I can't do it because I have to pick up my kid on Wednesdays." I want to demonstrate value first, and then we can talk about the logistics. Once they experience the value, they are more likely to see ways to incorporate the group into their schedule.

- Be curious about what made them willing to have a call about the group. This provides information on what's going on in their lives. I don't consider this person as a real, viable option until they start to emerge as one on the call(s). I don't start from a mindset of "This person is going to LOVE this so much; I know they are going to do it!" I'm in service and curious to discover for them and myself if this group will be a good fit for them.

And then? Rinse and repeat. Keep inviting. Keep having conversations, over and over, until your group is FULL. Keep your enthusiasm and inspiration high!

5. **Focus on the group.**

In my experience, when you're enrolling for a group, you want that process to be the main focus of your work. Talking to potential clients about your individual practice while you are filling your group is counterproductive, but coaches occasionally do this because they get scared, and because they don't have the cash flow to sustain them while filling a group. (If you do not have the cash flow to sustain yourself while filling a group, don't start a group.) When we start talking to and creating potential individual clients while we are also attempting to fill our group, it's almost certain that group will not fill. This is a competing intention. If you're filling a group, make it your top priority. The idea of both working on getting an individual client while filling a group can be seductive. It might seem like your group won't be harmed by your enrolling an individual client here and there as you are filling your group. Let me share: IT WILL BE. Anytime Michelle or I paused in our focus on 100 percent dedication to filling the group, we made the potential of filling the group less possible. And guess what? It's a painful learning experience. It's not fun to see that your group didn't fill because of YOU and your own self-interest in getting an individual client. It's like multitasking; that's not real—no one can really multitask. Same with enrolling: we want a single, relentless focus on what we say we want. I want my group to fill, and my every waking minute needs to reflect this—over and over until it's FULL.

6.   Creating content

Congratulations—YOU DID IT! Your group is filled. And *now* you can start working on content. The guideline I give coaches is "no working on content until your group is full OR two weeks before the launch date." Seem counterintuitive? Perhaps. But consider where you are now. In the process of filling your group you've acquired a greater understanding of your audience and what will serve them most. You will therefore be able to meet them where they are. For example, as you're filling your group for women in leadership roles, you may have learned that almost everyone wants to discuss communication with upper management. *Before* you filled your group that was one possibility out of a hundred that you'd considered. Now you know how important it is to discuss. You know your audience.

In fact, I highly recommend that you create your content

as you deliver the group. Meaning, if there are five live days with your group, only create content for the first day, then deliver it, then create day two. You are going to learn a lot from day one. Especially if it's your first time offering this group. Take your time and create day two after the experience of day one! And so on. This will make the group better, and you will customize the content of the group based on what the participants are bringing forward.

This doesn't mean that you won't have basic ideas or themes worked out for each day or call. It simply means you don't want to create tightly scheduled days early on. Be flexible and responsive to the needs of the people in the group. Serve and address those needs, not a generic group agenda.

Coaching

Last but not least, two more (obvious) thoughts. The first is that I'm sharing what's worked for me and many of the coaches I work with, and as you create your own groups you'll no doubt find your own nuanced ways of doing things. Go for it! And second, get coaching on filling your group! Don't do it without coaching. Make sure the coach who helps you has filled their own groups successfully, and that they have coached other coaches in to filling *their* groups successfully.

22

The Burrito Guideline

Converting Social Relationships into Professional Ones

Andy Petranek is a fantastic, very successful coach with whom I have worked in a variety of ways. I've coached him directly for more than six years; he did the University of Santa Monica (USM) Soul-Centered Professional Coaching Program I led with Steve Chandler, and he participated in the CFJ Coaching Success School for two years. After that, he was part of small groups for coaches I led with Devon Bandison and, most recently, Steve Chandler.

A former marine and gym owner, Andy was an early adopter of CrossFit, running one of the most successful CrossFit gyms in the U.S., here in Los Angeles. This is where I met him, and I liked him immediately, despite him saying that he wasn't sure how I'd do in CrossFit (I proved him VERY wrong—I was slow and not the strongest weightlifter and so on, yet I have a very strong show-up muscle).

CLIENT CREATION

Andy is a gifted coach because he's curious, deeply compassionate, and willing to be real with people about the ways they are holding themselves back. He's a true lifelong learner: Landmark, men's groups, meditation work, strategic coaching—you name it. Andy takes his personal growth and development very sincerely. You might think that as a former marine, he'd be very gruff and tough on people—if so, you couldn't be further from the truth. He has a huge heart, and in fact we've joked that he could position himself as "The Crying Coach" because he's moved to tears regularly.

So why am I telling you all of this?

Because: burritos.

Let me explain.

Andy has developed significant mastery in the art of connecting—that is, in reaching out and creating conversations, the kinds of conversations that come *before* a potential enrollment conversation (to understand more of what I mean, you can refer to Handout 5: Connecting, which we use in the school and which I've included in the back of the book).

At one point Andy was connecting with a fellow dad he's known for some time, someone from their kids' school communities. They were exchanging emails and Andy asked how the person was doing. He received a long response in which the dad said he was "doing okay"—and in which Andy also saw embedded a few key things, such as:

- He wanted more connection with his family.
- He was feeling a lack of purpose and a sense that "life sucked."

The Burrito Guideline

- He felt like he was drowning.

At the end of the email, the dad wrote: "It would be great to talk. Maybe we can get together over a breakfast burrito?"

Andy brought this email exchange to his next coaching session with me. He had a sense of what was needed, because he's not a new coach, and he wanted to confirm that what he saw was what I saw. Namely: this dad gave clear indications that there was a deeper conversation to be had, and that deeper conversation could *not* occur over breakfast burritos (as fantastic as breakfast burritos are).

Your accountant doesn't meet you for breakfast burritos when they need to tell you that you owe a lot of money to the IRS. Nor does your kid's teacher say, "Let's connect at Starbucks" to tell you that your kid is failing geometry. Your dentist doesn't meet you for cupcakes to share that you have gingivitis.

They meet you at *their* place of work. When there's something important to talk about, they know this isn't the time for hot sauce and guac or a gingerbread latte or a double-chocolate chip, gluten-free cupcake. They know this conversation needs to take place in a professional setting, one where they can lead.

Andy and I confirmed this—and then Andy replied to his email.

> I appreciate you, brother. Thank you for sharing all that you did in your email. There is A LOT here.
>
> Consider this for a moment . . .
>
> You could say that a good king of a kingdom ensures that all of his subjects are well fed, secure, taken care of, and feel

CLIENT CREATION

like they are making a contribution to the wellbeing of the kingdom. A thriving kingdom INCLUDES a thriving king.

If a thriving kingdom comes at the expense of the King, it's not really thriving, and whatever evidence of it doing well . . . it won't last for long. The king is a key component to the vitality of the kingdom. His needs MUST be fulfilled. He must eat well... and FIRST. His vision, leadership, actions, and wisdom depend on it. He must be connected to his lover, magician, and warrior. And he must take the time to satisfy HIS needs. The subjects of his kingdom can't really thrive without him thriving too.

You are the king of your household and family. If you are suffering, drowning, hurting . . . even if you don't pause long enough to really be with that . . . and even if it appears that you're "handling things for everyone else" and doing the best you can . . . the kingdom is sick and suffering. Your kids need YOU to thrive. It's very clear from your words that you're not.

I will most certainly make time for you, but this is definitely NOT a "burrito conversation."

When you're ready, I will block out 2 hours for you. You can come down to my house/office, where I see clients, and we will unpack as much of this as we can.

There are no strings attached to this. I don't have any expectations for anything beyond these two hours.

Let me know when you're ready and we'll schedule the time.

ap

The Burrito Guideline

I'm sharing the email with you (with Andy's permission) so that you can see what's possible in a response. Note, too, that my email responses aren't exactly the same as this, because I'm not Andy. Andy has found his voice and cultivated professional self-confidence as a coach after three to five years of doubting himself and his abilities. In other words, he's done the work. You can do the same, and you will also find your own voice.

The dad wrote back, thrilled that Andy was willing to give him so much time in a professional setting. There was a time when Andy's next question to me would have been, "What am I going to do with someone for *two hours?*" Now he knows what to do.

There's nuance to converting a personal/social relationship into a professional coaching relationship. It takes learning, serving, and practice to know when it's time to take a risk in the relationship and move it into a professional conversation. For example, if Andy hadn't had a relationship of a few years with this person—as a fellow parent—he might not have written so much or suggested the possibility that this person wasn't taking care of themselves. If he'd just met this person, he might have gone slower before writing back in this way. And knowing when it's time to do this, when it's okay to be more direct, when it's important to slow down and build rapport—this is all part of the learning and development of a professional coach.

You can learn to do this. And whatever happens, remember the burrito guideline.

23

Well-Paid Babysitter or Professional Coach?

Are you Mary Poppins?

You might not see yourself as a well-paid babysitter, yet that might be what you are. Mary Poppins may creep in at different times, and for some, Mary Poppins coaching is their main way of operating.

What I mean by this is some coaches play the game of "keeping clients" versus profoundly serving them. It can sneak up on us when our bank account is lower than we prefer or when we simply like keeping things in the "easy money" category. Most of the time, the coaches who are babysitting have a blind spot around this. In other cases you might not want to make your client "feel bad" for fear of losing them—and this gets in the way of you challenging them for their own growth.

Sometimes it happens through role reversal. Maybe the client is a high-level person with a big title—CEO, Owner,

Well-Paid Babysitter or Professional Coach?

Director . . . As their coach, you're thrilled to be serving someone at their level. You might even be nervous about doing a "good job," which might translate to unconsciously trying to please the person. Maybe you're mired in politeness and are too deferential even when it's not serving anyone. You might be concerned about your client getting upset with you.

Another way babysitting versus *difference-making* can show up is when we like someone. When we really like a client and can imagine being friends with them, we can unconsciously go softer on them and maybe not ask tough questions. Or we might ever so slightly justify a client's behavior to them or ourselves, like: "Well, they've got so much going on. Now isn't the right time to ask them about their lack of responsiveness or the way they judge their husband."

And there are coaches out there who would rather create a long contract and do the bare minimum. For example, there is "survival" coaching with a team. This is attempting to get a team to the next level of ownership, versus sitting down with the leader and sharing that the team is deeply unmotivated, along with letting the leader know that the team doesn't respond well to middle of the night emails that are filled with rants and upset. The team is not producing at the level they could be because the leader isn't showing up in the way the team needs her to . . . and you, as the coach, aren't being fully honest with the leader.

If any of this sounds familiar, it doesn't mean you're a bad person or a bad coach (although it tends to result in less effective coaching).

What it does mean is that you are more focused on comfort (yours and your client's), prestige, and good feelings than you are on the power and purpose of the coaching profession—namely, to make meaningful, often radical and almost always uncomfortable differences in your clients' lives.

Here are signs you might be babysitting instead of powerfully coaching:

1. You consistently do not challenge your client around behaviors, actions, and ways of being that you know are not serving them. You might be aware of lateness; unkindness and toxic behavior with employees, colleagues, and loved ones; unanswered communications; addictions (shopping, sex, screen time, alcohol); extreme debt; risky health choices; unaddressed health challenges; and much, much more. You know what your job is in these situations. You know you could support your client through transformation in these areas—even though it might be uncomfortable for both of you—but you resist doing it.

2. Friendship "plus" is occurring; each session has ample "chat" time. You're not requiring the client to bring a clear agenda, and there isn't consistent depth in the coaching. You're not sure what you got accomplished in a session, but you suspect it wasn't as powerful as it could have been.

3. The client has renewed one, two, three times and there still isn't any meaningful conversation from you about taking the coaching to the next level. Each new agreement essentially brings about more of the same.

Well-Paid Babysitter or Professional Coach?

4. When (uncomfortable) thoughts float through your mind about the quality of the coaching, you push them away, perhaps justifying why you aren't supporting the client the way you could using some of the reasons discussed above—for example, money, nervousness, wanting to be liked.

5. The client tends to lead the process in subtle and not-so-subtle ways. Maybe they tell you they don't want to talk about whatever you're bringing up, and you follow their lead without any conversation or an agreement to discuss the matter at a later time. Maybe, too, you can energetically *feel* them wanting you to agree with their stories/judgments/POV, and you give into this rather than gently (or otherwise) pushing back and helping them see new perspectives and possibilities.

When was the last time your client was uncomfortable in a coaching session with you? When did you last ask potentially confronting questions? Has your client ever gotten mad at you? That can be a sure sign you are stretching them.

If you're babysitting a client (or three) in your practice, there's no judgment. It can happen, especially if you yourself aren't getting coached in an intimate, rigorous way, and especially if you are struggling financially. What's important is that

Are you more focused on comfort and good feelings than you are on making a meaningful, often radical and almost always uncomfortable difference in your clients' lives?

you handle it. Not only because your client deserves it, but because the entire profession deserves it. We want the bar to be high, and we want the results that all of our clients experience to be deep, meaningful, and transformational.

We may be the only person in someone's life who can say what no one else is willing to in our role as a coach. We may be the only person in someone's life who has no agenda. Staying in the game of making a meaningful difference requires rigorous self-examination and openness to having someone else look at your coaching with you (as in, your own coach). So I invite you to slow down and ask yourself:

"Am I a transformational coach? Or am I Mary Poppins using too many spoonfuls of sugar?"

24

Situationships

Do you know the Taylor Swift song "Cruel Summer"? My teenage daughter is a true Swiftie, and she's made me an admirer too. We shelled out for tickets to her impressive *three-hour* show and her music has been at the top of my daughter's playlist forever.

So when we were listening to "Cruel Summer" I was trying to make sense of the lyrics, of what exactly was going wrong in the relationship she was singing about. I asked my daughter to explain them to me.

She said, "Well, they're in a situationship, and—"

"Wait," I said. "What's a 'situationship'?"

"That's when you're hanging out together, maybe kissing and stuff, and it's not defined. Nobody else knows. You might not want anyone else to know you're hanging out. It's not clear to you or the other person what you're doing exactly."

"Hmm . . ." I said. "I might need to steal that. Okay, go on . . ."

CLIENT CREATION

She educated me on the meaning of the rest of the lyrics, but what's important for us in this chapter is that new word: situationship. The reason it stuck out in my mind is because it's something we as coaches can easily fall into if we're not intentional about creating professional—paid—coaching relationships. Here are the signs you're creating situationships:

- The potential client does not have context for the conversations that are occurring.
- You are allowing conversations to keep going, and going, and going. That is, lots of "hanging out" and coaching without an end in sight. The potential client might be thinking, "Maybe this will go on like, forever, with no commitment."
- You are behaving friend-ish, meaning lots of social-self kinds of language in your emails and texts. "Hey girl, I feel you" or "Hey bud, how ya doing?"
- You keep not being paid.

Keep in mind that singing in angst or crying like Taylor is *not* a requirement to get situationships out of your coaching enrollment system. Here instead are four steps to undo situationships:

1. **Create context.** What does this mean? Start to frame the conversation in clear terms. Here's one good way to do that: "Today we are going to have a coaching conversation. It's different from the 'regular' conversations we have day to day. It's designed to have

you do two things: get altitude on your life and zoom in on the inside of your life—your thoughts, beliefs, and more."

2. **Be clear inside yourself on your limit for enrollment conversations.** Maybe it's two conversations if you've been doing this a while (more than two years) *and your practice is full.* Maybe it's three or four if your fees are high ($15-20k or more) and you really want to vet and demonstrate value (meaning, make the conversations so deep and impactful that they can't *not* continue). Then, communicate clearly to your prospect when it's the last conversation. A simple, "This will be our last conversation—let's make it as powerful as possible," will do.

3. **Professionalize yourself, your language, your way of being.** You don't need to be like a banker in a suit, *and* you do need to really slow down and get your communications cleaned up. If I read your texts or emails to prospective clients, would I know for sure that you are a professional coach and not an overly accommodating friend? Take a look at your last three emails to prospective clients and ask yourself, "Is it clear that I'm a professional coach?"

4. **Don't let what you do be a "secret."** Remember what my daughter said? Part of situationships is that nobody else knows you're in one. Too many coaches keep their profession secret. I don't mean that you should center yourself in conversations, as in it's all about, "I do this, I

serve these clients, I, I, I." I simply mean you can stand proud and share that you are a professional life coach, leadership coach, relationship coach, nutrition coach—whatever you are, *say it.* Share.

This is a dignified, important profession that more and more people are joining every day. You want people to know that you are part of this great profession.

What you don't want is to be creating and allowing coaching situationships.

25

We Are Never Ever Getting Back Together

Clients Who Disappear

Somewhere within the first five years of my practice I enrolled a fantastic client, someone I was really excited to serve. Then, before our second session, I received a whispered voicemail; it sounded like she was calling from a small cave, far, far away. In it she shared that she wasn't going to be able to continue with her coaching. There was no request for a refund, and she didn't offer any reason as to why she was discontinuing.

It drove me crazy for weeks. I called, left voicemails and sent emails. Nothing. No response. I was really bothered. What had happened?

And as I say, I really wanted to serve her—this was not a "Yay! I just made money with no work!" That's not how I roll.

I reached out to my coach, Steve Chandler, and asked,

CLIENT CREATION

"What do I do?"

"What can you do?" he said. "You've already called and emailed her. You've literally done everything you can. You can't make her respond."

He was right, *and* I still wanted to make her respond, to make it "right," to understand . . . Steve and I ran game film on my enrollment process, and what we came up with was there may have been an opportunity to spend more time with her, upfront. Get to know her better. Go slower. Would it have changed the outcome? Maybe, maybe not. Sometimes people are squirrely. Things happen.

This occurred a few (painful) times early on in my practice. Broken agreements and ghosting. When it happened, I judged and berated myself. I was angry. I felt like an idiot. I felt betrayed. I judged the client as self-centered. The client ignored my communications.

Luckily, my coach was there. He helped me see the value of clear agreements and showed me how to create them with a new client. He shared that moments like these are to be used for learning and to become more effective at enrolling and setting up agreements. We don't need fresh, new reasons to judge ourselves or others.

A little while ago it happened again.

One of my clients completely went away. Not on a vacation or a trip. They went away from their coaching. We'd hit the pause button for two months and had a clear agreement about when they'd be starting back up. Then, without explanation, *poof!* Gone into thin air.

This time I was able to look at what had occurred with

We Are Never Ever Getting Back Together

neutrality to see where I had created, promoted, or allowed it to happen.

And do you know what I discovered? It wasn't anything I did. Sometimes, people break agreements. And then they ghost you. And then they ghost you again. And then, maybe, they eventually respond, with no acknowledgment of the prior agreement or the ghosting. And if they do respond, it's often like they are on a different planet than the one where the original communications occurred. They are in a different place, onto something new. And from this?

There's no getting back together . . .

Like, EVER.

Life is like that sometimes.

The coaching business is like that sometimes.

Sometimes no matter what we do, a client situation gets wonky.

Sometimes people don't respond, even if we've served them well and had everything in place to create a strong container.

I share all this so that you know that nothing is foolproof in this profession. Even highly seasoned, successful coaches have stuff show up. The differences are (hopefully) that we relate to ourselves and the situation with greater ease and neutrality, and that these things occur very rarely later in your career versus at the beginning, before we've developed real business policies.

The takeaway is simply that sometimes humans don't conduct their communications at the highest levels. We can't control every single situation or predict how something will go, even if we've dotted all our i's and crossed all our t's.

And . . . at the same time, what you *can* do is make sure your policies and enrollment processes are airtight—so that when something occurs, you can know that you did everything you could. This takes practice. And along the way there are still learnings to be had.

Sometimes people don't conduct their communications at the highest levels. We can't control every part of the process, even when we've dotted all our i's and crossed all our t's.

In those early days when I was ghosted, what would have taken the sting out of it was knowing that I hadn't made any mistakes. The truth is, though, I *had* made some mistakes. What I learned from them, among other things, is that clear, upfront agreements between you and your clients make a big difference.

To that end, I'm including a sample agreement in the back of this book. I share it in my school, and you are welcome to mine it for ideas for your own agreements.

Note that these are not contracts; I'm not in favor of "contracts" unless you are doing coaching inside of a large corporation (they usually require it). The agreements here are reviewed after someone has paid, not before. We aren't trying to scare people with "contract" language. We want agreements. (Steve Chandler doesn't even send out written agreements to me or any client. He goes over agreements verbally, and that's it. His word is his agreement, as is the client's.)

So you will likely at some point find yourself in a situation with a client that hits you like a ton of bricks and you will think of the Taylor Swift song: "We are never ever getting back together." Yet the longer you stay in this business, the more you'll get in the flow of creating agreements that support you, your client and the coaching process—and which will serve to keep the professional relationship on an even keel. It also helps to come into acceptance around the truth that sometimes people are going to behave in ways we don't understand or like. Sometimes it's got nothing to do with us. It's simply part of maturing as a professional coach (and as a human being).

Serving Clients as a Professional Coach

26

Loneliness Is the New Pandemic

The Park-Bench Method of Connection

Recently, Steve Chandler and I were serving a large group of coaches when he commented that loneliness is the new pandemic, and coaching is the antidote. He's not alone in this observation. Loneliness is a global issue. In the U.S. the surgeon general issued a report, "Our Epidemic of Loneliness and Isolation."[4] In it, loneliness is compared to tobacco, obesity and addiction in terms of the harms it can cause. "Loneliness is far more than just a bad feeling," the report says. And unless we take serious steps to address it, "we will further retreat to our corners—angry, sick, and alone."

That's not overstating it. I wholeheartedly agree.

---

[4] Our epidemic of loneliness and isolation. (n.d.). https://www.hhs.gov/sites/default/files/surgeon-general-social-connection-advisory.pdf

SERVING CLIENTS

In Britain, they have created a formal position—a Minister of Loneliness—whose primary job is to create public awareness around the epidemic of loneliness and the new programs the government has created to address it. One of the solutions offered by the UK, Sweden, and Australia is actual park benches. The "chatty bench" is a park bench with a sign encouraging strangers sitting there to chat with each other. In a Northern Ireland town, the sign says: "Sit here if you are happy to chat with passers-by."

When Michelle and I used to do our complimentary events for women twice a year, more than fifty women would crowd into Michelle's family room. One day it was excruciatingly hot (Michelle lived in the valley in Southern California) and the air conditioning broke down before we started. Not one woman left our four-hour workshop, and it was easily upwards of 90 degrees in Michelle's house. This was way before the pandemic, and way before loneliness was at an all-time high around the world. When I look back at those events, I see that loneliness played a part in why people attended.

Michelle would say to me, "You know there are women who will never sign up for any paid offering we'd do. These events are important because some women come for the connection and community."

We are the Park Benches

Steve and I were recently asked a question by a coach:

"How do I connect and communicate with people that

Loneliness Is the New Pandemic

I'm a coach? Do I just start a conversation and slip it in at the right moment?"

Steve responded:

"When you are sitting on a park bench with someone, you aren't thinking about how to 'slip in' that you're a coach. You're just being with the person. There's no 'slipping in' anything. It's connecting and listening. This is a slow, relationship-building business that's intimate, not rushed—and when we are sitting on a park bench, we aren't rushing, right?"

As professional coaches, we are uniquely qualified to be the antidote to the epidemic of loneliness. Each of you, and all of us together, function as park benches for people—places where people can go to talk, to not be alone in their lives, to experience connection and community.

A paper by Ter Kuile and Angie Thurston called "How We Gather" shares that there's a general move away from organized religion. Secular organizations are creating deep bonds in ways they describe as "powerful, surprising, and perhaps even religious."[5] It's a worthwhile paper for professional coaches to read for a number of reasons—the paper speaks to the blind spots that are showing up in these created communities and what we want to watch out for, and it also speaks to the deep and positive experiences that are occurring for people who partake in these

---

[5] Kuile, T., & Thurston, A. (n.d.). *How We Gather*. sacred.design. https://sacred.design/wp-content/uploads/2019/10/How_We_Gather_Digital_4.11.17.pdf

different spaces.

These secular organizations, they explain, epitomize a combination of six qualities:

- community
- personal transformation
- social transformation
- purpose finding
- creativity and accountability

Sound familiar? It's what we, as coaches, do—we create groups, retreats, events, intensives, masterminds, courses (and more) that create these six qualities for people. For example, coach Tarita Preston is actively creating a Professional Women of Color community. Coach Amber Shirley has The Created Life, an inspiring community of entrepreneurs who serve powerfully from a place of love. Hundreds of coaches who have been through the CFJ Coaching Success School are creating communities—for women over fifty, for conscious fathers, for women who are childless by choice, for leaders, and more. You too are likely in the midst of building—or at least have a vision for—the community you'd like to create.

Steve Chandler is 100 percent accurate—coaching IS the antidote to the epidemic of loneliness. I invite you to take that in and use it as inspiration to become even more certain of the value of this great profession.

Remember Yourself

I'll leave you with something I learned at the University of Santa Monica. This is one of my guiding principles in life: Take care of yourself so you can help take care of others.

In this context, that means: don't allow loneliness to creep into your life as a professional coach, because it diminishes your ability to serve others. We can't assist humanity at large in creating intimacy and connection if we aren't doing it for ourselves, not to mention the fact that coaches tend to make more money when they are in community with other like-minded, like-hearted coaches.

I've written elsewhere in this book about the loneliness of entrepreneurship in general. In my experience, coaches tell me that they are alone a lot. While some thrive in aloneness, a majority share with me that if they aren't creating community in their lives, they gradually begin to feel the impact of their self-imposed isolation, and of having no place to be with other coaches to talk about their experiences in the profession, the joys and the challenges. As a consequence they can at times feel less inspired and enthusiastic about carving out their place in this

Don't allow loneliness to creep into your life as a professional coach, because it diminishes your ability to serve others. We can't assist humanity at large in creating intimacy and connection if we aren't doing it for ourselves.

SERVING CLIENTS

professional life.

If you fall into this category, I invite you to address it sooner rather than later. I'm here for you and for all of us in this great profession. We are a powerful and important community that makes a valuable contribution—never forget this! In no small way, we can help change the world.

27

Outrageous Acts of Service

The Universe requires action, not thought.

Are you challenged right now? Depressed? Anxious? Worried about your business or your own life? Is there a question lurking for you in a specific enrollment situation with a prospective client—an individual or an organization? Are you contemplating different things you *could* do, over and over?

If so, remember this: the Universe requires action, not thought. Action is what this business is about—specifically the action of serving others. In fact, my suggestion is that you try on *outrageous acts of service* for size. Not as a way to get a new client or impress a current one (though that might happen). Instead, do it without attachment to the outcome. Do it because serving is what we do as professional coaches.

As Steve Chandler says, "You can't out-serve the universe." So serve—do something outrageous for a client or prospective client today. You can even add on something for your spouse, your kid, your barista . . . *anyone* in your life.

SERVING CLIENTS

Outrageous acts of service can be an antidote to despair, fatigue, or fear—not just for you, but for whomever you're serving. When my business partner and best friend, Michelle Bauman, was in her first breast cancer diagnosis she worried about money (not that she needed to, but that's another story). Our coach, Steve Chandler, said to her, "I'll make money for you. You don't need to be concerned."

And he meant it. That wasn't just a line to make Michelle feel better. I said it to Michelle, too, and it wasn't a line. Steve never needed to make money for Michelle—and he would have done it if necessary, no question. His word is gold. Michelle and I both knew he was serious. Whatever else Steve's promise was, it was most definitely a commitment to an outrageous act of service.

You don't have to pay someone's bills to offer outrageous service. You can also:

- Send a current client a video or a handwritten card acknowledging them.
- Gift a current client a one-time session with a singing teacher/art coach/writing coach—something that gets them moving on something they want to do. I have gifted clients sessions with art coaches and with some of the best coaches I know, and it has had a profound impact.
- Choose to meet a prospective client at the beach, park or local hiking trail and do an outdoor walking session.
- Send a client a signed copy of a book that you know they want or would love (part of the outrageous service could

Outrageous Aspects of Service

be getting it personally signed by the author!).

- Have something made for someone. It could be a drawing of something you know they love (there are artists on Etsy who do amazing art for a very low fee).

- Add a bonus session, or access to you in a way you don't normally give access to a client, when they are walking through something challenging OR something big and new. I had a client dealing with a very, very difficult business situation. I let them know that they could text me as needed for the next month (this was a very intense situation). We'd get on spot calls too—whatever was needed. We spoke almost every other day for at least two weeks, with different spot coaching based on what was unfolding, and texted daily for almost a month. The client utilized this access in important ways. The level of service they experienced was very high, and it's something they often refer to as a major reference point for who they want to be in the world.

- Show up at something your client is doing in the world that they have been working on with you: a talk they're giving, a show, whatever. Get on a plane if necessary.

Outrageous acts are meaningful on a personal level. They astonish and make a difference—and they don't need to be "big." They just need to be *meaningful*. Thought out. Individualized. Considered.

Here are two examples from my own life, one in which I was the recipient of outrageous service, and another where I was

SERVING CLIENTS

the giver.

When Michelle died, she and I had been poised to start a small group for coaches. We'd already enrolled the goal of ten coaches. This was set to be a six-month group, and each coach was paying $12,000. The group was due to begin one month after Michelle died. I was not in the best shape emotionally, and I was feeling unsure of myself in general. I brought all this to my coaching session with Steve, sharing my uncertainty, wondering if I should cancel the group and refund the money.

Steve didn't hesitate. "I'll lead the group with you," he said. "No fee. You won't pay me. I'll show up and lead it with you. I'll pay for my travel for the live meetings. My only request is that you handle all the email coaching."

"What?" I said. "Steve, that's kind of insane . . . you'd really do that?"

"Yes," he said, in his very dry, very deep voice. "I wouldn't say it if I didn't mean it."

There's a little backstory to this. About five months earlier, when Michelle was very sick, Steve and I had breakfast during one of the University of Santa Monica Soul-Centered Coaching Program weekends we were leading. At this time it was slowly dawning on me that Michelle could, in fact, die. This realization was not easy for me. Even with all my training in Spiritual Psychology and my commitment to leading a life where my context was that we are divine beings using a human experience for learning and growth, I was starting to freak out. So over breakfast I suddenly said to Steve, without thinking, "You have to promise me that if Michelle dies, you are going to help me. You are going to help me figure things out, Steve, or with whatever I need to do. *You have to promise*

Outrageous Aspects of Service

me you'll help me."

He looked at me and said, "I promise you."

Fast forward to me thinking about canceling the group. I was not, at that moment, remembering his earlier promise. All I heard was Steve saying he'd run the group with me. He didn't say, "Well I made you a promise, Carolyn. Come on, don't you remember?" The original promise itself was outrageous service. The act of leading the group with me was outrageous service.

And he delivered on this promise beyond leading the group with me—in words, in action, in his time and in his dedication to me and my work. Steve made good on his original promise and then some. He has continued to be outrageously dedicated to my success and my life being good, and I can't think of a better person for me to model my outrageous service on.

We can do this for people. Therapists can't do this, because there are regulatory laws and such preventing them from doing this. Coaches are uniquely positioned to serve outrageously.

The other act of outrageous service I'll share here, the one I was able to offer, grew out of a heap of trouble two of my clients were in. When I say "heap," I mean *heap*—the kind of trouble that no one wants to be in, trouble that is self-created and very, very messy (in this case, for their business). The trouble led to a temporary but significant loss of business, clients, some of their team, and trust with each other. It also came with a loss of their inner and outer compass in terms of how to proceed.

In response I took ideas like the "number of sessions in our program" off the table. It was an all-hands-on-deck situation—my hands, their hands, my own coach's hands as needed, and the hands of anyone else I had access to who could assist.

SERVING CLIENTS

There were lots of phone calls, texts, emails, extra sessions and more. It didn't matter how often they contacted me. I made that very clear. There was no "too much." This was a very emotionally difficult time for them individually and as partners, on top of a very difficult challenge of looking at how to course-correct in the business.

Getting the job done took a year, total. The most intense period of focus was packed into about two to three months. Our time was spent resetting, re-grouping, getting clean and honest on all levels, and bringing back the clients who had left.

You might be reading this and thinking, "Give service to people for *free*? Give them books? Even if they might not hire me? *That's* what's outrageous, Carolyn! And not in a good way."

A life dedicated to serving without expectation of something in return is not for the faint of heart. Initially, it might feel strange. You might find yourself wondering, "When am I going to get *mine*?" These thoughts are natural as you undo the conditioned thinking that there always must be an ROI.

Yet it's the most rewarding life—in business and in *all* of life. I used to think that people who gave their time in service to the University of Santa Monica were LOSERS. I remember thinking in my first year, "Those people in the back of the room must be losers. Giving their whole weekend away as volunteers?"

I wasn't very "Christ-like." I didn't have any personal or spiritual reference points for service. My father had done tremendous service as part of being in Alcoholics Anonymous, yet he didn't talk about it with me until much later in life, after I went to USM.

Even so, you don't need a spiritual reference point to serve

Outrageous Aspects of Service

outrageously. I invite you to run an experiment. See if three months of outrageous acts of service don't create more clients for you—not to mention the perhaps more valuable side effect of greater joy and peace inside yourself.

Start with small acts—give a book you love to your barista, even though you know they will never be your client. Send a handwritten card of acknowledgment to a prospective client, just because. Anonymously give your kid's teacher or their gymnastics coach a $15 gift card. Get your spouse's car washed or fill it full of gas without telling them. The options are endless . . .

And the payoff is greater than anything you can imagine.

SERVING CLIENTS

28

Do You Let Your Client Think?

Back in 2014 my business partner, Michelle Abend Bauman and I spent three years training with Nancy Kline in the Time to Think model. This practice requires a coach to be silent for almost the entire time they're coaching, with questions asked only when the client indicates they are done.

Done doing what?

Thinking.

Even the questions we ask when they're done are very specific, along the lines of, "What more would you like to say?" They are not the more probing questions we might ask as coaches, such as, "How did you feel about that?" And there's no advice giving either—no, "May I offer you a thought of my own?"

The Time to Think model is based on the idea that *listening done well is generative.* That is, if we give our client (or anyone) time to think, and we listen as they explore their thoughts (out loud or within themselves), the process leads to new insights and understandings for them.

Do You Let Your Client Think?

In her work, Nancy Kline asks a radical question: "How do you know that what you are about to say is *more important* than what your client is about to *think*?" The fact is, we don't. How could we? If I'm listening to a client process their feelings about a relationship that's gone south, and I remember my cousin had a relationship like that, and I chime in with a comment, whether it's insightful or not, I've just derailed my client's own line of thought in favor of my own. What if they were about to come up with their own powerful, self-generated insight?

Most people are not being listened to deeply, with no agenda, and with love and generosity, on a regular basis.

As Michelle acknowledged about herself and coaches in general, "We like the sound of our own voices." At the same time, we know that as coaches that's not what we're there for. The last thing we should be concerned with is what *we* say. It's all about the client.

But how can simply letting our clients think be of any real value? Let's look into this, because it's something that can transform your coaching practice and your clients.

Early on in our Nancy Kline training, Michelle and I decided we'd include her work in our practice with other coaches. While we never said (nor do I say this now), "This is how people should coach," there's great value in getting experience with it. As coaches, our ability to be silent and create a container where people can think and be in their own inner guidance is what clients are, in large part, paying for.

SERVING CLIENTS

Here's what Michelle wrote about this at the time:

> In our training with Nancy Kline this week, we are giving each other lots of time, space, and generative attention so each of us can think for ourselves. We are creating the ideal conditions for the mind to do its magic. And we have been dazzled by the depth of transformation and also the speed at which the mind can work—given the proper conditions.
>
> We are also noticing how much we've become a "think for" society. That is, we all tend to look towards others (counselors, coaches, teachers, friends, parents) to do our thinking for us. To at least give us a clue about what they think we should do. But, really, how challenging and exciting is it to take full responsibility for our own thinking?
>
> Very.
>
> What's more, I'm moved by the experience of knowing what another human being truly thinks. And rather than being bored or impatient, it leaves me wanting to know even more deeply the truest and most independent thoughts of those closest to me, especially my husband and my kids. After all, what an incredible expression of love to be authentically interested and fascinated by the thinking of those we care about. And what an experience of intimacy to be privy to another human's thinking.

For me personally, at first I found being listened to in this way uncomfortable. I'm wanting to "do a good job" with my

Do You Let Your Client Think?

thoughts. My own people-pleasing is present at the beginning. I'm often making jokes about my "messy thinking" and questioning the value of any thought or feeling I have.

Then I settle in. My beautiful mind relaxes, and I go to places I don't often go to independently. No matter what, I'm thrilled to discover that my mind and heart know where to take me. In the presence of loving, high-quality, generative listening, the transformation and healing occur. Every single time—no matter what. If I give myself the time to do the work in the presence of a Thinking Environment coach, it happens.

Today the Time to Think model is what I use in the CFJ Coaching School for peer coaching between monthly classes. Peer coaching this way is rigorous. There's no interrupting, because, as Nancy Kline says, "When we interrupt we are viciously slamming a door on people's thoughts."

For the coaches in the school, the method is often challenging at first. Then they fall in love with the process *and* their own thinking. They experience the freedom and learning that come from being both the thinker and the listener. We have had coaches in the school share that they talked and thought about things they had never shared with anyone. It wasn't something they planned; it's just that in the presence of this kind of listening they opened up.

One of the most important things I can share with you is something Nancy Kline said over and over: clients pay us for the quality of our listening. The Time to Think model trains coaches to improve their listening skills many times over. And most people are not being listened to deeply, with no agenda, and with love and generosity, on a regular basis.

SERVING CLIENTS

Don't underestimate the power of thinking, your own and others. Don't underestimate the power of listening, your own and others. Be willing to risk experimenting with listening even more and talking even less. Beautiful things will happen.

29

Learnings from a CEO's Email

A new CEO-client of mine recently forwarded me an email that they had sent to their team. They were wondering why they had received minimal to no response. Within moments of reading the email, it was clear. They had not made:

- any clear requests
- a timeline for response
- an acknowledgment of the team or articulation of why their participation in the project made a difference.

To make the email even less effective, they had used "social self" language, almost friend-like in nature, and the message lacked any kind of inspiration.

Every person you coach is communicating in their professional life. Leaders, managers, small and large business owners, executives, and more are involved in written communications throughout the day. From morning until

SERVING CLIENTS

evening, there are emails, Slack messages, texts, and so on. They are communicating quickly, almost always without slowing down. Words play a HUGE part in our daily lives, and it's obvious that the same message can be conveyed in more or less compelling, professional ways. You can make a request that gets inspired responses, or it can die on the vine, or something in between.

When coaching a professional of any kind, I request they share with me the last ten written communications they sent to their team, direct reports, clients, and their bosses/senior leaders. I also ask for the last ten responses they sent to communications they received *from* their team, direct reports, bosses, clients, and so on.

This yields immediate data about a person's leadership capabilities, communication skills, unconscious biases, and more. It also gives immediate insight into how effective they are at building relationships, creating connections, and handling nuanced situations.

We hear and see a lot in our client sessions. We can't see and hear everything, and this is why getting a snapshot of our client's communications is highly valuable. You'll see things that you never would otherwise. I've experienced people who—given how they showed up in our initial conversations and sessions—I assumed were good communicators, and . . .

NOPE.

Written communications are a critical component of any professional's work (yours too, of course). As a coach, your email and Slack flow may be far less than your clients'—in fact, some of you may rarely use email or communication methods

Learnings from a CEO's Email

We hear and see a lot in our client sessions, but we can't see and hear everything. So getting a snapshot of our client's email communications is highly valuable. It's rare for a leader to have someone review their emails solely to support them in increasing their communication skills. You can be that someone.

beyond text. Regardless, as their coach you still need to be thinking about *their* communications, because doing so is a fast track to creating an impact in their professional life. It's one of the best ways to uncover how your client is being received by the people they work with.

I have reviewed a wide range of clients' professional emails and thought, "The people receiving these must be so frustrated, confused, screaming . . ." Rarely do I imagine the recipients are delighted or inspired, or think, "Wow—this person is a total rock star at communicating." And I've been doing this for more than fifteen years.

So when I receive a client's emails, here's what I do:

- Highlight the challenging sections and sentences on my own. This includes sections that might be too social-sounding, and (*gasp*) ungrammatical or simply incorrect.

- We then do a deep-dive session together where we go through the emails, often breaking them down, sentence by sentence. What is the person *really* communicating when they make a request? If they were the recipient of that email, how would *they* feel? Inspired? Disappointed?

Confused? Ashamed?

- I ask them to reflect on what was going on for them when they were writing and whether that influenced what came out in the email.

- I ask them what they *weren't* thinking about when they wrote the communication. How did that impact things?

- We delve into the emails that *did* work and explore *why* they worked.

- For communications where, if I were the recipient, I might have been confused, uninspired, or frustrated, we look at these slowly and discuss the impact and opportunities they present for greater effectiveness.

- We look at where they are assuming, where they aren't acknowledging specific people and teams, where they can make clearer requests, where they can be more curious, and where they can demonstrate greater leadership.

Communication is a key component of any professional's work, leadership, and impact. And it's rare for any leader, business owner, or manager to have their communications looked at by someone with no agenda other than supporting them in increasing their skills in this area. You can be that person. As a coach, you can assist your clients in becoming effective, inspiring, and clear communicators who get better results.

Now—as a professional coach, you also need to consider the possibility that knowing a thing or two about decent writing would serve your business. There's absolutely no requirement to

Learnings from a CEO's Email

become a full-on writer like me or Steve Chandler or other coaches who write books and articles. There *is* a requirement to be able to write a solid email or direct message, because it's not a great look when a coach can't put together a decent communication to a prospective client.

If you feel weak in this area, get coached around it, take a class, AND, of course, practice, practice, practice. Strengthening your ability to communicate in writing will serve you in the growth of your business, AND it allows you to serve your clients in new ways.

30

Your Client's Calendar

Not long ago a CEO client and I looked at his calendar. Not surprisingly, I saw back-to-back meetings, all day long. No space, anywhere. This was clearly fertile ground for exploration.

You can provide massive value by looking at a client or prospective client's calendar. I do this regularly—it leads to valuable conversations around what matters to someone and whether or not they're getting the results they want in their lives.

In the case of this CEO, I asked her to take me through one of her days, meeting by meeting. As she did so, I asked questions like these:

- What is this meeting?
- Why are YOU there?
- Is this the best and highest use of your time (is this where you can have the greatest impact)?
- If "no," why are YOU there?

- When do you think or create and develop new ideas?
- When do you eat or go to the bathroom?
- Do you decline meetings regularly?
- What message does your calendar reflect to you?
- What message does your calendar send to those around you, your direct reports, etc.?
- Is your calendar a reflection of your organization's values and culture?
- Is your calendar a reflection of what you value and deem important in your role?
- Are you actively creating your days/weeks or are others filling your calendar and making decisions about your time to which you simply acquiesce?
- If you want something different to occur in terms of the results you want, what needs to change?

If you coach any leader, a jam-packed schedule is not uncommon. In fact, the same is true of many of us in our daily lives. We don't have to be CEOs or coaches. We can be parents, teachers, truck drivers, entrepreneurs, baristas . . . There's a good chance that everyone you serve as a coach would benefit from a look at their calendar—aka how they are spending their time and whether it's allowing them to have the impact they want on their lives. Not everyone's calendar will be jam-packed, of course, and there's gold to mine from this data as well.

Creating a calendar in the first place can be a great

opportunity to examine what your client or prospect values. And from there they can make space to begin creating the lives they want.

Don't miss out on a highly valuable opportunity to move the needle in your clients' or prospective client's life in a significant way. You can play with adapting the questions I asked the CEO to explore with your clients how they are spending their time. You can do this with a prospective client in your second or third conversation if you sense it would serve.

31

Coaching the Uncoachable

Recently a coach named Ellen reached out to me after seeing a video interview I did with Steve Chandler as part of his Advanced Client Systems online school. I asked her to share a little more about herself and her business—what was working, what wasn't, and what she wanted to be different.

Ellen shared that she wanted to make more money. She was frustrated, because from her point of view she was having a deep impact, that people's lives were being transformed because of her work, and yet she wasn't making the money she wanted to make.

I asked her, "What are you charging now?"

"Eight thousand dollars for eight sessions."

"And where would you like to go?"

"Fifteen or twenty thousand dollars for the same number of sessions, to start, and then higher." She mentioned Steve Hardison as a coach with fees she'd like to emulate. Steve Hardison is also known as "The Ultimate Coach," and last I checked he charges $200,000 a year to work with him.

SERVING CLIENTS

Ellen was speaking fast with me, and I asked her how long her conversations with prospects were, on average. She said they were twenty to thirty minutes.

"For your consideration," I said, "that's very short. It's not much time to create context or value for coaching, in my experience."

"I don't want to talk to people for longer. I know a lot of coaches who don't either. We get right to it. I'm able to dive deep and ask them what's really happening. By the end of twenty or thirty minutes, they get that I know what I'm doing and they see that I can help. They say yes; everyone says yes."

"Just not to your higher fees," I said. "I hear you, *and* you are talking about wanting to at least double your fees now, and to eventually charge more like Steve Hardison's fees, in the area of $200,000 for a year of coaching."

"Yes" the coach said.

I shared with Ellen that when our fees go up, we want to slow down and create more context for what's going to occur in our sessions, which in turn creates greater context for our fees. The best way to do this is to give people a deep experience of what it's like to work with us. This can mean a ninety-minute conversation—or two to three ninety-minute conversations. In my experience it's not possible to do this in twenty to thirty minutes AND then have someone pay us $20k, $30k, $50k or more.

Ellen said, "I don't *want* to do two or three conversations for ninety minutes each. That sounds horrible. I can't even believe you're talking to me for an hour without us making a coaching agreement. Talking to people for longer is not in my personality. I mean . . . I don't know that I think it's necessary."

Are you noticing a trend? Everything I offered was met with, "I don't want to" or objections based on what other coaches are charging or doing. And, for the record, Steve Hardison is doing *Steve Hardison*. I invite all coaches to consider that being Steve Hardison is not an achievable goal, because there's only one Steve Hardison. Can you charge $200k for a year? Absolutely. And you'll need to do the work that creates that kind of value, as Steve Hardison has done. Even then, you still won't be Steve Hardison; you'll be *you*, creating your own path. It doesn't ultimately matter what Steve Hardison or any other coach is doing; you have to do *you*.

So, did Ellen's resistance indicate she was *un*coachable. Let's consider: what does "uncoachable" look like?

- A stance of "I'm pretty sure I know better than you."
- "I don't want to."
- "Yes, I'll go do that assignment." (And then they don't, repeatedly.)
- "I thought about what you suggested and then I decided it didn't make sense because of . . .[insert however they justify and argue for their limitation]."
- "It won't work for me. I tried it once or twice before and those things never do."

One of the benefits of having a coach yourself is that you can take "problems" like the one I was having with Ellen to them and get insights you might not initially have by yourself. And as I sat

SERVING CLIENTS

with Ellen, I remembered an exchange I once had with Steve Chandler, who said to me:

"Nobody is uncoachable. You just need to become a better coach—the coach they need."

The day he said that to me, I was *really* irritated. I had a particular client whom I was experiencing as uncoachable, and in my session with Steve I wanted him to agree with me that I was right. This person was definitely not coachable. It was them, not me, and I was off the hook.

So when he said, "Nobody is uncoachable," I thought, *I really don't like you right now, Steve.* What I said out loud, with a combination of aggravation and frustration, was this: "You really think that's true?" There was no curiosity in me for his response. I didn't agree with him. You might even say I was uncoachable at that moment.

Steve responded in his classic way. "Why, yes, I think it's true. I don't usually say things I don't think are true, just for fun."

Ugghhh! Now I have to be curious and find out what he means! I thought. I slowed myself down and, trying to disguise my irritation, asked, "What do you mean?"

"There's always a way in. You just need to become the coach who finds a way in."

Starting to feel like I was talking to Yoda, I asked, "How do I find a way in?"

"I don't know. Maybe it's about slowing them down. Or maybe you let them know you aren't being effective with them and that you'd like to be—what do they suggest? Maybe it's about only listening. It's a puzzle that you get to unlock. It's different for each person, and it really means that you want to get quiet and see. It doesn't mean you have to coach them—and, still, everyone can be coachable in the right environment."

I decided to sit with this after our session. I sat with it a lot. Here's what I came up with.

Coaching someone who occurs as "uncoachable" is a special challenge and opportunity. First off, realize that it's absolutely going to occur for you, because it occurs for every coach I know. It's an experience every coach is going to have, an important one in terms of growth and development. The keys to coaching the so-called uncoachable are:

- Looking at where you are judging them or making them wrong, because judgment and "wrong-making" contributes to them being less coachable. Clients and prospective clients *feel* our judgment, even if they can't articulate it.

- If they are a current client, there is always the opportunity to slow things down and ask them how they are experiencing the coaching. Listen to what they say. Perhaps they are not in the same place they were when you began working together, or they thought the coaching experience was going to be different.

- There can also be great value in offering to them what you are experiencing and noticing and getting really curious about it. You can ask if they've been in situations where they're given feedback that they aren't open to. Is that what's happening now? Or are *you* impatient and maybe not seeing what's really happening? How open are you?

- Someone being uncoachable is (ironically) an opportunity for coaching. It's an opportunity for sharing what you see, and in doing so greater connection and trust can occur.

This kind of exploration and experimentation might lead to the coaching ending, either because you decide to let them go, or they decide it's not a fit. Neither of these are the most fun or enjoyable parts of the profession, and yet there is still value to be had here. It will strengthen your enrollment process and what you pay attention to in choosing your clients. It will strengthen your coaching because it requires you to become more versatile—meaning deepening your listening, or changing the questions you are asking, or challenging someone when you experience them as not open.

Consider the possibility that you might be the first person who reflects to your client or prospect that they present as not open, or scary, or difficult. You might be the only person in their lives who has no agenda, no concerns about their reaction. This can be one of the most important and valuable conversations ever to occur inside of a coaching relationship, even if the person stops working with you or you decide to let them go.

If they are a prospective client, you have two options: assume that you are not the right or best coach for them at this time, or assume that there's a puzzle piece missing, and *you have the piece*. The piece could be more listening, or asking them if they are wanting something different, or reflecting to them what you are noticing in the conversation. Either way, your conversation can have tremendous value for both of you.

To return to my story about Ellen, I decided to slow down with her and really listen—and for the most part to simply agree with her. I shared that there

> "Nobody is uncoachable. You just need to become a better coach—the coach they need."
> ~ Steve Chandler

was no requirement for her to talk to people for longer times or to do anything different in her enrollment process. And I pointed out again that in my experience, as our fees go up, it can be necessary to spend more time with people, because they often need more of an experience with us when there's a higher level of investment.

Slowly, she began to warm up, and I gently offered that there might be an opportunity for her to slow down with her prospects.

Ellen paused and said, "Well, it's true, I've gotten that feedback before." Then, as we were finishing the call, she asked, "Tell me again, how do *you* work with people?"

I took this to be a request to explore the two of us working together, and I shared that we'd require more conversations before that became something for us to consider. I also shared my fees, because she wanted to know, and I wanted her to know.

Ellen said, "I'm really going to think about what you said today, and the fact that you spent a whole hour with me. It's really surprising to me. I probably would find out more if I played with this approach."

I smiled and let her know to reach out to me anytime if I could be of assistance. Within a few weeks, she did. What happens next remains to be seen.

32

Sacred Real Estate

Agreements between coach and client start in the enrollment process, when the container for transformation is being set up.

In my standard agreement with clients we both agree to keep our scheduled session time protected. We don't reschedule because we forgot we wanted to meet with a friend that day, or because it's the day before a long weekend, or because "something came up." The emergencies we allow for are the big ones, the real emergencies. Serious illness of the client or their kid. Death. Or maybe less traumatically, something truly unavoidable, like a delayed flight that leaves the client 35,000 feet above the earth at session time. Or sometimes I have corporate clients, for example, who must attend a major meeting that hadn't been scheduled when we'd set up our session time.

But rescheduling should not become a casual option. And if it's happening every few sessions, it's a sign to look deeper into what's happening.

Sacred Real Estate

This can be a tricky space to navigate for some coaches, especially when they're getting started. It raises a lot of issues we get into in this book: the desire to be liked, to people-please, to be easy to work with and so on. One coach said to me, "I don't want to appear rigid, so when someone calls and explains that they'd forgotten their friend was in town, or whatever, I just want to be helpful."

And, of course, it's *nice* to be accommodating. But accommodation for a non-emergency subtly (or not so subtly) devalues the session *and* the coach. It makes the work that will get done in that session take a backseat in the client's life. If it can be bumped around the calendar like a gym session you don't "feel" like doing, it says to the client, "It's okay that your commitment to this work and yourself is not a priority in your life." By extension, too, if you're so accommodating, it implies that your schedule as a coach is not as important or full as your client's.

Are these messages you want to send? Is this serving your client?

The same holds true if you as coach reschedule client appointments for non-emergency reasons. If you do this, you're effectively saying, "This is the way we do things around here." Not only do you thereby encourage the same behavior, you're also telling them that they and the work they've come to do isn't all that important. Our agreement is in place for both of us; appointments are sacred real estate on our calendars.

So what to do when this fundamental agreement is broken? It's fertile ground for coaching, even in situations where an appointment really does have to be rescheduled. The ensuing

SERVING CLIENTS

conversation can be around clarifying why the agreement is made in the first place, and what it means in terms of a client's (and their coach's) dedication to their transformation.

If a client agrees to a session time, they schedule everything else around *it*, rather than allowing themselves flexibility to change it for a non-emergency. If the client says, "Things have gotten so backed up at work and I'm out of my mind and I need to move the session," the coach might say, "Maybe now would be a perfect time to meet, so we can figure out how you get yourself un-backed up."

The commitment to a session also requires the client to make sure everyone in their life who needs to know *knows* that the client has a session at that time. If the husband is going to pick up the kids from school because of his wife's coaching session, he knows he can't decide to work late and ask her to pick them up instead. And so on.

This isn't being rigid. It's honoring the sacred pact you've made with your client to truly serve them. It shows them how important *they* are. It even shows them how to honor themselves by keeping the appointment *with* themselves, not to mention with you, the coach. And it points to the value of the work you're doing together.

So this is a foundational issue to get clear on with your clients up front. If a client has issues that you both know have a high likelihood of causing disruptions in the future—let's say an aging mother who may unexpectedly need immediate attention—you can create an agreement around that. You can even coach around that. If a client immediately starts talking about getting backed up at work when you ask them to agree to keep every scheduled session, you can dig into what they're really coming to coaching for. It becomes an opportunity to deepen their commitment.

Learn how to create agreements and keep agreements with your clients, and your practice will grow.

33

Build a Library

Successful professional coaches have vast libraries of personal growth resources they can vouch for. For example, besides reading *The Prosperous Coach* by Steve Chandler and Rich Litvin, I almost always recommend the book *Overcoming Underearning* by Barbara Stanny to any coach I talk to (and it's assigned reading in the CFJ Coaching Success School).

How do I know it's transformative?

Because I've read it myself (more than once), and it changed my relationship with money and earning. In fact, it was transformative for me. It made me different, and I can speak to *how* it made me different. I also made more money after reading it. I know a coach who reads it every year and who says she always makes more money when she does. That's the other thing with this book and many other resources I recommend—I've seen them in action helping other people as well.

I have all sorts of books I assign or give to prospective clients (coaches or non-coaches) based on what they are saying

Build a Library

gets in their way. I've read and used all of them in my own life or business. This is critical, because you want to know what you're assigning, what it did for you, and *why* it's valuable for the specific person you are assigning it to. You want it to work for them as well as it did for you.

It's important to match the resource with the person. Is it something that's relevant to a challenge they're facing? And—is there at least a reasonable chance they'll *use* the resource? If you know your client or prospect doesn't like reading books, gift them the audiobook instead, or send them a link to a supportive video like a TED Talk, or a movie, or a TV show. As nice as it might be to get a free book in the mail, if the recipient isn't going to read and get something out of it, there's not much point. So be familiar with what you're sending and who you're sending it to.

Do you have your own resource library? Resources you love and which transformed you? Here are some that I love:

- *Stutz* on Netflix
- Brené Brown on Netflix (and any Brené Brown book)
- Atul Gawande's Ted Talk on coaching, and his book, *Being Mortal: Medicine and What it Means in the End*
- *Leadership and Self-Deception* by the Arbinger Institute
- *Radical Candor* by Kim Scott
- *Authentic Success* by Robert Holden
- *Strength to Strength* by Arthur Brooks
- *More Time to Think* by Nancy Kline

SERVING CLIENTS

- Any book or audio by Steve Chandler
- One of my favorite things to assign to coaches and leaders is the Apple TV show *Ted Lasso*. It's VERY funny and a great way for people to deepen their understanding of what a good collaborative leader demonstrates.

If you don't have a library, you want one. If you have one and you aren't adding to it regularly, I suggest you want to be doing this for yourself and for the people you serve. Maybe it seems like you can just "think of things in the moment" as you coach—just wait for the right answer to bubble up in the right moment. Yet having a library makes life so much easier. Consider it your continuing education training as a coach. As you grow your library, you keep adding to your *inner* resources. You discover fresh perspectives and new ways to do things. You keep your options open and your skillset growing. You deepen your understanding. You become a better coach.

Our coach, Steve Chandler, sent Michelle a book almost weekly. She had a never-ending stream of books she was reading—and then, almost directly thereafter, she sent copies of the books to current and prospective clients if she thought they would be helpful.

And once you've created your continually growing library of resources, what do you do?

Give it all away! Successful professional coaches who know the value of service give it *all* away without hesitation. They send materials often, and without thoughts of, "Well, I should wait to give them this book until they become a client . . ." They know that through generous service, people start to

Build a Library

experience them as trusted sources of transformation. People start to ask them, "Do you have a book that would help me with . . . ?"

When you send a relevant article or other resource to a prospective client, say something like, "This might serve you right now." There's no need to add anything else. Nothing about coaching with you. Nothing about what would occur if you spoke again. Only the resource.

Do this with people you spoke to six months ago. Do it with people you spoke with six weeks ago. Do it with your clients.

And if you don't have the budget to buy prospects and clients books, that's totally fine! Send them articles or TED Talks or links to movies that might assist them.

Keep building your library—and yourself—and give it all away, over and over, and over again. In service.

(Please also see the Resources section at the end of this book.)

34

Judgment

When Steve Chandler, Michelle Bauman, and I developed the University of Santa Monica's Soul-Centered Professional Coaching Program, one of the segments we led was called "What Do You Listen for in Your Coaching?" These were our answers:

- Steve: I'm listening for the language of victimhood, the language of expectations.
- Michelle: I'm listening for hidden assumptions lived as if they are true.
- Me: I'm listening for judgment.

Now, you could say we were all listening for the same thing because, in many ways, we were. The language of victimhood IS essentially judgment, as are assumptions. And there are also subtleties for how we each might listen and work with what we've heard.

Judgment

Before reading further, you might ask yourself, "What am *I* listening for in my enrollment conversations or coaching sessions?"

Judgments are the biggest (and smallest) rocks along the path we walk as we learn to serve others effectively—as well as to experience more peace, joy and connection in our lives. It's difficult to serve and coach well if we are subtly judging ourselves and others for difficult relationships, poor money management, toxic leadership, not hiring you as their coach . . . and on and on.

Coaches judge. At least I do. In terms of our profession, I've found that a significant number of coaches are in judgment way more than they are aware of being. They (we) judge themselves, their businesses, other coaches, potential clients, situations and so on.

And people judge. It's what we do. Many of us are raised on judgments without knowing it. Probably our parents didn't know it either. All sorts of judgmental thinking: making others wrong, making our ways of being better, you name it.

I personally consider myself an expert on judgment because I did so much of it. Yet I had no idea how much I judged myself, others, and the world until I was sitting in the University of Santa Monica (USM) classroom as a student. I remember thinking, "Me, judging? I don't think so!?" Granted, I was often upset and angry about my parents, my brothers, my husband . . . but judging? Me? Aren't those just regular thoughts?"

Apparently not.

SERVING CLIENTS

I slowly discovered that they weren't "just thoughts"; they were judgmental thoughts, and they were hurtful to myself and others (mostly me, since they took up space and energy *in* me, and they didn't feel good doing so. Judgments are like filters covering your eyes. They make everything dark, muddy, murky . . . The filters of judgment create an experience of aloneness—when we are judging ourselves or others, we make ourselves separate.

I judged myself as a bad daughter. I judged my mom as a horrible mom. I judged my husband as unavailable. I judged my brothers as not loving me. I judged my dad as checking out. I judged my bosses as clueless. I judged the world as unfair. And, I judged the purple handouts at USM as *WAY. TOO. PURPLE.*

Not a fun inner life. It colored my outer life with sadness and dissatisfaction.

At USM, I started to unravel the judgments and the cost of continuing to hold onto them. USM introduces a tool called Compassionate Self-Forgiveness. It's designed to assist you in identifying your judgments and then to systematically forgive them. This isn't forgiving the person/act/behavior. It's about forgiving your judgments of those things. It feels awkward and strange at first, like learning a new language: "I forgive myself for judging myself as a bad daughter" versus "I forgive myself for *being* a bad daughter."[6]

Bit by bit, I slowly started to pull BACK the filters. Light and color started to trickle in. It didn't feel quite like light at first. It felt like the lyrics from Leonard Cohen's song "Hallelujah":

---

[6] See Handout 8: Compassionate Self-Forgiveness at the end of this book.

Judgment

It's not some pilgrim who claims to have seen the Light
No, it's a cold and it's a very broken Hallelujah

I, without an ounce of spiritual orientation prior to my USM education (other than little inklings inside), had the inner experience of a cold and broken Hallelujah. Love and possibility began to open inside of me as my judgmental orientation to life started dissolving.

There were judgments that took years and years to dissolve (and there are ones that I'm still working with!).

In particular, it required dedicated inner work and ongoing, repeated self-forgiveness when it came to the judgments related to myself and my mom. There were times I wondered, "What's the point? Is this doing anything? I mean, I just keep piling up judgments . . ."

What I didn't get at the time was that I was developing a practice of pulling myself out of the judgments, identifying them, and doing self-forgiveness. Slowly my judgmental way of relating to myself, others, and the world was dissolving. The repeat judgments and the new ones didn't "stick" for very long. I started to see that practicing self-forgiveness was a much better use of my time than hanging out in judgment or mentalizing and wondering about whether or not self-forgiveness was "working."

Identifying judgments and applying Compassionate Self-Forgiveness is a daily practice—something you can do throughout the day, or at the end of every day. And every day I continue to practice self-forgiveness, the freedom and joy I experience are like Hallelujahs, both small and large.

SERVING CLIENTS

This is a long way to say that judgment is a major roadblock for your clients, potential clients, and you—but there is in fact a way past it. There are the big judgments of parents and spouses, for example, and there are the everyday judgments of fellow drivers on the road, people who kick our seats on airplanes, and those who think differently from us. These add up—and they don't make our inner sanctuary a beautiful place to reside in, nor do they add to the sum total of loving on the planet.

> **It required dedicated inner work and ongoing, repeated self-forgiveness to develop a practice of pulling myself out of the judgment and doing self-forgiveness.**

The high cost of judgment in our world is plain to see. The polarization, the "against-ness," and all the wrong-making are eroding our goodwill and our ability to see the loving essence in ourselves and each other.

Learning and practicing the skill of Compassionate Self-Forgiveness isn't for the faint of heart. It requires a willingness to *see* and own one's judgments—because we can't forgive what we are unwilling to see.

This is an invitation. Listen for judgment in your own thoughts and words—if you clean up your judgments, your life will be better and your coaching will improve. *And* listen for judgment with those you serve. Or listen for subtle or not-so-subtle expressions of judgment by other names: victimhood, or hidden assumptions lived as if they are true. Listen for whatever

Judgment

is covering up the truth—namely that each person truly is the pure essence of loving.

(Please also see Handout 8: Compassionate Self-Forgiveness at the end of this book.)

35

The Art of Heartfelt Curiosity

Are you curious?

If I asked you to rate your level of curiosity on a scale of one to ten, with ten being exceptionally curious, what would you say?

How curious are you about the people you encounter in life? Not just your immediate family, friends, colleagues, prospects and clients . . . but everyone?

I've noticed a trend. When I attend an event at my daughter's school, or go to a party, the gym or the grocery store: heartfelt curiosity is dying. More and more it seems people are asking less and less.

Not, "How are you?"

Not, "What do you do?"

Not, "What did you think of the show *Squid Games*?"

Not, "Where are you from?"

Not, "Do you like what you do for a living?"

I was on vacation with my husband in San Francisco a few years ago. One evening we were having drinks in a hotel bar and we struck up a conversation with a waiter, asking him about the cost of living there (it's high, in case you were wondering). I asked him where he lived, followed up with, "Do you like East Oakland?" and then said, "Why are you a waiter?"

Now obviously this didn't come from a place of judgment or seeing him as having a problem he needed to fix. I wasn't thinking that someone as articulate as he seemed shouldn't "have to" be a waiter or anything else. It came from my genuine curiosity about the person in front of me. In the moment, it felt like a good question.

He looked at me for a moment and said, "Thank you for asking me that. I like being a waiter, and I'm also a financial advisor building my business."

"Oh," I said. "Interesting. Thanks for sharing that."

We talked a little more, exchanging thoughts about his business, about running your own business, about San Francisco . . . and that was that. I wasn't in client creation mode; I simply wanted to connect, and my husband did too.

Maybe it was because my husband and I had been together for nine days straight and were desperate for an infusion of new topics into our conversation . . . Or you might say that because I'm a professional coach, I "should" ask questions and be interested; curiosity is a job requirement. Yet asking questions out of obligation isn't very real or inspiring. On some level I think it's obvious to the person you're asking when you're faking curiosity. Our conversation with our waiter was a result of a genuine interest in him. My curiosity "muscle" might be strong because I've developed it over the years, but our interest in our waiter was real.

Curiosity reminds both parties in a discussion that everyone—including themselves—is interesting. We are all individuals with both shared and unique experiences. Curiosity—slowed down, authentic interest in other people—is a game changer. People feel seen and heard when we are curious. Curiosity in conversations opens doors that can lead to greater connection and discoveries.

In business it lets your customers know you care about *them*, not just about what they might spend with you. (And it *does* happen that a natural byproduct of genuine caring *can* be more business.)

Curiosity in Everyday life versus Curiosity as a Professional Coach

We benefit from getting more curious about the people around us. If we're too much in our own bubbles we do a disservice to our communities. Real people down the street matter. And our curiosity about them—in the local coffee shop or in the grocery store—also matters. Especially for older people who are living alone and may not be asked anything, much less even spoken to at all sometimes. Whenever we connect with someone it increases their experience of being seen. It might even increase the sum total of love on the planet.

We need to get connected to those in our direct worlds in service to humanity. Curiosity in everyday life is a way to gently share kindness.

Now, curiosity *is* a requirement for the professional coach. And as I wrote above, not the "fake" kind, but the true, authentic kind. Nancy Kline says, "People pay us for the quality of our listening." I'll supplement that by saying that people pay us to be genuinely, deeply curious about them and their inner landscape. Our job is to ask excellent questions—questions that unlock thinking, assist people in discovering how they truly feel and inspire new ideas, new ways of being, and new choices.

And then, of course, our job is to listen. Curiosity isn't just asking questions—in fact, I'll often point out that we don't want to stack questions like someone's taking an exam:

"How are you feeling about the conflict at work, is there anything you can do about it, and does it reflect challenges you're facing at home?"

Stick with a question or two. This allows people to explore themselves, to discover their own answers.

Ask one more question of someone today. A genuine question. Get in touch with your own curiosity, then look in someone's eyes, at the grocery store or in your house or at the gym.

And ask one NEW question in your work as a professional coach—a question you have never asked before.

As coaches and as fellow humans, let's revive the art of curiosity in our everyday lives. Genuine, heartfelt curiosity—in service to ourselves and others.

Curiosity reminds us that everyone is interesting. What's more, whenever we connect with someone it increases their experience of being seen. It might even increase the sum total of love on the planet.

SERVING CLIENTS

36

Stories Matter

Is it too early in *this* book to start sharing stories from my next one?

My current intention is for my next book to be about my mom, my relationship with her, and the process of healing I went through around that relationship. In it I'm going to share the story of an all-out verbal brawl we had in the back of a cab in Oaxaca, Mexico.

Now, I'm not planning on *just* sharing the parts where I'm in the cab, screaming at the top of my lungs, spit flying along with tears. Nor will I stop after telling how, in the hotel room after the fight, I was so upset I thought my body would never relax, and I was so angry I wanted to punch her in the face more than once.

That wouldn't be in service to myself or whoever reads the book.

Instead I'll keep talking—I'll share the process I went

through inside myself, in my hotel room, where I slowly asked for internal guidance and assistance, and I came back into balance, forgiving myself for the judgments against my mom and myself. I'll share how time slowed down, and I remembered that that was not who I wanted to be. Gradually, I came back into the truth of who I was, and who I wanted to be with my mom.

For me this story illustrates, among other things, where we—not just my mom and me, but perhaps you and others—can get to when we argue with someone we love. In sharing it, I am hoping that something resonates within the reader, and they connect to their own capacity for growth and resilience through challenges.

If you are a professional coach, your stories matter. All of them can serve and inspire, if used properly, with context. Every new story and occurrence in your life increases your ability to serve people in new ways.

I've recently been sharing more personal stories in the emails I send. Whether it's something that occurred with a client or my daughter or whatever. Not just in service, but sometimes as sources of hilarity. One of my primary goals is to make people laugh . . . because laughing is GOOD. Life is better when we laugh, and as professional coaches it's important that we don't take ourselves too seriously. There are a lot of coaches who have gone to the "This is SERIOUS business" school of thought, and it's not, as you can imagine, a fun school to attend. It's a dreary, uncomfortable place where everyone nods at each other in very serious ways and shares their concerns about the profession and life. They don't end up loving the profession, and nobody wants to hear their stories.

SERVING CLIENTS

As a coach, learn to be a storyteller. Share your triumphs and losses. Your stories can touch, inspire and amuse people. And maybe the most important thing they can do is move people to say, "If they can do it, I CAN DO IT."

It doesn't matter what the story is, as long as you learn to tell it moderately well. This means not sharing from the difficult part—that is, when you're not out of your own weeds yet in terms of emotional disturbance and upset. Michelle Bauman offered, "I don't want to share from the middle of my mess; I want to share when I'm at least two steps past it."

I don't share a story when I'm still triggered, angry, vindictive or judging. *After* this is handled, I can show the scars I earned in service to others. I can give all the gritty details, as long as I'm sharing from a supportive, constructive awareness of how it impacted me—and at least an intuitive sense of how it might support my client. I don't want to share a story just because it's important to me unless it feels in service to my client.

You might think you don't have any stories, but if you've got a heartbeat that's pretty unlikely. You just might need some brainstorming to get going. You could start with writing three of the most important stories in your life, the ones that shaped you and grew you into a new person, the one who is sitting here, reading this now.

Or you might explore what brought you to professional coaching (I share my story around that a lot). Or the story of your greatest fear coming to life, like losing a child or a spouse, and what occurred, and how this experience tested and served you. Or it might be the story of transforming your relationship to money.

Stories Matter

And a story might also involve a conversation you had with your child that morning, or a brief encounter with a barista, or how you felt when that guy stole your parking space the other day. It's not necessarily the monumental, earth-shattering quality of a story that counts; it's what can be drawn from it, what can be shared, what can serve in the moment.

Whatever the case, pick three stories and write them down. Write them badly, if you like; this is only for you. Then start inserting them into conversations with prospective and current clients, when it feels appropriate. Grow yourself into a storyteller. Stories—real stories of real, regular people—help us reflect on our own lives. They help us gather strength to do what we are called to do, to walk through the hard things in life. Stories serve because they show us the way forward, and they inspire us to keep creating.

SERVING CLIENTS

37

Be Gold

The following quote stopped me in my tracks.

It's a paragraph from the book *Educated,* by Tara Westover. *Educated* is a devastating, fantastic memoir about a woman who was raised by survivalist parents in Idaho. It tells the harrowing and powerful story of how she got out of one kind of life and created a totally different one. The following is what Tara's professor at Cambridge University tells her after she expresses wonder and a sense of inadequacy at being in the hallowed halls of the university.

> You must stop yourself from thinking like that," Dr. Kerry said, his voice raised. "You are not fool's gold, shining only under a particular light. Whomever you become, whatever you make yourself into, that is who you always were. It was always in you. Not in Cambridge. In you. You are gold. And returning to BYU, or even to that mountain you came from, will not

change who you are. It may change how others see you, it may even change how you see yourself—even gold appears dull in some lighting—but that is an illusion. And it always was.

What I love most here is that Dr. Kerry is giving Tara profound coaching about her current thinking and how it isn't serving her. He is attempting to show her the truth of who she is—proof of the unchangeable essence inside herself. He is pointing her inward, to where the truth is, and asking her to disregard any external reference.

What Dr. Kerry did for Tara is what we as coaches can do for our clients. His words, which took him less than a minute to utter, transformed a life.

And if they hadn't changed Tara's life, they would have at least changed mine.

I sent this paragraph to someone I was serving, reflecting to her that *she* is gold. She was feeling low, questioning her work, her life, and her place in the world. Now, if I could have, I would have come through the email and taken her by the shoulders and said, "Read this! Out loud! C'mon—we'll read it together." Because sometimes we need help being reminded of our true, essential nature: gold. Not fool's gold, but *gold* gold.

In this profession we get to send people things that move and touch us, in service to them and their growth. We can offer them support, assistance, tools for development. We can point out to them that they *are* gold, and that even though they are sitting across from us looking for answers, those answers are already inside them.

"Even gold appears dull in some lighting—but *that* is an

illusion." Every person walking around on this planet deals with this illusion to some degree or another—the illusion that they are anything less than gold. You can help your clients see this about themselves.

And you can know it about yourself too. We can only serve others to the degree we serve ourselves. If we are beggars at the table of life, living in scarcity and limitation inside ourselves and our business, we aren't going to serve effectively, and we are not going to be as strong a professional coach as we can be.

So be gold. Gold for yourself, and gold for others.

Communication as a Professional Coach

38

Letting Communications Die on the Vine

I recently coached another coach via email after he sent me his weekly report, in which he shared the actions he took to build his business. I asked him if he'd heard back from a prospective client he had mentioned in his prior report.

He said, "No."

"You didn't receive a response to your email?"

"No."

"Did you resend it, asking if they received it?"

He shrugged. "No. I stopped doing that because I didn't want people to think I was pushy or sales-y."

"So there's been nothing?" I asked. "You've let this person go?"

He shrugged again, this time a little sheepishly. "Well . . . yes."

COMMUNICATION AS A PROFESSIONAL COACH

I've seen this kind of thing happen again and again. Whether that email contains a proposal, a question, an idea—any of that. A lot of us can be one-and-done with emails, regardless of the response or lack of one. Yet when coaches don't resend emails, we let communication die on the vine for fear of being seen as:

- pushy
- bossy
- obnoxious
- salesy
- needy

Yes, I've been there, done this myself. Michelle did too. More times than our coach, Steve Chandler, could count.

Eventually, we learned that allowing a communication to die on the vine isn't helpful or necessary. When we allow it to happen, we miss out. We justify it by making up stories about what's happening on the other end: someone has decided they don't want our idea/service/assistance. They can't afford us. They don't like us. We said the wrong thing.

We project all sorts of stories onto the prospective client. And then, worst of all, we stop serving. We get mired in how we might look if we reach out again. Desperate? Needy? Or—gasp—salesy? What might someone think?

We also lose sight of the fact that most—if not all—of the time the prospect's lack of response has nothing to do with us. Most people process emails something like this: they answer the

Letting Communications Die on the Vine

five most recent emails in their inbox in a furious rush to get them handled so they can feel better. Then they stop—because they feel better—and move on.

If your email drops below those five, it's "buh-bye." It's not personal. Not about you.

Or . . . maybe they saw your email and thought, "I have to think about that." They might even think, "Gee, I really enjoyed that conversation with Carolyn, and she's asked me if she can support me around that issue we discussed. I'll give it some thought and email her tomorrow." Then they close their laptop or put their phone on silent and pick up their kids or go to the gym or meet with their client or . . . And tomorrow comes and goes and in the interim your email is buried under an avalanche of fifty new ones.

In either case—or any number of other cases where your email goes unanswered for unknown reasons—the opportunity for you to serve this person is going to be missed if you assume they don't want to talk to you again.

Freedom and Serving

When you release yourself from turning the mirror back on yourself and how you look, you are free.

Free to be curious.

Free to get back to making a difference and serving others.

Free to find out what's really happening.

Free to add value and drop the personalization.

I spent a *lot* of time in junior high and high school worrying about what people thought about me. I was anxious about being liked and accepted. This junior high school girl, the one inside of me, is not who I want running my coaching business. I *do* want her safe and cared for inside of me. Those younger selves, all present inside of us, don't go away. They wait for us to acknowledge their existence, and perhaps extend some loving care to them. They can even support us with their enthusiasm and excitement, their creativity. And, also, when we don't acknowledge them, or consider that they have been neglected, they tend to show up without our awareness and leak all sorts of feelings into our professional life, our adult relationships, and more. My inner teenager brings a lightness and joy to my life. She's important to my sense of self. But she's not who I want running the show when I'm sending communications—especially those that might take me just outside of my comfort zone—like deciding whether to resend an email with a simple, innocent:

"Did you receive the below? I haven't heard back from you."

Who's running *your* coaching business? The brilliant, efficient, superstar coach who is willing to risk a little rejection in the name of service and success—or your inner teenager, who makes rejection bad and scary?

Almost every time I email out a resend (or two) asking if someone received my previous email, I hear back, "Thank you. I was out of town" or "I was dealing with a challenge here" or "I was avoiding this because I know it would be helpful" and so on. And sometimes they don't even say what was going on. They just respond with, "Yes, I'd like to get on the phone, that works."

It's all good, because it all allows me to drop into service.

Letting Communications Die on the Vine

Consider this: instead of worrying about how you'll look, ask yourself what you have to lose. Is the worst-case scenario someone responding with, "Eeeewwww. You are so gross and pushy!"?

In all my years of coaching coaches and leading the CFJ School, this has never occurred. Not once.

Have people not responded? Yes.

Have I resent emails? Yes.

Have they declined? Yes.

Have they said yes? Yes.

Nobody has responded in a dramatic way that was shaming or embarrassing.

Can you handle this? Can you move through your fear of appearing pushy, salesy, etc., with the goal of truly serving the people to whom you are reaching out? I offer that you absolutely can. You can tolerate a no or a ghosting.

Even more importantly, if you are going to serve as a professional coach, tolerating no's and non-responsiveness in service to making a difference is a requirement.

39

How to Use Social Media

There's a Mary Oliver poem I love that begins:

> You do not have to be good.
> You do not have to walk on your knees
> For a hundred miles through the desert, repenting.
> You only have to let the soft animal of your body
> love what it loves.

Here's what I offer to you, in the same vein:

> You do not have to use social media.
> You do not have to make posts for hundreds of days, praying to the god of Instagram.
> You only have to do what is fun for you and what works for you.

For real.

There's nothing inherently "wrong" with social media. I use it, I like it. It's a super-fun, creative outlet for me to create

How to Use Social Media

interesting Instagram stories with fancy type, color and music.

Notice the word "I." I like it. If I didn't, I wouldn't use it. And my business would still have grown, because I connect with people a lot, almost all day long, in other ways.

Many certification programs out there include a short course on "marketing" to build your business, and it often includes social media. Lots of coaches encourage other coaches to post on social media as the best (only?) way to build a coaching practice. Yet there are plenty of coaches I know who have never stepped into social media and who have six-figure practices. All of their clients connect in different ways—out in the world, by email or referral, and so on. They don't spend any time on social media.

And at the same time, social media can also be used to create connections and clients if you dare to learn and get good at it. As I say, I'm not anti-social media. I'm just for using it in a way that serves you and your audience IF you want to use it.

What does it mean to use social media effectively (and responsibly) as a coach?

First, here's what it doesn't mean:

- Post after post of your (glamorous), somewhat Kardashian-like life, enjoying the beach with fabulous hair, your perfect family, your perfect work life, your perfect relationship and more perfect things that you created . . . and your immense gratitude for these perfect things. This isn't about these things not being real. You may have all of this and more in your life, and that's wonderful. The question is, do these posts serve people?

Are they helpful? Are they inspiring, or are they vaguely de-motivating, leaving people with the feeling that they need to lose ten pounds right now, and if they only did what you did, their lives would be filled with what YOU have? Maybe they even leave people feeling vaguely like there's absolutely no possibility that they can create what you have, because it's so far beyond them at this moment? Yes, people may respond to these posts, but are they helpful in meaningful ways? Not from my point of view. Enough with the ego-centered, "I, me, me, me and my fabulous existence that has no flaws or difficult moments."

- Posts of your coach-y quotes with no context. There's nothing worse than a coach, a quote and nothing else. Drive by quoting should be a ticketable offense. I'm serious. Stop quoting and start serving in real, depth-full ways. The only caveat here is for those of you who already have a robust community of people who follow you and who appreciate your (occasional) quotes; then it can actually be helpful to share them. You have already created a context for the quotes within your community.

- Posts of you unintentionally "shoulding" on people—that is, your posts are constantly telling people to "enjoy life" or "cherish the moment" or "don't hold back" or "be grateful." Nobody likes being told what to do. Do we all agree that gratitude and living in the moment have value? YES. Now find something real to say about it, something genuine that acknowledges we don't all feel gratitude

24/7. Nobody does (I'll bet even the Buddha had some low moments). And everyone has situations where they might be looking into the future or questioning the past. So if you are going to share about keys to living a more heart-centered, joyful life, consider the possibility of making it authentic, fresh and genuine. Be real—share about your own challenges and what shifted things for you; help us see you as accessible and real.

- Posts of you offering complimentary sessions to "anyone" because your calendar "has suddenly freed up." Seriously? The gig is up. We all know that your calendar didn't just free up. The truth is your client roster is low. Maybe it's always been low. And this isn't how to create a sense of confidence in you as a professional coach—either for yourself or for prospective clients. Raise the bar on yourself. Create a post that makes someone say, "WOW that was SO helpful. I'm going to put in the comments that this made my day." Get a comment like that and it's the beginning of a relationship you can nurture. That person STOPPED scrolling and wrote something to you. Private message them and nurture that. Slow down and connect.

- Posts that you haven't written, that other people are writing for you. I can almost always tell when a coach has hired someone to start writing for them. Sometimes it's subtle, sometimes it screams loudly, "It's NOT ME anymore!" There's a tone, a more marketing type of voice pushing through. It's tempting to do this, thinking that someone else is better at doing the work to create compelling content that brings people to you. Don't do it.

Now, if these kinds of posts have gotten you clients, then by all means, keep doing them. I'm 100 percent okay with being wrong. And if they haven't, STOP. It's not helpful to litter people's feeds with them.

On the flipside, what does it look like to be effective, compelling and useful on social media?

- Lots of experimenting with real, engaging communication that offers value to whoever reads it, whether or not they'll ever become a client. A gut check for this is simply thinking about if you were to see something like this, would you get value out of it or have your curiosity stimulated? Another way to think about it is to ask yourself, "What would be helpful to me and people like me? What would I want to see?"

- It's okay to be honest and to maybe even go a little out of your comfort zone. What is uncomfortable to share, within reason? This isn't a "let's use our pain as a marketing tool" kind of thing; rather, what's uncomfortable and TRUE that might be useful for others? To many people you may appear like you have it all together, so sharing that you're a human being just like them can bridge the gap and help them see what's possible.

- Be genuinely creative. That's not easy to achieve—it takes practice and lots of not-so-creative posts to find

How to Use Social Media

your voice. It takes experimentation, too, and sometimes that might result in an "embarrassing" post or three. Yet it's possible—and it can be fun and inspiring for you and your readers.

- Content that is immediately valuable. Yes, the aim is to have pretty much everything you post be valuable in some way, but here I'm talking about practical stuff like: "Three keys for shifting a difficult moment," "Two ways to create connection," "One thing you can do to ease your back pain right now." I might leave that last one for the more medially proficient poster, but you get what I mean.

Achieving social media mastery—or at least proficiency—isn't all that different from becoming a masterful coach. It takes time, effort, and attention. It takes a willingness to practice and be messy. So the question you want to ask yourself is: How much do I want this? Because if you want it and it's fun for you, great. And perhaps your time will be better spent becoming masterful at enrolling and coaching *first*. I don't think social media is going anywhere, and if and when you want to, you can lean into it.

I think many coaches lean into social media *first*, thinking it's the answer to client creation. It's not. Becoming a great coach and enroller is the very first step—only always.

And social media is—only always—optional.

40

What Will People Think?

At a certain point after Michelle passed, I started sending out videos on coaching topics like the money stories we tell ourselves and being okay with getting a "no" when you make an offer. The reception was . . . mixed. Or, rather, I assumed it was mixed because I lost a few subscribers somewhere along the way.

I received every unsubscribe request as if it were a little pointy jab in my heart. And I created, essentially from whole cloth, what I imagined these unsubscribers were thinking:

"Oh, geez . . . This woman's doing video now? Blech."

"She should stick to emails."

"She's so CHEEZY."

And the worst: "Carolyn's changed since Michelle was here. She's trying to be somebody else. It's not the same."

What was underneath all my thinking was a fear that people wouldn't like me anymore. My own self-judgments and discomfort with this new medium were naturally coming to the fore, because doing the videos and sending them out into the

What Will People Think?

world felt uncomfortable and vulnerable. (And I also acknowledge that you can't always hit it out of the park and that may have led to some unsubscribes.)

So should I *not* have sent out the videos? Of course not. I had a choice here—get exposed and work through my discomfort, or play it safe and keep doing what I'd always done. In my experience coaching hundreds of women, both with Michelle and on my own, we get concerned about "What will people think, and will they like me?" Especially when it involves putting ourselves out there in our business. We don't always think first about how courageous it is, how it will engage parts of ourselves we've only scratched the surface of, how it will open doors for ourselves and others, how it will allow us to serve people and do what we love. Instead we get concerned about what others will think. And when this happens we contract, we shrink, and we make ourselves small.

Taking a stand for our work is a requirement for growth. I'm not talking about an ego-centered, "I'm better than you" kind of stand. I'm talking about a heart-centered, deep place inside, where you know that you have something of value to offer, and you are willing, as Steve Chandler says, to "risk offending in the name of serving." Serving in this way means reaching out and connecting more—and in different ways—than it might feel comfortable to do. It also means doing so without attachment to whether or not someone works with your company or buys your product or service.

When we do this in the name of making a difference, we allow ourselves to expand into new ways of serving that stretch us out of our comfort zone. And this is where growth occurs—

both in terms of the bottom line and in terms of your own ability to be a leader and make a difference in your business.

The fact is, whether or not people were judging me and my videos, I'd already beaten them to the punch—I'd already judged myself. I'd already criticized myself or been embarrassed by myself. I'd already done all that—*then gently yet firmly walked myself through it.*

Self-judgment is occasionally present even today. I have grown (a lot?) . . . and I'm also human. Every so often I have a pang of low thinking and I look at who unsubscribed. Shock! My ego gets ruffled and I think, "Why don't they like me anymore?"

Then I remember that ego-centered thinking is not where I want to come from. I want to come from elevated, heart-centered thinking. From this place, there are no concerns, there's no wondering. It's all okay.

What about you? Do you find yourself wondering what people are saying or thinking about you, your emails, your videos, your invitations, your enrollment conversations? Does this wondering keep you out of action for fear of being seen as pushy, or needy, or some version of too much?

Welcome to the wonderful world of professional coaching and the ongoing opportunity to practice turning the mirror away from yourself and holding it up for the person you're serving. Your number one job is remembering that this profession is not about you and how you look. It's about risking offending in the name of serving. Your thoughts about how you appear, or what people will think, are natural, and you get to choose if you are going to believe them, much less act on them.

Will people sometimes think less-than-flattering things

What Will People Think?

about you? Probably, and that's none of your business. There will be many more people who will think, "This person sees me. This person is willing to connect with me and notice me and say something to *me*."

Playing small doesn't serve. Nor does judging yourself, or hiding out because of what people might think. This is true for you as well as for your clients. We serve others by stepping beyond the small self, beyond the people-pleasing, and beyond the self-doubt and fear, in the same way we serve ourselves by doing it. This is how we learn to thrive.

41

The Crime of Slime
Cleaning Up Your Emails

I read hundreds and hundreds of emails from professional coaches (male and female) to their prospective and current clients. It's not always pretty.

Here's an example from a coach who is writing to a neighbor with whom they've started to connect more deeply:

> Dear Maria,
>
> It was great talking with you and hearing about your challenges at your new job—and about your new Pomeranian! I forgot to mention that when I was growing up my neighbor had a dog like that and it would always dig up the flowers in our yard!
>
> Anyway, if you'd like to talk again, my schedule is pretty open next week and I'd love to connect. I think I could really help you with what we talked about, so let me know if you're interested.
>
> Loads of love,
>
> Dave

The Crime of Slime: Cleaning Up Your Emails

You might think, "What's so bad about it? It's their neighbor. It's friendly, nice. What's the matter?

On a scale of 1-10 of sliming (10 being the most slimy), I'd put it at a 7.5. Why? These sentences:

> "I forgot to mention that when I was growing up my neighbor had a dog like that and it would always dig up the flowers in our yard!"

> "Anyway, if you'd like to talk again my schedule is pretty open next week and I'd love to connect."

> "I think I could really help you with what we talked about, so let me know if you're interested."

And to get even more specific, these words:

> Anyway
> Love
> Interested
> Loads

As professional coaches we have opportunities to communicate with clarity, focus, curiosity and service. The coach in this email is communicating from their social self and shows a kind of mushy, tentative salesyness. I suggest they don't have enough professional confidence, because rather than being direct there's at least a little feeling that they're beating around the bush as to why they're writing in the first place.

Here's a revised version; what do you notice?

COMMUNICATION AS A PROFESSIONAL COACH

Dear Maria,

It was great seeing you in the neighborhood today and hearing about the challenges at your new job. I appreciate your honesty and your fierce tenacity around getting the challenges handled—it says a lot about you and who you are. You mentioned wanting to talk more. If it would be useful, we can put some real time on the calendar and meet. Is this something you'd like to do? Let me know either way, and if yes, I'll send options.
I'm also attaching an article, "Maximizing your First 90 days in a new Leadership Position," that might be valuable.

Warm regards,

Dave

PS: Your new dog is amazing!

Now if you are mired in more social-self kinds of communicating, the above could feel wildly different, maybe even not as "nice." It's true that every communication is different, because every relationship and the context for every relationship is different. Often as coaches, we know people in more social, personal contexts, and our job is to convert a relationship from a social context to a more professional context. It requires skill, nuance and ongoing practice and development.

If you have never had any coaching around your email communications, the kind done with a fine-tooth comb from a strong coach who's further down the path than you—you are doing yourself a profound disservice. Because it's almost 100

The Crime of Slime: Cleaning Up Your Emails

percent certain you are dealing with—cue horror music—Coaching Slime Syndrome. Thousands of coaches are unknowingly engaged in Coaching Slime Syndrome. Michelle and I were, too, at the beginning of our coaching careers. At the time, our coach Steve Chandler reviewed almost every one of our emails. The level of cluelessness we had about our communications was often hilarious—and definitely not pretty.

This came as a surprise to us, because Michelle and I had a lot of experience writing communications in our former professional work; she was a lawyer and I was a university admissions director. We thought we knew a thing or two about writing professional emails. And we did; but in the context of sending coaching emails, we had a lot to learn. One of us would send Steve an email we were about to send and think, "That one's pretty good!"

Then we'd get his response. Picture your high school English teacher's red-ink corrections on the paper you wrote at the last minute after only skimming the reading material and forgetting to proofread for grammar and spelling errors.

For example, Michelle used to write in her emails:

> I'm looking forward to talking!

Steve wrote back:

> How do you know you are looking forward to talking to this person? You don't know this person. This is a social-self "nicety" that is not necessary.

He continued:

COMMUNICATION AS A PROFESSIONAL COACH

> You're communicating with a bubbly effusiveness that can be misinterpreted to mean you're not the strong, successful coach you are. Remember that you are writing to leaders, and while they know you from your work as a lawyer, it's different when you're writing them as a coach. You need to establish who you are from the first communication. Save the extra warm effusiveness for AFTER they pay—then you can be as warm and effusive as you want.

Our minds were blown. We were women who were socialized to be "nice" and "friendly" in professional settings, and this often translated in our communications to a "softening"—lots of "please" and "thank you." Steve was pointing this out, and it was both shocking and freeing. We thought we had our communication skills down because of our previous careers. We were completely wrong.

Our former professional experience did not translate into the coaching world as seamlessly as one might think (which I think is the case for many coaches coming from different professions—in particular, corporate executives, professors, and marketing professionals). It was different to be the mouthpiece for an institution offering Master's Degrees in Spiritual Psychology; this required a high level of professionalism, but of a different type. And when she was a lawyer, Michelle could be more directive and explanatory in her communications; again, she was not using email to serve and enroll new clients into working with her in the way coaches do.

As a professional coach, when I write an email to a prospective client I want the emphasis to be on the prospective

The Crime of Slime: Cleaning Up Your Emails

client. But because it's "just you" behind the emails, it can be easy for you to become riddled with unconscious neediness, people-pleasing and role-reversal. And perhaps worst of all, the email can be about you and not the recipient.

One of the "golden guidelines" of coaching communications is to *always* provide value in your emails, texts, or calls. What does this mean? Ask yourself: if you received the email you are about to send, would you feel you got something valuable out of it? Caring, thoughtful, curious and useful? Or is it you attempting to get something?

Steve kept pointing out the times we did this. And slowly, after many, many hilariously botched emails, we learned how to stop sliming and spot the following slime behaviors in our communications to prospective clients.

- Neediness and desperation:

    "I know you couldn't make the last meeting, that's okay. You also asked if I'd ever coach someone and only meet once every 3 weeks for 15 minutes . . . I would, if that's the only thing that works for you."

- Putting the prospective client in the driver's seat:

    "We can meet whenever you'd like. Tomorrow? Tomorrow night? During my grandmother's funeral? What works for you?"

- Lack of service and no value:

    "Hi, I'm checking in to see if you are a go on paying me the $5k for 6 months of coaching. I haven't heard from you.

- Social self:

    "Hi, how are you :-)? Did you have a good 4th of July? Any BBQ's? I hope you and your husband are loving the new season of *Property Brothers*—OMG, did you see that barn door!!!! Hey I was thinking about you (I'm always thinking about you) and what you and I talked about in the jacuzzi meeting. I know you and I are still talking about you and your life—let's do it again!"

- About us and not them:

    "Dear xx, I was talking to a client the other day who had a similar challenge to yours. I suggested to the client that they start doing breathwork. I have been doing breathwork for years, and it's been a HUGE game changer for me. Now I'm actually going to offer breathwork as part of my practice, and I was thinking you might want to try it with me."

- Attachment AND righteousness (as in, the email is loaded with the energy and subtext of "you should meet with me/be my client/work with a coach/etc., and something is obviously wrong with you if you don't"):

    "I realize that you said now is not a good time for you to start coaching. I get it, and given everything happening in your life, might it be an important time to re-consider everything we discussed? Your taking on these challenges alone seems like a big misstep—and I share that with a lot of caring for you. I don't want you to end up in something you can't handle—the very thing we discussed. You really aren't set up for doing this without a strong coach in your corner, and I want you to think harder about it. . . ."

The Crime of Slime: Cleaning Up Your Emails

Take the Slime Test

Look at your last ten emails to prospective clients. Review them through the lens of service, leadership, and strength—and remove any traces of slime. Better emails, texts, and private messages lead to more people saying yes to sitting with you. They also lead to more people wanting to work with you, because the prospective client doesn't feel the unconscious "slime" of your attachment, or "social-self-itis," or the overall "smell" of selling vs. serving.

Even if you're a seasoned coach, if you haven't had anyone review your emails in a while, there's a good chance they could improve. It still helps me to have support in this area now and again. I still love discovering my own slime—and I invite you to discover yours!

Always provide value in your emails, texts, or calls. Ask yourself: if you received the email you are about to send, would you feel you got something valuable out of it?

42

A Coach Who Dared to Stop Being so Agreeable, "Nice" and "Friendly"

Let's look some more at how our social self can creep into our emails.

Once upon a time I worked with a coach in my school who didn't know how to communicate as a strong professional. His emails were riddled with people-pleasing pleasantries and lots of "friendship" kinds of communications. People often responded with phrases like, "It would be so nice to talk again." He wasn't getting clients and was confused as to why this was the case. So I did what Steve Chandler had done for Michelle Bauman and me. He ran his every email past me, and I responded with notes.

A few red flags pointing to social self were showing up in his communications:

- Thanking the recipient for responding, as in: "Thanks for

A Coach Who Dared to Stop Being so Agreeable

responding. It's wonderful to hear from you." Brain surgeons don't thank their patients for taking their calls or responding to emails; they know the work they do is life-saving. Coaching is no different. Your work is life-saving. Time to act like it.

- Lots of "sloppy" words and sentences like, "Let's try to start right on time for your next session" or "We can attempt to get to all 5 of your agenda items. I'm not sure though . . ."

- Sharing personally at a level that creates "friend" confusion, as in, "My jiu-jitsu class ends at 4, how about we connect at 4:30?"

This coach was willing to slow down and really take in the coaching. He was undeterred even when at times it felt uncomfortable to do so.

Slowly, his emails started to change. He shortened them. He made them more efficient, used less social-self language and made fewer attempts to be "nice" with his words. He started learning how to serve in emails. He was more curious, asking questions like, "Tell me more about what is happening with your boss. You mentioned it's been bumpy." He stopped using sloppy language, like, "Let's try to make sure we start on time for the next session" and "I hope we can get to your agenda items right away."

He created policies and communicated them to his clients. "All coaching sessions start on time. We respect each other's time, and this is demonstrated by arriving on time, ready to work."

His income doubled in six months.

His professional self-esteem?

From my point of view, it *quadrupled.* He was a completely different person in his email communications and way of being.

If you haven't looked closely at your communications in your practice (emails to current and prospective clients), you are missing a potentially huge way to grow yourself and your business. The same is true virtually *any* time you meet with your clients, in person or on Zoom one-on-one, or in front of groups. Listen to what you're saying and ask yourself: Am I being direct? Am I serving? Am I taking neediness out of the equation? Am I acting in my and my client's best interests? Remember: people are not served simply by you being "nice" and "agreeable" with them. They are served by your honesty, integrity—and sometimes by your "disagreeableness" in addressing issues no one else will take up with them. That's your job.

Becoming an economic powerhouse requires digging into the ways you might be leaking, and looking at those places where you're people-pleasing, where you're in social self and diminishing your professional strength as a coach.

My greatest days in growing my business were those when my own coach pointed out where I'd collapsed into wanting to be liked. And now one of my favorite things to see is someone going from being a leaky, people-pleasing, wanting-to-be-liked coach to a coach with professional and personal policies and an ability to communicate with clarity, care, and professionalism.

When that happens, you know what results? Stronger income, more clients and a happier life.

A Coach Who Dared to Stop Being so Agreeable

(Please also see Handout 9: Being a Great Professional Coach vs. Wanting to Be Liked at the end of this book for additional support.)

Becoming an economic powerhouse requires digging into the ways you might be leaking, and looking at those places where you're people-pleasing, where you're in social self and diminishing your professional strength as a coach.

COMMUNICATION AS A PROFESSIONAL COACH

43

Who's Answering Your Email?

For a good chunk of my professional life—from age twenty-one until I was thirty-eight—I behaved like my bosses were my mother.

I didn't do this intentionally; it just seemed to play out that way. I'd receive emails from a boss and be afraid to open them, afraid I'd find out I was "in trouble." If I proposed a new idea for something, I'd be scared, afraid my boss wouldn't like it. Sometimes I held back from sharing the idea, and other times I'd preface it with, "This probably won't work, but . . ." If a boss gave me feedback that I hadn't executed something the way she'd wanted me to, I'd collapse into despair, feeling like I needed to find a way "back into her good graces." Just her name in my email inbox could strike panic in me.

What does she want?
What did I do wrong?
Is she mad at me?

My professional life was often emotional, challenging, and

uncomfortable. I had periods of feeling invisible, underappreciated and disregarded.

If you had been watching me from the outside, all you would have seen was a true professional. In fact, for a long time before I became a professional coach, I was in a key leadership position. Yet inside me all those feelings constantly churned away. So even though I excelled at my job, I still experienced inner fear and judgment. And my mood was dependent on my status with my boss. If I received positive feedback, I felt connected to her. The world was a good place. If I made a mistake or my boss didn't like an idea I offered, I was sad and frustrated, and I felt as if I didn't matter. I was cast out.

You might be thinking, "How the heck does this relate to your mother? Carolyn is one messed-up coach!"

Consider the possibility that until we have done the internal work to resolve our relationships with our parents, we are often re-creating those relationships in our world, in service to surfacing the unresolved material so that we can handle it. Professional relationships often mimic relationships with one or both of our parents. Authority figures, like bosses, are fantastic for this. For you, it might be father issues or abandonment issues, or it might be expressed as fear of getting things wrong, feelings of inadequacy, or any number of other things. Welcome to the club! The point is we carry these things with us until we work through them.

My mom was complex—amazing at times, and at other times, well . . . very complex. I was often afraid of her moods growing up, and as a little girl I decided that the best strategy was to do my best to make her happy, because she seemed *so* unhappy. We do this as little kids; our parents are our Universes, and we often decide we are responsible for their happiness—or, as in my case, it was a double-edged sword: I decided I was responsible for her happiness *and* her unhappiness. This relationship dynamic ended up being played out for me with my future bosses—particularly female ones.

Tiny Hands Shouldn't Send Emails

As I worked with all of this, I realized that the little girl inside me was the one reading the emails from my boss, and often the one writing the responses. I began the process of taking her tiny hands off my keyboard and lovingly letting her know that not only did she not have to respond, she also hadn't done anything wrong. One by one I worked with the old hurts, judgments, and decisions I had made as a little girl about who I was and my illusions of unworthiness. I began to mother *myself* with tenderness and compassion. This was a process over time of slowing everything down, of using the Principles and Practices of Spiritual Psychology and applying loving to the parts inside that hurt.

Over time, my experiences in my workplace transformed. I became more effective and productive in my work. I was less driven by my emotions, and I stopped taking things personally. I started appreciating my ideas and sharing them more readily, without collapsing if they were not implemented. And this led me to a realization: my boss was actually . . . great. She no longer scared me. She was no longer a source of disturbance or upset or approval (at least not most of the time). *She was just my boss.* A

Who's Answering Your Email

woman I worked for. She wasn't mean or punitive. She was, in fact, a wonderful boss.

Our bosses, our colleagues, our clients—they all provide us with opportunities for growth. How many times have you been bothered, frustrated, irritated—triggered—by a colleague's or client's comments? Experienced yourself feeling left out or desperately wanting to prove yourself somehow? Maybe you find yourself upset and angry at your coach, or your boss, or your spouse for not acknowledging you or seeing all the ways you are demonstrating leadership.

You can learn how to use these experiences for healing and growth. Our workplaces, our professional lives, our professional relationships are some of the most fruitful places for us to grow in inner leadership. It simply requires that we slow down and explore our reactions—instead of just acting on them and writing an apologetic or angry or overly pleasing or . . . *whatever* kind of email that little child inside us thinks it needs to write.

Who's answering your emails, talking to your boss, serving your clients, parenting your children? The empowered, strong, awake and conscious adult? Or the little kid inside? Are you seeing your clients, colleagues, everyone in your world with clear eyes, or are you walking around with tinted glasses on (not the rose-colored kind), playing out your family-of-origin issues, like a dramatic play in which you are both the protagonist and the audience?

As professionals, we want to do this important work with ourselves. It makes a profound difference in our worlds and the ways in which we can contribute with greater clarity, peace, and ease, as well as joy and enthusiasm. And it helps us serve our clients even more powerfully—especially if they're facing the same kinds of challenges.

Our professional lives and relationships are some of the most fruitful places for us to grow in inner leadership if we slow down and explore our reactions instead of just acting on them

Utter Coaching Nonsense to Avoid at All Costs

44

Thought Leaders and "Coaches of Influence"

Do you want to be a thought leader? How about a "coach of influence"?

There seems to be a new trend in various professional coaching circles about making a conscious choice to become someone to whom others refer to as a leader of the industry or touchstone for what this business is all about. The coaching field is not alone in this; in fact the idea likely came from other industries first—think Apple with Steve Jobs, Tesla with Elon Musk and so on. Articles abound on the internet sharing how to go about becoming a thought leader through a series of actions, like producing content and coming up with a distinct and authoritative platform. In the coaching arena, another criterion might be only coaching the truly greatest people in the world and turning "regular" people away.

Cards on the table: you've probably already noticed the

distaste I have for this trend. To my mind it's becoming yet another thing that coaches "should" be thinking about in their business like it's an important, valuable, viable goal.

If you've added becoming a thought leader to your plate, allow me to offer that it's 100 percent NOT necessary. Will there be thought leaders and coaches of influence? Yes, for sure. I'll share a few current ones below, with the important caveat that I very much doubt these people set out from the beginning with the intention of being one.

For example, you can be sure that Steve Chandler wasn't sitting around twenty years ago thinking, "My goal is to become a massive coach of influence." Nor is he producing content today with that intention, despite the fact that in certain spheres he is most certainly a thought leader and coach of influence.

I'm pretty positive Brené Brown didn't start her career with thoughts like, "How do I crack this 'thought leader' thing? Because I could REALLY rock that; it's my purpose in life."

Nancy Kline didn't say to herself, "I'm totally going to kill it as a coach of influence by making sure that people everywhere THINK for themselves."

Robert Holden wasn't holed up in his house in London a few decades back, writing his books *Loveability* or *Authentic Success* and musing, "Yep, right here; this is thought-leader material."

These people are all thought leaders, it's true. And other coaches will naturally emerge as authentic thought leaders. And I believe this will happen through the gritty, unglamorous time and effort they spend developing themselves, serving and sharing insights, *because these ideas are burning inside them.* They are

Thought Leaders & "Coaches of Influence"

called to share. They *have* to share, whether it's with two or twenty or twenty thousand people. Whoever reads or listens to their words. *They don't care about influence.* They aren't talking about influence. They care about making a difference with whomever they can.

We don't need to chase the idea of becoming thought leaders in this profession. Our egos (mine included) might be drawn to such grandiose thoughts, but we don't have to listen to them. This idea does a disservice to the profession, because it gives the impression that *influence* is the currency that moves the world. But it's not—*unless you are in the context of ego.* In an ego-based context, influence seems like something we need (or desperately want) in order to get into the spaces where "big things" are happening.

The true currency that moves the world is the currency of the heart. Love is the true currency. And not just any love. It's the big, unconditional love that is available to all of us, at any time.

Michelle's favorite quote was from Mother Teresa, and it's up on my own wall:

> "Not all of us can do great things.
> But we can do small things with great love."

Now I'm not correcting Mother Teresa when I also offer that doing small things with great love IS doing great things, especially in our profession.

Being a coach who serves profoundly, someone who has a beautiful practice where people's lives are transformed—even the lives of "regular" people, like parents, small business owners, teachers—AND making the money you want to make along with having a fulfilling life is available to ALL of us. In my mind, *that's* what we're here for in this profession.

I'm not saying to you, "Don't become a thought leader." There's nothing in and of itself that's bad about that, if it happens. And if this is your calling, you have my encouragement and support in doing all the gritty, laborious, and sometimes lonely work to develop your thoughts and share them courageously.

What I don't want to see in our still young profession is coaches running around thinking that becoming a "coach of influence" is somehow "the ultimate and best goal," that it's something to strive for. Because what I see as really worth striving for is creating deep transformation in the lives of your clients, one person at a time, over and over again, and making your own life a beautiful masterpiece.

45

AI Is a GREAT Coach
(you should hire them/it)?!

Is Albert the AI coach coming for you and your job?

There's a lot of noise in the world about AI and what it's going to mean for our lives, our work, and humanity at large. I'm not here to weigh in on the overall possibilities of what is going to occur with AI over the next twenty to thirty years. I don't know enough, nor am I an expert in the technology arena.

What I *can* share about is the profession of coaching and the potential impact of AI on it—and specifically on you.

Ready? Little to none, with one caveat: the impact it's having on your thinking.

I'm not naive. I'm aware of the programs being created where organizations can have real-time "coaching" provided to leaders via their computer as they are on a call or in a meeting. Based on what AI hears in the communication of the leader, it will offer different prompts/coaching to "auto-correct" the leader, if you will, on their language, tone, and more. (And if you're reading this say ten years from when it was originally published, there are likely even more sophisticated AI programs providing "coaching.")

So maybe these processes will be useful to some extent. But I believe that what AI cannot replace is one human being's ability to attune to another human being. AI cannot create a container of trust and safety into which a person comes and brings their biggest challenges or deepest dreams and starts to unpack them, one by one. AI can't share real, personal experiences of failure, loss, judgment, upset, and possibility as truly their own. AI can't lovingly call you on your BS in the same way a human who gets to know you and your blind spots can.

In other words, it won't be a real, human relationship; it will be a facsimile. It will only go so far, and it only does so much.

AI is nothing to be afraid of *if* you are committed to being a truly masterful coach. Because truly masterful coaches can't be replicated by AI. Can certain, more basic, goal-oriented, physical-world reality coaching be replaced by AI? Maybe. If a client needs help staying on track in the morning, I can imagine that certain computer algorithms might come in handy. AI can ask: Are you getting enough sleep? Are you eating nutritious foods? Are you experiencing stress? And then it can recommend standard activities to

AI can't lovingly call you on your BS, and it's not a replacement for your own vital nature. Your thinking and creative generativity matter.

correct any imbalances in those areas. But when a client is in a nuanced and difficult leadership conversation, or a complex personal situation where sensitivity and deep questions really matter, AI will be at a distinct disadvantage. So it *might* be true that if you are not growing yourself as a coach and you want to stay in the world of goal-line coaching, maybe—just maybe—consider what it will take to rise above the AI noise (that will get loud). I offer to you that this could be a GREAT time to consider deepening your coaching so that no one can touch it, not even Albert the AI coach.

But Are YOU Coming for AI?

AI can spit out ideas for you: outlines for workshops, retreats, coaching exercises on intimacy or goal-setting, titles for articles, social media posts, and more. Are you going to use AI for this? This is obviously your call. There is no one answer, no one-size-fits-all. You *could*—and I also offer that you might not want to. I've played with AI to spit out a wide range of titles for this project—it was the first time I'd ever touched AI, and it was useful. The titles became a jumping-off point that stimulated me to think harder. It helped. And in the end the final title was all mine, no AI, and *this* was useful to discover as well.

It's a slippery slope to use something as a jumping-off point and then slowly, bit by bit, get reeled in. "I'm just going to use this exercise on goal-setting that AI created using all the other exercises that are spread across the internet. It's a really good exercise."

UTTER COACHING NONSENSE

It might be.

And at the same time, if you aren't connected to the content in a real way—that is, if you can't speak to the content from your own life—it won't ring true. And it needs to ring true when you're sharing it with others.

As I'm writing this, the Hollywood writer's strike is just wrapping up. One of the writer's biggest concerns was studios using AI to write scripts. The writers weren't just concerned about the financial impact of this on their livelihoods (which was significant); they were concerned about the overall artistry of writing being diminished. AI is creating *its* content by pulling *other people's* content from across the internet. It's not taking into consideration what's new, what's dated, what's thoughtful, what's creative, what's redundant.

And most important of all, it's not being birthed from inside of you. It's missing that magical element that we don't fully understand, the mysterious aspects of creativity that shine when we come up with "something from nothing."

Do I sometimes see another coach do an exercise and say to myself, "*Wow*—that was good, I'm going to try that at my next live event, with a slight tweak"? YES. I'm seeing how the coach used and presented it. I'm paying attention to the responses in the room and thinking about what I might do differently, given who *I* am and how I like to present. So, although AI can give you a ton of options, it can't tell you where and from whom those options are coming. It can't share where they were used, what the response was from people in the room, how the coach used it, or what the context was.

AI Is a Great Coach!

I'm not suggesting you don't use AI. I'm suggesting that if you do, you use it with caution. Use it carefully, and don't get swept away in the ease of it—don't lose your own unique ideas in the process. AI is a tool, not a replacement for your own vital nature.

Remember that your thinking and creative generativity matter. When we take the time to think and create, our creativity grows. So if you want to use AI to spur your creativity and your ideas, that's wonderful. When you use it as a replacement for your creative thinking, that's where your creative muscles get weaker, and the profession gets weaker, and people start to think, "AI is a great coach—just use AI."

UTTER COACHING NONSENSE

46

Hell No to the Hell Yes

Before we begin, a disclaimer: the following may not really be an instance of "complete and utter nonsense," but I think it IS something that seems to be getting out of control, and which I think we can benefit from looking at more closely.

You likely won't be surprised that we get a LOT of "no's" as we are filling the CFJ Coaching Success School each year. Here, too, no's are good. In fact, they're important, because the school is not for everyone—it is only for coaches who are very sincere that this is *their time* for major growth and upleveling in their business.

Recently though, Jonny Roman, the director of the school, and I had a few people share with us that they were not, in their words, a "Hell, yes!" Meaning, they weren't absolutely, 100 percent certain that this school was the *perfect* fit for them, and they had zero questions about signing up.

I got a little suspicious—not of them, but of the "Hell, yes!" narrative itself. "Hell, yes!" is a kind of rallying call in our profession. It speaks to people's enthusiasm to seize the reins and transform their lives. Some coaches think you need to be a "Hell, yes!" in order to be all-in.

Is this high level of enthusiasm useful? It definitely can be. And it's also *not* always an appropriate gauge for determining where a client or prospective client is in their deeper feelings around coaching. Don't misunderstand: I'm all for a *clear* "no." And . . . can an average, maybe even nervous "yes" be good enough? Is it always the case that if it's not a "Hell, yes!" then it's a no, or even a "Hell, no!"?

This is often the criteria in the context of hiring a coach, paying for coaching/a group/a school, taking a specific job, leaving a specific job, choosing a profession, deciding to get married or divorced, deciding to have a child or not have a child . . . All these and more of the seemingly large decisions in life. The message seems to be that in order for something to be a yes, it has to be a HUGE and BIG and LOUD yes if it's a real, deep and true yes.

I disagree.

In my experience, this isn't accurate or required, and it's possibly not even helpful. In other words, I'm calling BS on the "Hell, yes!" (A gentle, firm, non-agressive BS). And I'm taking a stand for a different yes.

A simple yes.

A quiet yes.

Dare I say, a nervous, even tentative yes.

Upon reflection I realized that the most important decisions in my life have not been "Hell, yes!" For example:

- Choosing to marry my husband of twenty-nine years was not a "Hell, yes!"—nor even the kind of emphatic yes that my best friend, Michelle Bauman, gave to her husband Scott's proposal. My yes was pretty quiet and simple. It was abundantly clear because of a voice I heard inside, and it is, hands down, one of the very best decisions I have made.

- Choosing to apply to the University of Santa Monica and earn a Master's degree in Spiritual Psychology was the furthest thing from a "Hell, yes!" that I think I could get and still ultimately say yes. It was a nervous, doubting yes, an "I don't know if this is a good idea, maybe this place is a bizarre cult, yet something inside is saying 'do it'" kind of yes. Again, it turned out to be one of the very best and most important decisions I have ever made.

- The same was true for deciding to work at USM two years later. This was, again, a nervous, "What if I find out this place is a #@x! show behind the scenes" kind of yes. And yet this was one of the most precious, positive decisions of my professional life, a decision that led me to speaking and facilitating, and to the profession of coaching.

- Hiring Steve Chandler as my coach? It was an "I'm nervous and I think this guy can help me" yes. If I had required a "Hell, yes!" of myself I'd be living a different life, because it's likely I wouldn't have hired him.

- Michelle Bauman: our whole relationship and working partnership was a fun, not-knowing yes. It was a, "Yes, let's spend time together and see." Michelle said to people that she had no idea if we could make money together, and that on paper the decision looked pretty bad ("Why would I give half the money to Carolyn?"). For us it was a yes in our hearts, not a "Hell, yes!" There were no crashing cymbals.

- Teaching at the University of Santa Monica? Developing the Soul-Centered Professional Coaching Program with Steve Chandler, Drs. Ron and Mary Hulnick and Michelle? New levels of terrified and yet certain yes. For Michelle? "I'm not so sure . . . I'd better text Carolyn in the middle of the night questioning the yes" yes.

- Helping Michelle through her illness and then her passing? A terrified and absolutely solemn yes tinged with deep despair.

- Then there's one of the most significant decisions of my entire life: deciding to lean into getting pregnant, not knowing the outcome, not sure I wanted it and not sure I didn't want it. This was a deep, certain, freaked-out, WTF am I thinking and this is important" yes. With the magnificent result of my daughter—my amazing daughter—despite my sacred ambivalence.

- Oh, one other. Deciding to start a school for coaches. This was a "Really? Me? Can I stand forward and say this and do this?" yes.

There you have it.

Every key decision in my life thus far has really *not* been a

"Hell, yes!"

"Quiet certainty" yes. "Disturbing, nervous, flipped-out" yes. "Fun" yes. "WTF" yes. "Inner guidance" yes.

If you've been in the "Hell, yes!" or *no* camp, then realize that the conversation can shift. Remember that your yes is yours. Quiet, loud, nervous, certain, intense, prayerful, big, small—it's yours. The same is true for your clients. Their yes is their yes, and it may not be a "Hell, yes!" Like with my decision to coach with Steve Chandler—not a "Hell, yes!" but a yes I'll be grateful for forever.

Maybe the mindset of "it's either a hell yes or it's a no" is more of an ego thing, a brash, pumped-up state we think we need to to make the yes feel "good" or "right" or more certain. Yet as I've shared, my best yes's so far haven't been brash or big. They were simple, nervous, quiet, slow, laughter-filled, shaky, heart-centered . . . These were the yes's that were good enough for me.

Consider running an experiment in which you make room for your own quiet or nervous yes's—and for your client's and prospective clients yes's of whatever shape and size. This requires more nuance. How does one discern the yes when you aren't looking for crashing cymbals and drums pounding out, "Yes! Yes! Yes!"?

It requires greater listening inside. It requires distinguishing between fear (never a good enough reason not to do something) and the voice of excitement, which can be very similar. It also requires asking deeper questions, as in, "Would this serve my greater good right now even though it's (wildly) uncomfortable?"

When I'm working with a client and they are not sure regarding something that's a "yes" or "no" answer (especially one that seems big), my primary response is almost always, "You'll know. Be with it, get quiet, and the answer is there."

When it comes to coaching and someone is unsure about saying "yes" to working with me or another coach, that usually tells me that they either need more time with me—being served by me—or they might be a no. When it's me, and I want this person as a client, I usually give them more time—like another conversation or two (if I really want them). Or I let them be, serving them through sending a book or something to watch. When I'm coaching a coach who has a prospective client who is also unsure, I offer the same coaching. My experience is that if a person really feels safe and is served by us profoundly in ways that transform them, it's often a yes. People sometimes need more time with us, in the experience of being served by us. And . . . if it's a no, and you gave them more time, there are usually great learnings in there that you can mine for the next time. There's no specific set of rules, no one recipe that works for every person—it's nuanced, every time.

I'm not here to say your no or your client's no is really a yes. That's not for me to decide. I trust your inner guidance, and theirs. What I *will* say is that in my experience, my yes's are often quieter than my clear no's, and maybe it's possible yours are too. So maybe we can take the pressure off and not require what occurs like a more aggro version of a yes?

Here's to more nuance, more listening, more gentleness and more room to have different yes's.

47

Six Figures in Six Weeks

On paper (or in your Facebook feed) it sounds good: "Take your coaching business to six figures in six weeks!"

There's a lot of ridiculous stuff that coaches get bombarded with on the internet all day long, and this is one of the most egregious examples. It's so unfortunate. It's also a totally unreasonable proposition, and yet it continues because some coaches are drawn into it. And someone who talks a really good game does a good job of selling and manipulating a coach's dreams and fears and—boom—a coach pays $25k to be in a program that will get them to "six figures in six weeks" or some similarly "the sky's the limit" proposition.

New enrollees receive detailed scripts (ugghhh) of exactly what to say to people. They tell coaches to do a thirty-minute (or shorter) discovery call, and then . . . MAKE AN OFFER.

A coach I spoke with recently was in this kind of program. She paid $27k and it wasn't going well. She hadn't made any money, and she was struggling. She didn't really understand serving and was instead caught up in the steps this program outlined. In short, she was following the "rules," but she was not winning the game.

We slowed things way down. I shared that in my experience no coach gets to six figures in six weeks. Most don't get to six figures in six months or even a year. I asked her, "If you wanted to be a doctor and you saw an ad saying you could become a doctor in six weeks or even six months, would you believe that?"

"No," she said. "Absolutely not."

"So what made you think it was true of this profession?"

She shrugged and said, "I don't know. I just kept seeing ads from well-known coaches who said it could be done."

I shared that in every profession there are people who will feed on those coming up after them—without integrity. Maybe, maybe somewhere there's a coach who has made six figures in six weeks or six months; I certainly don't know any of them, and I know a lot of coaches. What, I asked her, might it be like to treat the business of becoming a professional coach like learning to become a doctor, an accountant, an engineer—any professional position that requires not just skill but practice, personal growth, and dedication?

She said, "It would take time."

"And learning, and focus." She agreed. I asked her if she'd considered the possibility that it could potentially take one to three years, maybe more, to consistently earn six figures.

She was quiet for a moment, then said, "I hadn't considered that. I've been feeling a lot of pressure to make it work quickly."

Becoming a successful professional coach is a project, one that can take time, depending on where you are in the process, who you are and what you bring to the table to start with. For example, if you're coming from a corporate job, your trajectory and timeline may be different than if you're coming from a therapy or teaching background. There's also the matter of learning the kind of material you're reading about in this book. And there's practice. It's an intentional process, and the more time and attention you bring to it, the more likely you can accelerate it. What's more, if you take on this project on a timeline that takes into account all of the above, you can relieve the enormous pressure you might be feeling to make it work in six weeks or six months or whatever.

I shared all this with her, and she started to look and sound more relaxed. And that's how I want you to feel.

Coaching is a profession like any other. It takes time and effort to become financially successful. You want to be prepared for this, whether that means having enough money in the bank before you start, a part-time job to support you while you make it work, or being okay with tolerating some uncertainty and smaller balances in your bank account for at least one to three years.

Don't buy into the hype of six figures in six weeks. My encouragement is to buy into the fact that creating yourself as a professional coach is a project that requires a dedicated, no B.S. project manager who doesn't let you off the hook—aka *you*.

48

Hiring Other People to Get You Business

(Nightmare dressed as a daydream?)

A n email I received recently (one of many similar versions):

Dear Carolyn,

You've never heard of me. Hi, I'm Aaron.

I got your email by asking ChatGPT, "Who has the most amazing business in the world, and why is it Carolyn?"

Ok, I got it from a lead-finding tool.

Let me get right down to it . . . are you running monthly promos for your services or having anyone get great leads for you?

If not, you're leaving between 20k and 200k/mo+ on the table. I don't know if this is a problem you have, but I help busy businesses run monthly promos and find great leads, working on a pure commission basis.

No retainers. No upfront fees. No hidden costs.

I'll handle everything, writing promos in your voice your audience will love . . . finding the right people for you to talk to and then coach! You ONLY pay me a small cut of the sales I'll bring in each month.

If I get zero results, you don't owe me a thing.

I'm not sure if this is something you're interested in.

If it's not, totally cool. If so, reply "more info" and I'll shoot over a short message that details everything.

I promise it'll be the best thing you've done all year. Cheers!

Cheers to Aaron and their corny marketing copy, which feels to me both disingenuous and ridiculous (no judgment; they are doing their best). And . . . maybe this kind of thing excites you. Reading it, you might heave a big sigh of relief and say to yourself, "HALLELUJAH! My nightmare is over! No more enrollment! I get to just coach and do what I do best!"

Not so fast.

This might *seem* like it would be *so* great. And I know many coaches who have gone down this path, only to discover one of three things:

- It was too good to be true, huge waste of money and energy.

- The leads that did come were NOT even close to strong or appropriate.

Hiring Other People to Get You Business

- The cost outweighed the return (when the service charged in advance for it). Often.

This approach appeals to coaches who "hate" sales, who despise enrolling and who pine for the day when "my whole business is referrals and I never have to connect and invite again!"

I hear you.

And I offer that you are missing something vital: the value and importance of learning how to enroll effectively, and how much this improves and deepens your coaching.

Plus—it's a blast.

A blast? Meeting people, connecting, and enrolling is a blast? Did you fall and hit your head recently, Carolyn? No. The joy of creating a client yourself, from scratch, is unparalleled. Michelle would often say to coaches, "When I look out into the world, see someone I know is up to something, and begin nurturing and then ultimately enrolling them as a client? These are the clients I love the most!"

There's no "hack" for connecting and serving. Some of the most meaningful work happens in the early stages, when you are building trust and rapport, and someone is starting to share their challenges or heartfelt dreams with you—maybe things they have never shared before. Michelle would also say that some of the deepest coaching occurs in these early conversations, where the foundation is set for the work ahead.

Is that something you want to *skip* in your practice?

Now, if you're like me and you have a school, could someone do this *with* you? That is, could you enroll together, as

> **If you're hiring other people to get you clients, you're missing out on something vital: learning how to enroll effectively improves and deepens your coaching.**

a team, so that there's a group effort around connecting and bringing people into your practice? Yes. And, of course, the two people who did this with me—Amber Krzys for the first four years of my school, and Jonny Roman now—both knew me and the school very, very well. Amber had been my client for many years. I coached her in her own enrollment practices in her business, and Michelle was her coach before me. Jonny went through the school as a coach, and so he has firsthand experience of the school and what it does for people. This kind of sharing of enrollment *can* work. But I would not bring a stranger in off the street to help me enroll for the school, someone who wasn't intimately connected with who I am and what the school is all about.

There's another angle too: having someone else get you business tends *not to work*. Probably because the prospective client needs that sense of connection and support to enroll the first place. They are, after all, ultimately enrolling with *you*, not Aaron.

I haven't seen this work effectively. Are there coaches for whom it's worked? Probably some—I just don't know any. And as I say, I don't think this approach is for coaches who want to create deep, intimate coaching relationships with their individual clients.

Maybe for more goal-line kinds of coaching than soul-line (although again, for an individual coach my point of view is that

Hiring Other People to Get You Business

it's a strange and not ideal thing). And perhaps it could help in enrolling for larger programs—perhaps people like Martha Beck and Tony Robbins have people enrolling for them for events?

And, when it comes down to enrolling for my practice, and likely for yours as well, consider this: Aaron doesn't know me from Adam. Aaron cannot be in my voice, can't ask questions I would likely ask spontaneously and in response to something that happens in the moment. Aaron doesn't get the sheer pleasure of the beginning, of the early stages of building a relationship that can result in deep and powerful personal transformation.

Aaron doesn't understand these things—especially the ways in which they arise from within the space that is created between myself and my client or prospective client. And *I do*. I know when to slow down or speed up. I know the resources that might best serve the person. And one of the reasons I know these things is because I've been practicing enrollment and connection for a long time.

I don't want Aaron handing people off to me, because that sends a message to prospective clients that "I don't do the early stuff. It's beneath me. It's not important enough. I'm too busy and important to enroll."

We've talked about this idea elsewhere in this book, and I'll share it again: Turn enrollment into the thing you love *as much* as coaching. Because one deepens the other. See enrollment as something you *get* to do rather than dreading doing it. If you're struggling with this, find someone who can coach you into this understanding, and you won't need Aaron or anyone else to fill your practice.

Serving Yourself: Personal Growth as a Professional Coach

49

Coaches Adrift Without Coaching

The other day I was in a conversation with a new-ish coach who said he wanted to be coached. He knew it was "a good idea." He wanted to be making more money in this profession, and he wanted to be expanding what he did, who he served. He was struggling, trying to make it work, and he felt like he wasn't there yet.

I also recently spent time with my own coach, in a room with four other dedicated coaches, looking at my business and personal life and at what's calling to me from both. I came out of the room different, clearer, with some actions to take, and feeling different inside.

Then I had another conversation, this one with a not-so-newish coach who ran groups and did other kinds of work as well. She wanted to expand her work, and she had concerns about providing for her family. She had never worked with a coach.

Another coach, someone who had been coaching on and off for years, told me he was frustrated and angry that he couldn't seem to make enough to earn his living solely from coaching. He told me, "I haven't found the right coach to help me."

All this reminded me of what my business partner, Michelle, said to a room full of USM grads at an evening we facilitated for the University of Santa Monica's Soul-Centered Professional Coaching Program. We were talking about this profession of coaching and how there's a low bar to entry. Michelle explained,

> I'm a product of coaching. There's my USM education, which is important. It's my foundation. There's my coach, Steve Chandler, who helps me in all areas of my life. Now, we don't need much to get into this profession. A phone, a computer . . . that's not really the point though. So getting *in* isn't the question. The question is, how do we become great at what we're doing? Not great in the ego sense; great in the *mastery* sense. How do we get great at something? I can tell you something *I* do: I have my coach, and every year I put myself in something where I'm learning and growing. I'm growing so that I have more to give to my clients and to my business.

What Michelle (and I) are saying is this: *All we have to give to others is our own consciousness.* That's it. That's all we have. And all we have to give to our business is our consciousness. You could say what we put in is what we get out, by which I mean that whatever we take in and process from our lives and our coaches and the programs we participate in and our own coaching of others is what we have to give to others.

Coaches Adrift Without Coaching

So in terms of building a coaching business, when it comes to having your own coach, here are some very basic equations:

No Coach = Less Effective
No Coach = Less Growth
No Coach = Less Income
No Coach = More Floundering

Coaches want and need to grow. Newer coaches, especially when they are in the first five years of their work in this profession, *need* coaching. Real coaching, on their business and themselves. My own point of view is that coaches need coaching throughout the course of their careers—in service to their own growth and the growth of their clients. That's just me. Breaks between coaching programs are great too—and I'm committed to ongoing learning and growth.

Don't get me wrong. The coaches I mentioned at the beginning of this chapter are fantastic people, and they are also helping others. Yet they're in a real dilemma. They haven't chosen *in* yet. Not really. Not fully. Not to themselves, to their business, or to this profession.

How do I know? Because they aren't being coached. It's evident in their speaking, in their thinking—they are in the land of uncoached thoughts and an uncoached way of being.

I love this profession. I love that it's not regulated and that people are required to choose *in* or *not in* when it comes to growing themselves and their business—because it separates out those who are in this for the duration. Since there's a very low bar to entry, the profession welcomes all . . . those who stay, and those who put in the work of showing up, of being taught, of being served so that they can serve in greater ways—in other words, of being *coached*—those are the ones who create mastery.

There's no way to know that out of the gate. You can't know it until you are in the room. Until you have made the investment. There's no way to know what it's like to share your own underbelly, what can occur when you let someone see your own perceived messiness. Until you are in *your own* container of learning and expansion, there's no way to know what is available to you *and* your clients.

Furthermore, there's no way to know what you are asking others to do if you have not done it yourself. We can only assist others to the degree we have assisted ourselves. So when you are offering coaching to others and aren't making the same (or greater) investment in your own coaching, you may help, but it's unlikely you'll be as effective. Maybe you won't know when to go deep. Maybe you won't risk asking an uncomfortable question because you've never had to answer it yourself. On the other hand, if you *know* from experience what you're asking your client to do, you can be more present for them and support them more deeply since you've done it yourself.

So I hope to see you on the other side. On the other side of growth, of expansion, of a stronger business mindset and an even more joyful life.

I hope *you*, too, become a product of coaching. And not just because the best coaches I know are products of coaching. But because your whole life will be better. You will serve more effectively. You will create a stronger, more financially successful business. Your days will be more joyful. You will be expanding.

Coaches Adrift Without Coaching

You will know what it means to be coached powerfully, and because of this, your clients will too.

There's no way to know what you are asking others to do if you haven't done it yourself. So when you're offering coaching to others and aren't making the same (or greater) investment in your own coaching, it's unlikely you'll be as effective as you could be.

50

My Barbie Dream Camper

Let's talk about Barbie—and specifically, Barbie Dream Campers. I had a Barbie Dream Camper growing up and I loved it—I could make a little barbecue on the fake grill. Barbie and Ken would hang out, talk, roast marshmallows, you name it. It was a perfectly safe and fun place to spend time.

And without realizing it, as I came into adulthood, I created my very own *inner* Barbie Dream Camper. I did a great job at it: my camper had a fancy built-in bed, coffee maker, mini-fridge . . . everything I needed to ensure I didn't have to go outside and speak up for what I wanted. My inner camper was where I hung out during all the times I said yes because I wanted to be liked or approved of, even though inside my answer was no. Those times I didn't negotiate for a higher salary right at the start. The instances when I was afraid of being perceived as "difficult" if I disagreed with someone. When I stayed longer, even though I wanted to go, when I watched others experience greater opportunities because they could say the word "no."

My Barbie Dream Camper

Too many of us sit inside our inner Barbie Campers or our Dream Houses and don't come out "for fear of" something bad happening. Sometimes we let other people—and ideas—move in. We let them put up their pictures and play their music, and we think we just have to put up with it. We take their offers instead of creating our own or asking for more. These choices happen in an instant—and over the course of a lifetime. Each one leads to another plastic panel in the Barbie Camper. For me they became another way to keep myself in Barbie Land, not getting messy, not communicating my ideas and vision. I made these choices myself more times than I can count, stopping myself from experiencing greater freedom, empowerment, and abundance—not just financially, but also in terms of my own personal and professional growth.

This only stopped when I stopped looking outside and started looking inside at the choices I was making. It stopped when I hired a coach. It stopped when I decided that the only thing, the only person keeping me in the Barbie Dream Camper was *me*.

My assumptions were along the lines of, "I'm not able to be a business owner," "I can't manage or make money," "I need to work for someone; it's the only way to make a living." In addition to these, there were the assumptions of, "I need other people to do this," "I can't do it alone," "I won't be okay if Michelle dies."

I've not completely stopped either—I still bump up against ones like, "You can't write a new book, Carolyn," "You can't do new things, new and *bigger* things," "You are getting older," "You're done."

Now I know the low hum of these limiting beliefs. With

SERVING YOURSELF: PERSONAL GROWTH

attention and intention I can break through, sometimes even before I've fully bought into them. This is my job—not just as a coach who needs to keep growing herself, but as a human being. And this is what we as coaches help other human beings do. Everyone has an inner Dream Camper that they are hanging out in, accepting as "enough"—we can help them drive it into new territory.

How about you? Is your Dream Camper truly yours, or is it Ken's Mojo Dojo Casa House? Are you willing to take back the keys to YOUR camper, and drive it wherever YOU want to go?

Consider that the inner structures we build—whether we're talking about Barbie Dream Campers, glass ceilings or something else—contribute to the outer ones that exist in the world. If we think our salary is out of our hands, that women can't get a certain job, that creating a successful coaching business is impossible, we join a chorus of other people who think the same, and we reinforce these beliefs, regardless of whether there's any actual truth behind them. The more we accept the fact that the steering wheel is already in our own hands, the more likely it is that we'll go where we want to go. And the more we drive our Campers with confidence, the less others will be able to backseat drive using *their* map.

And as we courageously do the things that are uncomfortable, the outer world is challenged to change.

There is no assumption that's immovable.

There is no story that can't be dissolved.

Where might we GO if we didn't buy into these plastic facsimiles of a life well lived? If we own the houses of our hearts and minds, if we develop enough self-esteem to speak up even if we might not be liked, what new ideas will be seeded and nurtured? What new leaders will be born? What new ideas will be created? What lives will be transformed?

We are responsible for the choices we make and the ideas we buy into. And the best part is that we can *still* love our Barbie Dream Campers—and transform them into powerful, inspiring and unstoppable vehicles.

Consider that the inner structures we build—whether we're talking about Barbie Dream Campers, glass ceilings or something else—contribute to the outer ones that exist in the world. The more we accept the fact that the steering wheel is already in our own hands, the more likely it is that we'll go where we want to go.

51

Grow Yourself

Successful professional coaches are regularly doing something to *grow themselves*—new experiential work, new programs, different kinds of personal growth work. In my own life, I'm committed to something new every year. This could include working with a different coach (in addition to my current one), a workshop, a training course, and so on. It's important for my work, because the more I learn and grow, the more I have to give to my clients. And it's important for my life!

You might exclaim, "You mean I need to keep investing time and money in workshops, coaches, trainings, even *after* I've made it as a successful coach?"

Yes!

Here are some of my own examples as to why this is so important. As I've already mentioned, Michelle and I went and studied with Nancy Kline and learned the Time to Think approach to coaching. We did this while we were being coached by Steve Chandler. Guess who recommended Nancy to us?

Grow Yourself

STEVE. He sent Michelle her book, *Time to Think*. Michelle read it (almost immediately) and said to me, "We have to go work with her."

So we did, and it was *amazing*. Nancy changed us. As I share elsewhere in this book, we took her work back to our clients and shared it with them, and they got even more value from our work with them because of it. I started working with Nancy individually again after both my parents died. I wanted to go deeper into the Time to Think work, and I wanted to be with Nancy.

Another example: when Michelle passed I did enormous amounts of research and studying about grief (I was wondering why I felt crazy, had insomnia, and was eating almond croissants daily). I found the work of Megan Devine,[7] which helped me profoundly in my personal grief *and* made me a better coach. Her thirty-day grief writing course was beautiful and challenging. I've shared her work with clients and prospective clients over and over again. They know I walk my talk, that I've done my own work and continue to do so.

I also went to a Three Principles intensive a few years ago. So many people around me were getting into the Three Principles that I knew I needed to experience it myself.

This is all part of the idea that you can use *everything*—all the challenges, life events, teachings, workshops, experiences— use it all to *grow*, and then turn around and share it in your work. Becoming a trusted source of transformation for others is a process, not an event.

---

[7] www.refugeingrief.com

SERVING YOURSELF: PERSONAL GROWTH

And it's the NUMBER ONE thing highly successful coaches do.

Steve Chandler the godfather of coaching is *always* taking a course, working with a coach on some new thing, reading books and watching movies or talks. Always.

We become better coaches every time we do something to grow ourselves. Our consciousness is what people are buying. The more we grow, the more we expand, and the more valuable we become. We bring everything to our clients: our life experiences as well as all the trainings, workshops, coaching sessions, therapy and everything else we've done in our lives.

Every person I work with gets the benefit of the very first thing I did in terms of significant personal growth—my Master's Degree in Spiritual Psychology from the University of Santa Monica. People benefit from it even if I never mention it. It's alive inside of me, and I lean on it every time I serve someone. And every session I've done with Steve Chandler, Nancy Kline and others is in me to use as I work with someone.

Michelle's passing pushed me into new, painful growth. It was one of the greatest growth opportunities in my life, and despite the pain, I'm grateful for it. My parents' passing led me to research and read about the phase of life after both parents are gone, which led me back to working with Nancy Kline more deeply. And so on. I pass all this and more on to clients and anyone else who crosses my path, as appropriate.

I want to keep adding to my inner awareness and learning as long as I'm around to do so. And I suggest you will want to as well if you are clear about gaining mastery in this profession.

52

I Can Build Anything

I recently volunteered at my daughter's high school to make sets for their spring musical. My husband, our daughter and I went; we really like doing service as a family. I figured I'd be working on something straightforward, like painting backdrops. When we arrived, the woodshop teacher introduced himself, showed us around and gave us suggestions for what we could do. He talked about saws, creating a chair where spikes could rise up through the seat (it was for *The Addams Family* musical), building a fence and more.

Here's what I began to hear myself saying, first in my mind, and then out loud, with an appropriate dose of self-deprecation:

- "This is not my wheelhouse."
- "Umm, measuring? I thought I'd just be painting some wood..."
- "I'm not the woodworker—that's more my husband's jam."

SERVING YOURSELF: PERSONAL GROWTH

- "This is not the best use of my skillset."
- "Is there something else I can do? I'm really good at creating money, ha, ha, ha. I don't think I can do this."

The technical director for the show didn't miss a beat. She looked at me and said, "You can learn to build anything."

I was instantly thrilled—and slightly embarrassed. Here I was, a leadership and life coach, vomiting up limiting beliefs in rapid fire, one after the other. Thankfully, this kind woman woke me up to my own inner soundtrack of contraction.

I said to her, "You're totally right! We can learn to build anything! *I* can learn to build anything!"

How quickly I was labeling myself as someone who "can't build sets"! Someone who "doesn't measure/can't use a staple gun/won't be able to help in this instance." Creating a really solid, immovable argument for why I should stand around and look at my phone, or maybe get water for people instead of getting in there and doing something.

That is not who I want to be. Labeling myself as someone who can't build anything is *not* the example I want to set for my teenage daughter, or for any other teens in the room who happen to be listening. So I changed the narrative: "I can learn to build anything."

And guess what?

I made stuff! I MEASURED the lid of a coffin and then used foam to glue it to the lid. Following the teacher's instructions, I learned to use a staple gun; it was deeply satisfying to *wham* the staple into the wood (while I held my fingers out of the way).

I Can Build Anything

I felt awkward, nervous, and clumsy a decent amount of the time, and embarrassed that I was the ONLY person who didn't bring work gloves (my husband brought his, but I don't even own any). I still made some self-deprecating jokes . . . and I had a great time. It helped that I made the awkward, clumsy feelings okay. I was encouraging within myself: "You're doing so great, Carolyn—look at you!" This kind of thinking tends to make me laugh inside, and it feels way better than, "You are such a fx@ing idiot, Carolyn . . ."

There's simply not a good enough reason to withhold loving from myself anymore. There *never* was, only now I'm clearer on the consequences of self-talk. I don't want to pay the price of feeling bad and have to do the work it takes to rebuild my own self-trust. I would prefer to simply *know* I can count on myself for kindness and caring, to be good to myself.

Are you a label maker? So many people walk around with labels slapped—boom!—right on their forehead in big capital letters—without any awareness of it. "I'm not a money person," "I'm a hugger," "I'm not timely," "I'm a sushi person," "I'm bad with numbers." The list goes on. (And, of course, we all slap labels on *other* people's foreheads as well—imagine if we could let those fall away too.)

What kinds of labels do coaches put on themselves? You might be more familiar with a number of them than you would care to admit. Here are a few, along with their potential consequences if you go on believing them.

- "I'm not good at dealing with no." *Consequence:* fear of rejection leads to fear of asking, of putting oneself out there.

SERVING YOURSELF: PERSONAL GROWTH

- "I can't require someone to do an assignment, pay in full up front, not move a session, etc." *Consequence:* not being in leadership means not fully serving the client or yourself.
- "I'm not someone who can charge a higher fee—it's not in me." *Consequence:* you remain stuck at lower fees.
- "Nobody will pay a higher fee." *Consequence:* see immediately above.
- "I could never fill a group, lead a retreat, stand in front of a room, tell a client they're fired, etc." *Consequence:* you won't *try* to fill a group, lead a retreat, stand in front of a room . . .
- "I'm a great coach—I'm not a good enroller." *Consequence:* you resist enrolling and struggle when trying.
- "I can't invite people—my practice was built through referrals and other work. Inviting isn't my thing." *Consequence:* you will struggle to fill your practice.
- "I don't know how to connect on my own. It's not in my wheelhouse. I'm SO much better when someone refers a person to me. Then I can really be with someone." *Consequence:* missed opportunities at the gym, at the grocery store, at the PTA meeting, etc.
- "I can't build stuff." *Consequence:* not building stuff . . . Okay, this one's mine, but maybe it fits for other coaches too.

I Can Build Anything

Labeling creates limits in your life and business. You end up acting as if these labels are permanent features on your forehead. But they're not. And the best thing about becoming aware of your labels is that *now you can start peeling them off!* You can remove those labels and discard them. And you can help your clients do the same thing.

AND! If you *are* going to label, since you know they can be disarmingly effective, why not try new, more expansive ones on for size?

I can do ANYTHING
I can PRACTICE
I can GET BETTER
I can learn to INVITE
I can handle [XYZ]
I can GROW

And they're *all true*. I'm not talking about chanting affirmations that you *wish* were true. This is about literally rewiring your brain. The negative labels, those things you're saying to yourself consciously or otherwise, are tanking your ability to move in new directions. I invite you to slow down and really look at the quality of your thoughts. Are you allowing your thinking to dictate what you are willing to do and not do? At what cost?

As for me—I can learn to build anything. I can even use a staple gun!

SERVING YOURSELF: PERSONAL GROWTH

53

Coaching, Loneliness and Community

Entrepreneurship can be lonely. A 2018 *Forbes* article[8] cites the Gallup Wellbeing Index, *Harvard Business Review* and the Self-Employment Review for the UK in sharing data around how entrepreneurs experience loneliness. In some instances at least 30% of them cite it as a "problem." That's not surprising, is it? No hanging out, drinking coffee together. The setting for Monday morning is pretty much the same as it is for Sunday evening if you work from home. Coaching in particular is a business where you can isolate, barely leave the house, work (or pretend to work) in pajamas (or at least pajama pants), and have poor hygiene. You can even do it for multiple days in a row.

---

[8] Agarwal, Dr. P. (2021, June 29). *It is time we acknowledged loneliness in entrepreneurs and did something about it.* Forbes. https://www.forbes.com/sites/pragyaagarwaleurope/2018/07/12/loneliness-as-an-entrepreneur-heres-something-we-can-do-about-it/?sh=20d209107f0c

Coaching, Loneliness and Community

Not that I ever did . . .

Think about what we encourage our clients to do: get out there! Connect! Go do stuff! Stretch!! What are we modeling if we stay huddled in our apartments, scanning social media to see what people are up to?

The truth is, coaches do better with connection. All entrepreneurs—and all *people*—do, too, at least with *some* degree of connection that brings us out of ourselves and into community with others. Whatever your profession, it's too easy to get stuck in your own thinking when there's nothing to balance it out. And one of the most important things a coach can do is hire their own coach and get into community with other coaches.

I had the privilege of having Michelle Bauman in my life for more than ten years as my business partner and best friend. She and I were our own community, the two of us. At the beginning of my (our) business, I had someone in lockstep with me. We bumbled our way through uncomfortable conversations, and we reported in to our coach, Steve Chandler. We could be uncomfortable, messy and needy together. We could bounce ideas off each other, share fears and goals, and support each other every day in more ways than I can count.

Steve would point out to us how rare this was, and how lucky we were, but I didn't believe him at first. "Really?" I'd say. "Other coaches don't have people to do this with? I mean, forget about business partners, even as friends?" Steve would shake his head.

When Michelle was gone, I was alone in a way that I could never have imagined. She was someone who understood the journey of growing oneself in this profession—who not only

SERVING YOURSELF: PERSONAL GROWTH

knew me but who really was my true peer in growth and learning and experience. Her loss was devastating.

I still appreciated my work and my clients. I still had my coach . . . and yet, I didn't have Michelle.

For a time I didn't *want* anyone else, much less a group. For a long time I felt like I was on an island. Every once in a while, I let people visit for short stints. Nobody really understood the loneliness I was experiencing, this double-edged, gaping wound of losing my work partner and best friend with whom I had once been able to talk about anything. When Michelle passed, it was as though I went from being in a community of hundreds to . . . nothing. *That* was the level of connection Michelle filled. We'd grown something significant together—a partnership in business and deep friendship—and just like that it was gone.

Time and inner work started to soften this. So did coaching my clients, because serving others is one of the best ways to get out of your own stuff. Then my coach suggested that I join a different group of his, a very small one. He thought it would be good for me. I didn't really want to—and I said yes anyway, because (for the most part) I listen to my coach, and I am wildly coachable.

And to my surprise, it helped. As part of a group of other coaches I could feel myself opening up again. Slowly, I started feeling less alone in the profession. World-class coach Devon Bandison became a true and cherished friend through this group. In addition to his excellence, Devon brought unexpected joy, fun and laughter into my world that I didn't ever think I'd experience in a professional relationship again. Other groups followed, and gradually I shifted to a new understanding, one that integrates my relationship with Michelle into who I am in a deep way. I was able to receive in community, be with peers and benefit from this. Michelle's place beside me is not filled, because there's no filling it (and I don't yearn for someone to fill it either). I still have moments where what I want is her presence, her unique intellect and wisdom. I'm pretty sure I always will—and now it's there inside of me, always available.

> **Don't wait; stop going it alone. Make sure you have your own coach. And find people dedicated to growing themselves in this profession, who are open to who you are and what you have to share.**

This is my very long way of saying *we need community*. The University of Santa Monica was where I first experienced the benefits of deep community. Then I participated in a number of groups with Steve Chandler, and with a few other coaches. Community makes a significant difference in the growth of a coach and their business. Even though I come from a transformative educational model that was all about community (the University of Santa Monica, which I loved) I am still learning how vital community is in this profession. I see what happens in my own school, how the community makes everything better for a developing coach or a seasoned, successful coach who's simply been on their own and has become isolated. In the first month, people get connected and through that process feel less alone. The foundation becomes one of rooting for each other, of choosing to see every individual win

SERVING YOURSELF: PERSONAL GROWTH

as a community win. As with any good school, it is a space where you can make mistakes and be messy and vulnerable—and be there for each other. Many coaches return several years in a row to support their business growth and earnings, and because they know that when they trip and fall, hands will be extended to help them up again, and everyone will move forward together.

Michelle would often say that she and I would only work with newer coaches in a group setting, because you can learn faster in a group. The questions people have and the situations they share typically reflect something many others in the group are working through. "Oh, right . . . me too" becomes a common refrain. Obviously this accelerates the learning process—and it also makes it easier to see you're not crazy, you're not broken—and you're not *alone*.

I mention the CFJ school because it's infused with the loving and learning Michelle and I shared; our connection is part of the soil in which the school grows. At the same time, community is available in *lots* of places for coaches. Seek out the programs and schools that resonate with you. What's important is that you recognize the importance of community. It is the antidote to loneliness. And beyond that, it can accelerate your personal and professional growth.

Don't wait; stop going it alone. Make sure you have your own coach. And find a place that will lift you up and teach you things you can't learn on your own. Find people dedicated to growing themselves in this profession, who are open to who you are and what you have to share.

54

The Universe Has My Back

A Context for Living

Twenty-four hours after I landed in L.A. from Dublin, I was getting ready for my first day back at work when something dawned on me: I couldn't remember having taken my computer out of my backpack when I unpacked it.

Mild feelings of disturbance trickled through my body. It was 8:00 at night. I looked in my backpack again; it was empty. I looked in a few more places where I might have set my laptop in the hours since I'd been home. Nothing.

I started to feel a slightly heightened disturbance. "I have a Zoom call tomorrow," I thought. "And my whole life is on my computer."

I called to my husband John. He came into the living room looking as glazed over and jet-lagged as I probably did (our bodies thought it was 4:00 in the morning). I said, "I think I left my computer on the plane. I don't remember putting it in my

SERVING YOURSELF: PERSONAL GROWTH

backpack."

"Let's look in your office."

I knew it wasn't there, and I went through the process anyway. Then I Googled, "Left computer on plane" and got a bunch of suggestions. I called the airline and left a message with their lost and found. Then I said to my husband—with a tone of what you could charitably call "relaxed high anxiety"—"We have my backup right?" Because I was writing my second book and I had other things I was working on for the upcoming CFJ Coaching Success School on my computer. Nothing I wanted to lose or have to recreate.

He looked at me, deeply tired, and mercilessly said. "Yes, and you last backed up 500 days ago."

Now, you can judge my very poor computer backup protocol. Go ahead. But before you start sending me emails about getting my computer back, or hacks for backing up, or how I could use the Three Principles or breathwork to regulate myself, I'll finish the story.

Within ten minutes of John and I Googling, he came back into the living room and said, "I just got a call from the airline about your computer." I called the number and the person on the other end asked a few verifying questions, then told me where to pick up my computer. John and I smiled at each other, tired and grateful.

As a friend of mine later said, "The UNIVERSE had you backed up."

Yes it did.

Now let me ask you a question: who or what do you have backing up you and your business?

Are you backing yourself up?

For real—do you have human backups?

A coach?

Community?

What about a life context that backs you up inside when life becomes more challenging? One of my favorite questions to ask a prospective client is this:

"Do you have a context for life? A way of viewing life and the world that you utilize and practice?" Sometimes I'm met with a blank stare in response, or I'm asked, "Do you mean a spiritual foundation or . . . ?"

"It could be," I often say, and I also share that a life context could be something that's taken on unconsciously or otherwise from our parents and the world. For example, in my family, the unspoken context was "Life is for arguing, being alone in your room, and being upset at those around you. That's love."

Other people have contexts like, "Life is hard and we don't get the good stuff" or "Keep your nose down and don't be noticed" or "Work is life."

There are all sorts of life contexts.

When I sat in the University of Santa Monica classroom and heard, "You can use everything for learning, growth, and upliftment" I nearly fell out of my purple chair.

Then, "How you relate to the issue IS the issue" and "Mistakes are for learning." I almost thought I was in a prank TV reality show. Could I really learn to experience the world that way?

Yes.

It was life-changing for me to live into and experience a

different life context. Context is everything. Your context for life, and the growth of your business, is everything.

Is the Universe for you?

Does life love you?

When you don't get a client, were you spared? Is it a good thing in disguise? A learning opportunity? Was your enrollment process lousy? Or are you just lousy? Do other coaches have things go easier for them than things go for you?

If you don't have a created, conscious context you live by, you will live by your default, unconscious context—generally, whatever you developed and didn't question as you grew. The same is true for your clients and prospective clients. Understanding and getting intentional about this is a big way to help ourselves and our clients create our lives.

The Universe Had My Back (and so did Aer Lingus)

I didn't back up my computer. I made a mistake and I left my computer on the plane. My husband went with me to the airport to get my computer. My editor had all the recent writings on his Google Drive. Life would've loved me (and still loves me) whether or not I lose my computer.

I invite you to practice a more loving-life context, one that always has your back. Play with asking your clients and prospective clients about a life context, about what their operating beliefs are informing them about how life "is"—and whether it's worth shifting to something more wonderful.

Conclusion

We complete where we started, in a boat. Hopefully your boat is different now—sturdier and more robust, able to withstand any kind of waters you encounter. More importantly, my hope is that you have now claimed yourself as the captain of your business and are charting your direction and taking the initiative in serving and creating clients.

I wish you "fair winds and following seas." This phrase is a nautical blessing used to wish someone good luck on their journey. "Fair winds" speak to favorable winds that will carry you home, and "following seas" speaks to the waves pushing you in the direction of your heading. I hope this book pushed you into more financially successful and personally and professionally satisfying waters!

And no matter what, remember that in this profession (and in all professions) we do better with assistance . . . first and foremost in the form of coaches, with community, and with ongoing learning and growth.

I'm rooting for you and all of us—always

Handouts & Sample Coaching Agreement

Download full-size versions here:

carolynfreyerjones.com/lps/tcs-book-handouts/download

Handout 1

Anatomy of An Enrollment Conversation

THE ANATOMY OF AN ENROLLMENT CONVERSATION

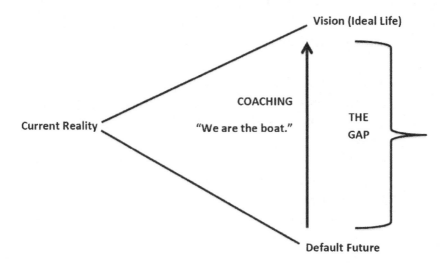

The Default Future—What happens if you do nothing? Where will you be in six months, a year?

The Vision (The Ideal Life)—What would you like to have happen? How important is this for you? Could you wait?

The Gap Conversation—The space between the Vision and the Default Future. Our job as coaches is to discover the landscape of their life and the Gap(s) so the Client's decision is whether to close the Gap(s) or not.

The Gap Conversation generally takes place within the first longer coaching conversation. It provides a structure, a "roadmap"—allowing the coach to create context and assist someone in getting an overview on their current life along with their unlived life.

We begin this conversation by "gathering data"—meaning, we want to get a picture of the person's current life. Where do they spend their time? What are the "categories" of their life—for example, they might have the categories of:

- **Health and well-being (exercise)**
- **Creative endeavors/hobbies (carpentry, pottery, singing, art, sports, race car driving)**
- **Work**
- **Family**
- **Relationship (marriage or significant other)**
- **Spiritual practice**
- **Friendship time**
- **Parenting or elder care**
- **Volunteering**

Some people may have only a few of these categories, some may have more (the people with one or two categories may be coming to you because they want to create more depth in their life, more engagement outside of work and family, for example). Your job is to capture, through questions, the landscape of their life. As you are in this discovery process with the person, you can draw it on a white board as a circle with segments—some coaches refer to it as, "This is your current life as an island—and we are going to put the segments of the island into your life. Let's call this Island A." Some coaches describe it as your current life pie (who doesn't like pie?).

Once you have fully developed their current life on the white board, you are going to then create "Island B" or "Pie B"—this is the "ideal life" or "life the way you always wished it would be." This is where we discover what's not working—where the opportunities or gaps are.

This can begin with a simple question, "So—if this were life the way you always wished it would be, what would be new or different on this island? What categories would be deleted, or just different—maybe better, richer, or . . . ?"

For example, someone might not have relationship in their current life—and in their "ideal life" they really want a relationship! This is where you can look for areas to do some coaching around. You might ask, "Tell me about your marriage—what's that like?" You might discover it's not so great—that this person is unhappy with the level of connection in their marriage. You are going to ask some more questions around this, to uncover more. Rather than completely stop here and start coaching around the marriage, you want to note this and then keep going, as in, "OK—we are going to come back to this would that be alright with you?" Get to more of their life. What else is not present that they want (maybe they really want more spiritual connection—or maybe they are yearning for a better relationship with their dad). Your job is to uncover the deeper landscape of their life that is not the way they had hoped. This is where you get to start assisting them in looking at what an ideal life could be, both inside and out.

There are many directions a Gap Conversation can go in. As you grow as a professional coach you will become more adept at knowing when to stop and look at a particular area, when to pause and say, "can I offer you some coaching on this?" and when to slow down and ask more questions. This is also a time of determining how willing a person is to share—are they staying on the surface? Are they revealing more about their child than just, "We don't get along"?

The purpose of a Gap conversation is to assist both you and the person in SEEING where the gaps are in their inner and outer life, and then to assist the person in determining if shifting this is

important enough for them to invest in themselves with a coach and dedicate time and attention to it.

Note: some people are willing to stay in their current life, their "default future." They may not be ready to go into the work of creating new possibilities, or they simply may not be in enough pain. We are seeing where they are at, we are getting into some coaching with the person, we are moving the needle with them in one or two areas that have been identified.

We as coaches are the boat to move across the Gap. A strong enrollment conversation demonstrates an experience of how coaching works as a process for partnering together to close the Gap.

Another area to consider is that there are two components you can look at with someone—their outer life and their inner life. Many people will not have any reference point for an inner life or an inner experience of life; i.e., what do they experience inside throughout the day—regardless of what happens on the outer? This can be a fruitful area to explore.

Said another way, most coaches are focused on exploring the outer life with someone—the goal line. The goal line is about physical world reality—as in jobs, housing, or health. This is all fine, we all have things we want to create in the world.

The inner life (the soul line of life) for most humans is rich with opportunity. How are we being with ourselves day to day? Is our inner dialogue rife with self judgement? Comparison? Overthinking and deliberating about things that might never occur? Do we have a connection with our heart vs. just our minds?

As professional coaches we can assist people in both the goal line of life and the soul line of life. The Gap Conversation is a vehicle through which you can discover the deeper opportunities that someone might not have even considered.

Practice the Gap Conversation. Practice getting their current life up on the white board, and then the life they are yearning for. Once we become more skilled at the Gap it gives us a wide variety of directions to take someone in, serving them deeply and giving them an experience of coaching.

Handout 2

Coaches and Money

COACHES AND MONEY:
An Opportunity for Growth

Here's one thing I can say with full certainty:

Yes, you CAN do well as a coach AND have money fears.

Here's another thing I can say with full certainty:

Getting your relationship to money more cleaned up and handled will make you a FAR better business owner and coach.

Here's how I used to relate to money:

I figured if I didn't look, listen, or SAY ANYTHING about money or to money, all would be well. . . or it wouldn't, and I wouldn't know anyway. My basic premise was, "LA LA LA LA LA YOU AREN'T HERE I DON'T NEED TO LOOK AT YOU."

I pretended it didn't exist. I was afraid of it and all things related to it—taxes, managing bank accounts, setting up tracking, EVERYTHING.

The irony here is my dad was a banker and financial advisor . . .

I'm sure he loved knowing I was (basically) financially illiterate until I was in my late 30's. The good news is as I became more willing to focus on money, clean up my money stories with the help of my coach, Steve Chandler, and learn how to make more of it, he could be proud that I made excellent money as a professional coach. By the time he died, he'd known for some time that I was 100% okay—he was not concerned about my financial life one iota . . . and that makes me very happy.

Maybe your relationship to money is different? Maybe you treat money like a lousy romantic partner: you get mad at it when it doesn't show up for you, you stomp your feet and yell, and then when it is there, you are thrilled, and you spend it all on fancy dates and things. Then you repeat.

Or—maybe you are the lousy partner, who ignores money and simultaneously hordes it, never takes it out, only buys things you absolutely need, never anything you want.

Maybe you treat money as purely transactional—i.e., *you* do this, and I'll do that. There is nothing more, nothing less.

Whatever it is, there's room for growth—because the moment we are setting fees as a new coach (or raising our fees as a more established coach), or offering a larger proposal to a corporate client, our money "stuff" appears in our thinking and our conversations.

11 PHRASES COACHES SAY or THINK REGULARLY REGARDING MONEY

1. I'm afraid to share fees with a potential client—I'd rather just not have to discuss money at all, it's SO uncomfortable.

2. If I raise my fees my people might go away—I'd rather keep my fees lower and know for sure I'll have clients (even though I'm working with as many people as I can and I'm not at the earning level I'd like to be at/need to be at to make my life work well).

3. This organization can't afford me/my coaching/won't like my fees.

4. I'm outraged at these coaches who charge high fees—it's disgusting, we shouldn't ever charge so much. And yes, I know I'm in judgement.

5. I lowered my fees three times and I offered an easy payment plan. Now I'm resentful, I'm almost doing it for free.

6. Coaching should be free—charging for transformation feels very wrong.

7. Nobody has said yes in the last 10-15 conversations . . .and I'm not lowering my fee.

8. There must be an easier way to make money. This profession is hard and I'M NEVER GOING TO GET OUT OF DEBT.

9. You are going to pay little ol' ME?

10. I don't like it when someone says that they can't afford my fee.

11. I enrolled 3 clients and I'm afraid this is all a fluke and there's no way I can earn a living with this fee. How can I raise it when I just started?

There are probably another 11 statements coaches make regularly about money—and you get where I'm going here.

NOISY THINKING

We need to get our thinking about money quieter and more relaxed. When we are anxious about money, about the current state of our bank account, whether or not someone is going to pay us, or wondering if we are going to survive, we are not at our best.

And when we aren't at our best, and we are focused on our own money stuff, we aren't serving. We aren't making a difference, and we are generally not able to be present with the person in front of us.

THE PATH TO A MORE RELAXED AND PRODUCTIVE RELATIONSHIP WITH MONEY (and more clients)

It's like Candyland, only different (your relationship with money may be like Molasses Swamp—and YOU can get out!) . . .

FOUR STEPS TO TAKE

1. **If you don't have enough money to pay your rent or mortgage for three months, don't attempt to ONLY make money as a coach.** For most of us, this is STRESSFUL and it will leak into our conversations. People will feel it and likely not hire us (nobody ever says, "The coach I met with seemed stressed—they

were sweating and picking at their nails so I hired them!")

2. Is it true that some people can tolerate $20 in their bank account and still show up relaxed and present and serve beautifully without attachment? Yes. If this is you, great—and for the rest of you don't make this a requirement. Get a part time job, take out a loan, **do something to ease the financial pressure so you can show up relaxed and present when you are in conversation.**

3. **Consider that anything you feel regarding money is not a fact—it's a feeling, and feelings are NOT facts.** Required reading for all coaches in the CFJ Coaching Success School is, *Overcoming Underearning* by Barbara Stanny. The requirement is to read it whether you have read it before OR not, and for coaches who return to the school (~50% return each year) they re-read it. If you haven't read it, get this book NOW. Read it, with an agreement that you'll do all the exercises in the back of each chapter (FYI—even if you are earning the income you want to be earning you can be an underearner—we can be underearners at $500k or $2 million—because underearning is a mindset; it's not about the number).

This book is not for the faint of heart if you do the exercises—and it's a gamechanger.

4. **LOOK at getting a handle on your relationship to money as a way to learn about your clients' relationships to money.** Your clients are going to want you to help them with how they relate to money—so you'd better get going on this for yourself. Your judgements about people who you perceive "make a lot of money" or "spend frivolously" or "don't deserve the money they have" all need to get cleaned out. Your fears of making money and who you might become *with more*, or your fears of not ever having enough, need to get brought into the light of day and dissolved with compassion. If we judge those who make money as "bad" or "capitalist pigs" it's going to get in the way of our ability to earn a good living, and if we are in the limiting belief that "poor is pure" this will impact our ability to thrive financially.

5. **Ultimately you want to put money in its rightful place.** It's not good or bad, evil or nirvana. It's a tool—and when we clear up our relationship to money four things tend to occur:

    - We earn more money.
    - We are clear that it's about the WORK. Meaning . . . it's about the value of a transformed life, a transformed relationship with one's child/spouse/boss, the value of becoming a stronger, more effective leader who can make a bigger impact inside an organization.

- We are less attached to money in general—it's no longer an indicator of our worth and value (because our worth and value is infinite, no amount of money can ever come close to our true worth and value).
- We give more money to those around us and to causes that speak to our hearts—helping our loved ones, our communities, and more.

IN CLOSING

Our relationship to money is one of the most valuable sources of growth and learning. It's a critical area for business owners to get conscious about. Don't wait. Make it a priority NOW to clean up your relationship with money.

PS: This is SO vital for coaches that every live class session at the CFJ Coaching Success School has a section on upgrading your relationship with money! We get at the stuff going on underneath and bring it to the surface so YOU can be more effective.

PSS: Another step to take—do a session or two with a real financial coach! Someone who can help you look at your current situation with clear eyes and assist you in seeing what practical steps you need to take so your accounts are in order and you know what's what.

Handout 3

Professional Coaching and Your Professional Self

PROFESSIONAL COACHING AND YOUR PROFESSIONAL SELF:
A KEY TO YOUR LEADERSHIP

Professionalism is often defined as the skill, good judgment, and polite behavior that is expected from a person who is trained to do a job well. Also included is the adherence to courtesy, honesty, and responsibility when dealing with individuals or other companies in the business environment. This trait often includes a high level of excellence going above and beyond basic requirements.

Coming from our Professional Self is a service to others. When we are in our Professional Self, we can make a positive difference — setting up a strong container for transformation to take place, sharing the truth as we see it, supporting clients in seeing their blind spots, and assisting in someone's transformation. When we are in our social self, we limit our opportunities. We are in the small self, wanting to be liked, unwilling to be in leadership for fear of what a prospective client might think—all ego-referenced thinking. The qualities of the Professional Self are Integrity, Clarity, Leadership, Focus, Loving, Confidence and Attunement. When in our Professional Self we are not concerned about whether someone likes us or whether they think we are coming off as "too strong."

This skill provides us the opportunity to strengthen who we are as professionals, wherever we are. As professional coaches we want there to be as little in the way as possible for us to make a difference in the world. Growing and strengthening our professional selves allows others to experience trust and a sense of being able to count on us as a reliable source of transformation.

Handout 3: Professional Coaching / Professional Self

<u>EXAMPLES OF COLLAPSING INTO YOUR SOCIAL SELF/ROLE REVERSAL WITH CLIENTS OR PROSPECTIVE CLIENTS:</u>

1. Allowing a client to be late (repeatedly) without addressing it.

2. Letting a client cancel sessions/move sessions (repeatedly) without addressing it.

3. Socializing in a session; i.e., starting to talk more personally, "friendship lite."

4. Allowing a client to eat breakfast/lunch/dinner while in session.

5. You have assigned a client reading/an action/written assignment. They don't complete and you don't address it.

6. A prospective client moves an enrollment conversation 1,2,3 times and you continue to book new dates without addressing it.

7. Your client misses a payment and you don't follow up immediately—and you do another coaching session without correcting this.

8. A client texts or calls you late at night and you respond regardless of the time or if you are involved in a personal endeavor.

9. A current or prospective client is overly affectionate when saying hello or goodbye—long hugs, lingering glances, and you don't address it; rather, you participate.

10. You meet prospective or current clients in more social places—coffee shops, bars, restaurants, etc.

11. You move sessions with your clients/prospective clients — and you share personal information; e.g., "I have to move our session because my juicing cleanse didn't go well."

EXAMPLES OF HOW THE SOCIAL SELF CAN SHOW UP IN COMMUNICATIONS (EMAIL, VOICEMAIL, TEXTS):

1. Using the following salutations with clients/prospective clients:

    a. "Hey XXX,"
    b. "Hi XXX!"
    c. "Hi Sweetie,"
    d. "Yo bro,"
    e. "Hey Dude,"
    f. "Dear Brother from another Mother"
    g. ANY USE OF EMOTICONS WITH PROSPECTIVE CLIENTS

2. Using the following signatures with clients/prospective clients:

    a. "hugs and kisses"
    b. "xoxoxo"
    c. "lots of love"
    d. "with eternal loving and gratitude"
    e. "Thanks (show smiley face emoticon"
    f. ANY USE OF EMOTICONS WITH PROSPECTIVE CLIENTS

Handout 3: Professional Coaching / Professional Self

3. Phrases that can be indicators you are in your social self/role reversal in communications:

    a. "I look forward to meeting you."
    b. "Let me know if any of these dates and times work for you."
    c. "If it works for you I can meet with you at XYZ, or ABC, or 123, or LMO, and if these don't work I can do . . ."
    d. "I would love to meet with you . . . "
    e. "I'd be happy to have a conversation with you . . ."
    f. "If you can't afford to work with me now, we could talk about a lower fee, or a payment plan, or maybe we can talk about a trade . . ."
    g. "Yes, it's completely okay—take as much time as you need to make the payment."
    h. ANY USE OF EMOTICONS WITH PROSPECTIVE CLIENTS.
    i. Your communications to current clients are almost exclusively emoticons of smiley faces, hearts, rainbows and thumbs up.

EXAMPLES OF PROFESSIONAL LANGUAGING:

1. Instead of "Does that work for you?" Using, "Please confirm."
2. Signing an email, "Regards or Sincerely," or simply signing your name.
3. "If it would serve you I am willing to offer you time on my calendar."
4. "If it would serve you I am willing to have a conversation with you."
5. "I'd like to discuss working with you."

6. "As soon as I receive payment, we can book our first session."
7. "Is having a conversation something you'd like to do?"
8. "Do I have your permission to share with you what I see?"

Handout 4

Your Calendar Is Everything

Wake Up and Look No Further

WAKE UP AND LOOK NO FURTHER:
Your Calendar is Everything (EVERYTHING)!

Like most professions, we are in a profession where our calendars are a tool. They are also our "report card."

What . . . a REPORT CARD? That's horrible. That makes most coaches want to gag (except for the coaches who loved report cards and were externally grade-motivated (that would not be me).

Prepare yourself—this could either be one of the most useful handouts you ever utilize or one of the most challenging . . . so much so that you throw it out before you even finish reading it.

DO YOU DARE UP YOUR CALENDAR GAME?

If you want to . . .

- **Increase your income, your calendar is going to matter** (whether you are a new coach or 3 years +)
- **Make a bigger difference, your calendar is going to matter.**
- **Fill a new group/add individual clients to your practice/create a new video or post—your calendar is going to matter.**

First—GRADE YOURSELF

Answer the following:

FULL TIME COACHES:

1. If you are a full-time coach and your practice is not full (or you are not at the income level you would like), count the number of new conversations on your calendar in the last 3 months and the number of hours you have set aside for enrollment activities.

   Before you read the following, be aware: <u>this might be uncomfortable</u>. It's intended to be. We cannot change what we don't look at. Getting real about the actual numbers is an opportunity to course-correct and create the results we want.

   GRADING for FULL-TIME COACHES:

   14-16 (or more) conversations with new people in a month = A
   10-13 conversations with new people in a month = B
   6-9 conversations with new people in a month = C
   5 or less conversations with new people in a month = D

   GRADING FOR PART-TIME COACHES (HALF TIME):

   9-11 conversations with new people in a month = A
   7-9 conversations with new people in a month = B
   5-7 conversations with new people in a month = C
   4 or less conversations with new people in a month = D

You might be reading this thinking, "HEY—who made you the judge and jury on how many conversations earns an A, B, C, D?"

My own early experience showed me how many conversations it took to grow a coaching business. My coach, Steve Chandler, showed me, guided me, and pulled me back from the denials and the pretending into as-is reality and what was required to create a strong coaching practice.

In my own work coaching coaches for over 12 years, these numbers are a solid gauge for what leads to results—i.e., converting conversations to clients. Are there variations? Sure (if you are a newer coach with little to no practice coaching or enrolling, it will take more conversations to convert, and likely more months to get results).

Note: if you do not like what you are seeing in your grade and you are finding yourself angry at me, you are free to discard this grading system and make up your own—one that makes you comfortable with what you are doing or not doing with your time, one that keeps you in the blissful bubble of, "I'm doing okay, it will happen and I can still hang out and do yoga all afternoon 3 days a week or go to long lunches with friends or scroll through social media . . .).

That's the challenge and the gift of this profession. You can do whatever you want—the only person who knows what you are doing is you (unless you have a coach or are in a school or program where there's agreed upon accountability—if you are, way to go!). If you want to hide, you can hide—nobody will know except your calendar and

your bank account. If you want to excel, it will be reflected in both places.

Consistent conversations with new people where you are practicing coaching and enrolling will lead to paying clients. I can't predict how long it will take—and if you keep doing it month after month, it will happen.

For those of you who are willing to use this handout and consider this a road map to what is more likely to create financial success, continue reading.

MY GRADE IS NOT WHAT I WANT—NOW WHAT?

Time to pivot and course-correct. You've had a cold dose of reality about the number of conversations each month that tend to create results.

**What will you do to create more conversations?
How will you connect with more people and begin the process of nurturing and building relationships?
What steps will you take to grow your community and serve more?**

All these questions need to be looked at and slowed down, one at a time. Then determine your next steps and <u>get into action</u>.

USE YOUR CALENDAR to UP YOUR GAME!

Put time on your calendar for connecting. Look at all the open space on your schedule—and if you don't have people to invite, put time on there for connecting. If you are full-time, minimum 4 hours a week. Create places to connect—

join things that YOU are interested in—pickleball, art classes, meet ups, toastmasters, group surfing lessons, book clubs . . . libraries, go volunteer somewhere. GET into the world, get committed to being places, connecting and being warm and curious.

THIS IS A PROFESSION, NOT A LIFESTYLE

This is real. Too many coaches are not putting in the time and they are walking around stunned that their business is not coming together in the ways they'd hoped and imagined. They are in debt or they are simply not living in the way they would like. They are scrambling to make ends meet, and they are frustrated or in denial that it's going to happen; they think, *Just a few more posts on social media and it will start to occur* . . .

If this is you, WAKE UP! I love this profession and all of you who want to make a difference too much to sugar coat this . . . get to work.

There are coaches who tell me they are "drained" by conversations, or they want their summers to be more open with time for travel or personal interests.

Totally fine . . . except you won't make the income you want, or the community you want to do the fun things you want to do, making a difference in the lives of others.

FOR COACHES WHO ARE 3+ YEARS IN THE BUSINESS WHO ARE MAKING A SOLID LIVING AND WANT TO TAKE THEIR PRACTICE TO THE NEXT LEVEL AND INCREASE THEIR INCOME

GRADE YOURSELF

Answer the following:

1. Count the hours you have had open weekly for the past 4 weeks. Assume a 5 day a week work week with a 10am-4pm work schedule. You are counting the hours not engaging in any work activities; e.g., conversations, enrollment activities, or client coaching sessions. These open hours might be time you are working out, spending time with friends or family, on social media, watching Netflix, doing laundry, staring at your screen, etc.

   GRADING for FULL TIME COACHES:

   10 or less open hours a week: A
   11-13 open hours a week: B
   14-17 open hours a week: C
   18-20 (or more) open hours a week: D

2. **GRADING FOR PART-TIME COACHES (HALF TIME):**

   6 (or less) open hours a week: A
   7-10 open hours a week: B
   11-13 open hours a week: C
   14 or less open hours a week: D

Open hours where we are coasting along are NOT our friend if we want our practice to go to another level. This can occur when we are "good" with our income. We want more, we have new ideas we'd like to put in motion . . . and the comfort of the now easy $150k or $200k a year, when we don't have to work particularly hard to maintain this income keeps us in cruise control. We have a "good flow"—and we

have a lot of time to not do much; we are not as inspired or alive, and we aren't making the contribution we have the capacity to make.

RISE UP and MAKE YOUR DIFFERENCE

There will be many who stay low earners in this profession, never making it past $25-$50k. Some of this will be due to not getting to work. They will stay in low gear, not getting the connection between conversations on their calendar and what's in their bank account. Another contributing factor will be not getting beyond more basic goal-line coaching—they'll stay more focused on the external, not venturing into the deeper waters of soul-line coaching.

There will be coaches who continue to coast, who do well and who don't turn up the flame on themselves and their capacity to serve and thrive.

You read this. Now you know, and you get to decide. Don't put your hands over your eyes and ears and pretend you didn't see what it takes.

Grade yourself once or twice a year. Be honest. Be brave. Make your calendar a tool that you come back to again and again to see what's real, and adjust accordingly.

Get coached, get coached, get coached. Never let your calendar be a blind spot—the coaching profession and the world will benefit from us rising up and getting to work.

Handout 5

Connecting

CONNECTING:
It's time to get BETTER at This Critical Part of the Coaching Profession

There's a lot of conversation in the coaching profession about finding new people, connecting with new people, and getting clients.

JUST THE FACTS (6, as a matter of fact)

> **FACT 1:** Most coaches (especially new ones) have wobbly or no skills of connecting and building a relationship beyond an initial meeting.
>
> **FACT 2:** Most, if not all, coaching certification programs have nothing in them about the skills of connecting and building relationships.
>
> **FACT 3:** Most coaches don't initially think of the profession of coaching as a relationship-building business.
>
> **FACT 4:** Many coaches avoid connecting—and would prefer to not "have" to do it.
>
> **FACT 5:** Many coaches are insecure, inexperienced conversationalists.
>
> **FACT 6:** This is one of THE MOST VITAL aspects of our business, and one that can be not only a source of real clients—it can be a joy-filled act of service.

OKAY, CAROLYN, SO I'M WEAK AT CONNECTING (AND I DON'T WANT TO DO IT)—NOW WHAT?

STEP 1 - STRENGTHEN YOUR ABILITY TO CONNECT AND BUILD RAPPORT

Right after you meet someone, it's time to shift into rapport and relationship-building. What does this mean? It means that you want this person to feel connected to you in a real and personal way. Here's the secret:

DEMONSTRATE THAT YOU CARE ABOUT THEM AS A FELLOW HUMAN BEING (NOT A POTENTIAL CLIENT)

The number one way to energetically push someone away from you is to make the connection exclusively about business. The number two way is to be looking at them with dollar signs in your eyes. Want to know why? Because they can see and feel this—even if you think it's subtle. It's NOT. Energetically people know when you are being shark-like—and it's a turn off.

CARE ABOUT PEOPLE

I remember being in a meeting with CFJ Coaching Success School faculty member Devon Bandison and he asked a coach, "Do you care about people?"

It was a good question (we both weren't sure what the answer would be).

You need to care about people. For real—beyond anything.

STEP 2—ASK QUESTIONS THAT GO BEYOND THE BASICS

I have a pet peeve. Almost any party or gathering I go to I'm rarely asked anything—and I mean anything. As in nothing.

These are parties or situations where I don't know people and they don't know me.

Guess what?

People everywhere are losing the art of conversation and connecting.

Guess what?

The profession of coaching NEEDS TO BRING THIS BACK. Our business depends on it (and parties and other situations will become much more fun and meaningful).

What do I mean by going beyond "the basics?" Here are a couple of the most common basic (and sometimes insensitive) questions NOT to ask:

- **(if you are at a party/gathering) "Are you so-and-so's wife/husband/partner?"**

    This is pretty narrow—as in, you must be here because you are in relationship with SOMEONE. Lots of people are not in relationship (by choice or not). Don't assume.

- **"What do you do?"**

    Do? Lots of people don't "do" in the context you might be thinking, as in work in a formal job. This question can create disconnect if someone isn't "doing" in the context you are thinking. I'm not saying don't ask—just ask better. An example might be, "What are you up to in life—what's

important to you right now?" We have all been asked the "What do you do?" question so much (so tired)—it's time to sunset it and ask an upgraded version.

OKAY—so those are the two main ones to NOT ask, or to ask differently.

BETTER CONNECTING WHEN WE DON'T KNOW PEOPLE AT ALL

"Passengers, as we begin our descent, you may now suddenly act open and friendly to the person beside you."

This is the connecting when we don't know people in various settings: on airplanes, in coffee shops, in line at the DMV, at the Back-to-School night for our kids, and so on.

The best connecting with brand-new people who you don't know at all starts slow, and gently (I do mean *gently*) goes down deeper, paying attention to the response and calibrating accordingly.

Questions can be fun. Questions can be warm and bring people closer. Questions can create intimacy, sparks of aliveness, and new thinking. Before you read the following, keep in mind that questions can start with being contextual. As in, if I'm at the DMV, I might be talking to the person behind me about the line, if I'm in the correct one, or how slow or quick the line seems to be going. I don't start with, "What's your life like?" If I'm at my kid's back-to-school night and I'm meeting another parent, I might start with, "Who's your kid?" If I'm at a coffee shop, I might ask the very deep and life-altering question of, "Are you getting iced coffee or hot?" (This is a very important question for me.)

After that, it can progress. Start small and go bigger one question at a time, seeing how the person responds.

A few questions I like are:

- **Are you satisfied with (what you are up to)?**
- **Do you do the things you love to do in your everyday life?**
- **What's the least fun/inspiring/meaningful thing about your life (or work)?**
- **What's the most fun/inspiring/meaningful thing about your life (or work)?**

These are not the most groundbreaking questions—and you don't necessarily need groundbreaking. Come up with questions you'd like to be asked. That tends to lead to good questions. And don't ask like a robot - remember that your warmth matters.

What do we need? Slowed down, generative listening. A lot of coaches listen with an agenda; namely, "I'm listening to gather

information so I can possibly invite you to a conversation" versus listening because you are someone who enjoys connecting deeply with people for the sake of connecting deeply with people. People can feel when we listen with an agenda. It feels *"blech"*—stop doing that. People want to feel like you care because you care. Period.

STEP 3—KEEP CONVERSATIONS FLOWING WITH CURIOSITY

Becoming a strong conversationalist is of great value in this profession. Now, you don't need to be highly verbal with lots of wonderful, witty things to say. In fact, this is less valuable.

Great follow up questions include:

- tell me more about that
- tell me more
- Oh, that's interesting—what brought you to wanting to do xyz?

"Be interested, not interesting."
- Steve Chandler

Being interested is of much greater value in this profession than being really interesting.

BETTER RE-CONNECTING WHEN YOU ALREADY KNOW SOMEONE AND IT'S BEEN A WHILE

This is the other kind of connecting—i.e. reconnecting with people that you knew from another time in your life . . . people you worked with before you became a professional coach,

people you went to college with, people you knew from your child's school community.

When we re-connect with people, we want to *want to* reconnect. Don't reconnect because you are a coach and you want something. Re-connect because you liked this person, because they were fun to work alongside of and because you are taking a stand for being someone in the world who doesn't just think about people—you actually re-connect with them.

This is an area of opportunity to grow into—to become someone who reaches out to people, who remembers people and who acknowledges them for who they are and who they were in your life. If someone was there for you when your parents were getting divorced, if their folks drove you places, you can reach out and tell them you'll never forget this.

Re-connecting is a way to grow your world. Some people might become clients and some might never—and isn't it great to simply re-connect for the sake of reconnecting?

A FEW MORE FACTS

FACT: If you practice the art of connecting and being in conversation, you'll get better.

FACT: People will be positively impacted by your caring attention and focus on them. It will mean something to them (especially because so many people are not good at conversing with care).

FACT: Done well, with genuine caring, it will lead to people feeling good and wanting to talk to you more.

FACT: When you are meeting and connecting with someone you'd like to coach, you'll be relaxed because you have been practicing. You'll be able to connect with grace and ease. This will allow you to create a conversation that makes a difference to someone.

FACT: Trust and rapport-building is a process, not a one-time event. This cannot be rushed, this cannot be bypassed.

STEP 4—START

1. Pick 5 people you are going to re-connect with. They can be from prior jobs, prior communities, or people you used to see at your gym. The guideline is you remember them as someone you liked/admired/were inspired by—**and you'd love re-connecting with them regardless of your work as a professional coach.** Send a heartfelt, private message on social media or an email. Start slow, be real, be genuine. Ask them how they are doing—find out what's happened in their life since you were last seeing each other. Be slow, be gentle, and start getting into conversation. Don't rush to invite them into a conversation—because that's you wanting something (a client). Maybe after a few messages you suggest a 20-30 minute zoom coffee. Practice building a relationship again. You'll know over time if there's something that you can help them with—it will naturally emerge in the connection and conversations.

2. For the next 2 weeks, practice connecting with people you don't know. A minimum of one a day—whether it's at your local coffee shop, or when you make a call to set up a

medical appointment. Start practicing the art of conversation—one gentle question at a time.

Are you willing to take this on?

STEP 5—KEEP GOING—LEAN IN, NOT OUT

We are in a relationship-building business—that's what coaching is. The privilege of coaching someone does not come without trust and rapport being built. Build this muscle—treat people like human beings, not bodies with dollars on their heads. Take this on as part of your job and get on it. Be part of making life better by becoming a heartfelt, real conversationalist who demonstrates caring and interest in others.

And who knows? Maybe parties across the globe will get better!

Handout 6

Invitations

THE ART OF INVITATIONS for PROFESSIONAL COACHES

This is a profession where you can create clients—not passively "wait" for them to come to you, hoping and praying for referrals.

I have heard professional coaches say, "I can't wait until I don't have to create clients—it's going to be so great when all I do is get referrals."

I kindly challenge coaches who say this. I challenge us as a profession that this is NOT the end-all be-all, the golden ticket many in the profession think it is. . . .

WHY NOT?

Because creating clients is fun. It's creative. It's important.

Important how?

Important to know HOW to do so a way that is not salesy, or creepy, or desperate.

Important because we want to be empowered business owners who are not fantasizing about "Someday, maybe this will all get EASY and I'll be able to put my feet up and drink champagne as the referrals flow into my inbox…."

That's as BAD as "Someday my prince will come and all will be well; I'll never have to think about money or a home again."

I'm not interested in being rescued—are you?

I'm not interested in putting my business in someone else's (pretend) hands, **waiting for my business to grow.**

I offer to you that you don't want to be either—that this approach is not only a mistake, it's an immature stance in your business.

Please don't misunderstand—referrals are a beautiful thing and are something we as professional coaches can cultivate through serving our clients so powerfully and well that they share about us with others. We can, as professional coaches, learn how to create more referrals.

And we can also learn how to invite people into our world with genuineness, with creativity, and will no attachment to the outcome.

Welcome to Building the Muscle of Effectively Inviting for Professional Coaches

You can create them starting today—through the process of invitations. Invitations are so special. In essence, you are opening your heart to someone who inspires you, someone you are curious about, someone who seems fun that you may want to serve by inviting them to talk with you.

The key to this process is paying attention to where you are coming from as you compose your invitation. Are you coming from needy and creepy—i.e., *I need a client!* Or, are you coming from your heart and your genuine desire to be of service?

What you are about to read is referred to in the CFJ Coaching School by one coach as "paper gold." <u>This coach read this handout prior to coming to the school because her beloved husband, who was already in the school, shared it with her. She</u>

utilized it and within weeks had created new clients and $40k in new income.

I share this both as a way to emphasize the possibility this opens up for coaches, and I also share this with caution.

This handout is not a golden ticket to clients. It's like anything—it can be mis-used, it can be misunderstood, it can be ripped off or superficially (or badly) implemented and it can lead to NOTHING. And then a coach can toss their hands up in the air and say, "SEE THIS DOESN'T WORK."

This handout does not take the place of being coached.

This handout does not take the place of having a coach help you see your blind spots, your neediness, your attachment, your less than effective service communications.

You are invited to both experiment with the below AND proceed with optimistic caution, knowing that in the beginning it's likely that unless you are being coached by someone who has become skilled in this you will likely experience messiness and discomfort (which is one of the most fun things I experienced early in my business).

Read on!

CRAFTING AN INVITATION:

Step 1: Acknowledgment—this is one of the most valuable and important skills a professional coach can strengthen in their work—not only in enrollment, also in coaching.

Most people walking around in the world are sorely underacknowledged. Most people don't grow up in families or experience school environments where true, heartfelt acknowledgment is practiced.

Acknowledgment is one of the most beautiful demonstrations there is of another's gifts, presence, words, or actions.

Acknowledgment at its best is, most importantly, REAL. It's thoughtful. It is delivered in such a way that the recipient feels seen and heard with no strings or agenda.

Slow down and reflect on this person. What's making you want to invite them? What do you see in them? What stands out? What do you see that perhaps they don't?

Don't think they get acknowledged all the time or they might have heard this before—because chances are they haven't. The most accomplished, successful people are walking around feeling less than (because it's something most people deal with across the planet).

Share why you want to offer this person time on your calendar. What stands out about them? What draws you to them?

Step 2: Invite—This section is where you'll invite them to a conversation. You can get creative if you like and come up with a name for your conversation—a strategy call or something like that—based on what you do. Note: This is not a requirement. I don't have a name for mine.

Step 3: Context—This is where you set the tone for what's possible and share a little about what they can expect. You want them to

know that this isn't a chat or just a random conversation. This is a time where powerful things—life-changing things can happen.

You'll also want to include details about the session—length of time, in person or phone, that it's complimentary. You need to give them that information so they can make an informed decision.

Step 4: **Permission to Say No**—It's so important to give them an out. Not everyone is going to want to take you up on this offer, so letting them know they can say no is so valuable.

Step 5: **End with a Question**—Is this something you'd like to do? Let me know either way.

Know this process will grow and evolve as you grow and evolve. You will ultimately find your own voice.

Note:

The sample invitations included in this handout were written by myself and CFJ Coaching Success School
Faculty Member Amber Kryzys.

SAMPLE INVITATION 1

Dear Tom,

How are you doing?

The last time we connected you were starting to think about leaving your position at YY . . .

I'm wondering if you are still in this inquiry?

If yes, I want to offer you something—and that's us dedicating two hours to you and this question that's percolating. We'll slow down and unpack it, looking at it from a variety of angles in the light of day.

This time is a gift—no strings, no discussion of anything further—if we handle this question in our two hours together that's great. I'm offering this because you are one of the most dedicated, thoughtful people I know. You have inspired me since we met—and I want to serve anyone who inspires me at the level you do.

Tom is having a conversation something you'd like to do?

If yes, I'll send options—and, if this has already been settled inside of you, or it's not something you are up for, responding with no is totally fine. Either way, know that I hold you in high regard.

Regards,
Carolyn

SAMPLE INVITATION 2

Dear Monica,

You have been on my mind. Donna shared with me about your Russia trip—and, of course, a smile came to my face!

Monica you continue to be one of the women who I see in my mind's eye as spectacular on every level. And my commitment to myself is when a spectacular person will not leave my mind, I invite them to come sit with me in my office.

This is an invitation—which means you can, of course, say NO if it's not something that brings enthusiasm and excitement forward for YOU. This invitation is personal, only for you. This time is for you ... we will focus on your life, your heartfelt dreams, and what is calling to you.

This may be the only time we ever sit together, and that is totally fine with me. And—please say no if it does not line up for you. You stay spectacular to me regardless of whether we meet or not!

Let me know either way—and if it's a yes, we will get it scheduled.

Regards,
Carolyn

SAMPLE INVITATION 3

Dear Heather,

It was FANTASTIC to have you at the Inspired Leadership complimentary event—you demonstrated such willingness and openness in sharing the challenges your organization is facing—bravo.

Heather, I don't do this very often—and when someone stands out to me, I honor this. I'd like to offer you time on my calendar. This time is a gift: we can sit together and get deeper into what's happening—the challenges, the opportunities—whatever would serve YOU. There's no requirement for anything further beyond this meeting; this is my gift to you. And it's completely fine to say no.

If this is something you'd like to do, we'll get it on the calendar. And know that regardless of whether we sit together or not, it was an honor to serve YOU at the event and I'm rooting for you—always.

With loving,
Carolyn

SAMPLE INVITATION 4

Dear XXX,

Happy New Year! I hope you had a fantastic shift from [year] into [year]. I can only imagine the joy and celebration inside as you welcomed the New Year. I know 2015 was a big year for you—and I so admire the way you supported yourself in walking through it.

This morning I was remembering our conversation from XXX's party where you shared your desire to lean into coaching. Given it's a new year, I'm wondering if having a deeper conversation would serve you? Would leaning into coaching be valuable starting now?

There is no pressure here XXX and no strings attached. This is only if you want to go ahead and start gathering information and possibly leaning into enrolling clients. What I can promise is that our conversation will serve you. At least, that is my commitment. We'll slow down and get a full scope of what's in your heart— where you are now in your life and what you want. Just that alone can be quite illuminating.

If this sounds good to you, we'll set aside a couple hours to really dive in. To be clear, there is no fee for this conversation. And, if it doesn't sound good or feel like a fit right now, that's totally fine too.

I just wanted you to know I'm thinking of you and really support you in taking a stand for the life you want—and how you feel called to serve. What I do know is you got it—if you choose to use it!

Let me know what you think.

Sending you so much love,
Amber

SAMPLE INVITATION 5

Dear YYY:

As I was exploring the bodyheart for Business Owners email list today—occasionally I like to see who's out there and what they're about—I couldn't help but reach out to you. I absolutely love your voice and your message. YOU come through in your writing. That's a gift.

What a cool journey you've been on! I love that you took life into your own hands and did research to learn more about the people you looked up to—and how that led to you being a life coach. I have never heard anyone come to this work that way.

From time to time, I invite someone to sit with me for a complimentary coaching session, where we get into your life, your challenges, your opportunities.

I don't do this very often—my coaching practice is generally full and I mostly work through referral. I only invite people who I see as up to something meaningful in the world.

You are one of those people. Please know, it's totally fine to say no. These sessions are deep and they are not for everyone; if you want to get into an area of your life that isn't currently working to the degree you'd like, we'll go for it. A lot happens when people sit with me—I don't hold back as a coach—so I want you to know it's completely ok to say no thank you.

Is this something you'd like to do?

Let me know either way—and if yes, we'll get it scheduled. FYI—this will be a 90 minute to 2 hr session, so if you'd like to do this, plan on setting aside that much time.

And, either way, know I so support what you are doing—and who you are being in the world!

Amber

SAMPLE INVITATION 6

Dear XXX,

I came across you and your website via XXX on Instagram? You have such an exuberance and joy for life! I can still picture your photo in your pineapple pants, jumping in the air.

I browsed around your website. Your comfort zone adventures are awesome. Such a valuable way to serve people, grow your following and keep you stretching. I'm curious about your coaching. How is that going? I also had a couple ideas for you about your website that may be supportive.

Wanna hear them?

Totally fine if you don't.

Know that I think what you're creating is awesome! Keep going!

Love,
Amber

SAMPLE INVITATION 7

Dear ZZZ:

It was so great seeing you at [CONFERENCE] in February. You, of course, were your bright, delightful self! I wish we could've gotten more time to catch up. Will you be at [DIFFERENT CONFERENCE]?

I know a while back we explored working together, and it wasn't the right time or investment. I'm reaching out today because I'm leading a women's group starting April 3rd that may be a beautiful fit for you.

The program is really designed to support women in transforming their relationship with their body. I don't know of a single woman who couldn't use a little more love in this area of her life! Besides, I've found over the years leading this program that there's a ripple effect—more peace, less criticism, more joy, less fear, tend to ripple out into every part of life.

Does this sound like something you'd like to know more about?

If so, we'll set aside some time (about an hour) to talk more deeply about how you feel about your body and how you'd like to feel about it. We'll slow down and explore putting yourself and your body first—and what's in the way of that. We'll look at how your life might be different if you loved your body and yourself even more.

And, if this doesn't resonate, I want you to know it's totally ok to say no thank you. I'll still love you the same no matter what.

You are one of those people who stands out to me. You are so smart, alive and heart-centered. You are the kind of woman I want

to support, so I look for ways to make that happen. This may or may not be one of them.

Let me know what you think.

Love,
Amber

SAMPLE INVITATION 8

Dear YYY,

I've been thinking about you so much this year, especially with all the changes at [JOB LOCATION]. How are you?

Last year you attended the Life workshop I led—and you contributed so beautifully to the day. I wanted to let you know about another complimentary workshop I'm leading on Sunday, February 26th from 11-3pm.

This workshop is devoted to your relationship with your body. We'll honestly look at your current relationship with your body— where you are, what you want, and what's keeping you stuck.

Benefits to this day include: Seeing and believing your own beauty. Walking away with more confidence and greater willingness to speak your voice. Attuning to your body's wisdom and so much more.

I suspect you probably have a solid relationship with your body...and there's always room to deepen, right? Plus, I just love you and want to see you.

Wanna come?

Let me know either way.

Love,
Amber

INVITATION EMAIL PROCESS GUIDE

You are the leader in this process. As a leader it's your job to make this process as simple and clear as possible, so in each email only ask the prospective client to do one thing. See below...

Email 1: Invitation. All you want to determine here is—Do they want to talk with you? Do they want to set up a conversation?

Email 2: If you haven't heard back in 48 hours after sending email 1 you'll want to send a ? email. The ? email is where you strip out the subject line of the email you had originally sent and replace it with a single question mark. In the body of the email, above the prior one you sent, write something like: "Dear XX, I didn't hear back from you on the below. Did you receive?"

In writing this, we want to be innocent. Do not make their silence or lack of response mean anything. We live in a modern world. People don't get their emails or they delete them while waiting in line at the grocery store. Holding in your neutrality is key in sending the ? email.

If you have heard from them and they want to continue, move to Email 3.

Email 3: Give dates and times that work for your schedule. All you want to do in this email is set the date and time and add, "I'll share call details once we set the date."

Email 4: Once the date is agreed upon, share the logistics for the session—phone number, etc.—AND start working with them now by sending pre-work. Get them engaged from the get-go. Ask if

they are willing to do the pre-work and return their answers by a certain time.

Email 5: If you haven't heard from them, you can send another ? email after 48 hours.

IN CLOSING

As with anything, inviting is something that we get better at with practice and attention. It's not a "one and done" kind of thing—it's a skill that we can develop, and it can be something we can do for the rest of our professional lives as coaches.

My beloved business partner Michelle Bauman often said to coaches, "The clients I created are some of my most favorite clients. These are people I saw out in the world and thought, 'I'd love to coach them, I might be able to help them.' It's one of the most fun things to do to create a client from scratch and bring them into your world."

I invite you to take this on as a practice and a skill that you can master over time. Enjoy the process of inviting—it's one of the best actions a coach can take to grow their business AND make a difference in the world!

Handout 7

Enrollment Questions

ENROLLMENT CONVERSATION SAMPLE QUESTIONS

NOW: Looking for pain / what's not working.

- What's happening now?
- What prompted you to reach out to me?
- What's an average day look like for you?
- What's your greatest source of stress?
- What's missing in your life?
- What do you complain about?
- What's not working to the degree you'd like?
- Where are you out of integrity? Where have you made a commitment that you're not really committed to?
- How's your family, relationship, friendships, work, health?
- What's that like for you?
- What are you ignoring?
- What are you tolerating?
- Is there anything else you want to share?

IDEAL: Looking for pleasure / possibility—what's the goal behind the goal?

- If you could create anything, what would that be?

- What do you want?
- What else?
- What would that bring you?
- What would your ideal day be like if you could live any way you wanted?
- What would you want if you knew it would be ok if you got it?
- What would you wish for if you had a genie in a magic lamp?
- What would you want if you knew you couldn't fail?
- What does your heart long for?
- How do you want to be remembered?
- How will you know when you've got what you want? What will you see, hear and feel?

OBSTACLE: What's in the way?

- If this is where you are, and this is where you want to be, what's in the way?
- How do you keep what you want out?
- Where do you hold back?
- What stops you?
- What are you afraid of?

COACHING: Give an experience of coaching / the work.

- How is that working for you?
- What/Who will you lose if you live your Ideal Life? What will it cost you?
- What's the upside of staying where you are?
- What do you feel is the real issue here?
- When you believe the thought _____ how do you respond/react?
- Who would you be without that thought?
- What are you waiting for?
- If you did know, what would you do?
- Is that really true?
- What does _____ mean about you?

COMMITMENT: What's their number?

- How committed are you to creating your Ideal Life?
- How important is this to you?
- If commitment were on a scale from 1-10, where 1 was *I'm not committed at all* and 10 was

  I'll do anything to create this life, what's your number?
- What would it take to go from a 7 to an 8?
- What's in the way of being a 9?

DEFAULT FUTURE

- What if you do nothing?
- Let's imagine you do nothing, what's life like a year from now? Five years from now?
- If you didn't change, what would your life be like?
- Is that ok with you?
- Is there no urgency?
- What are you really committed to?

PROPOSAL

- Is this something you'd like to do?
- Is this something that's worth drawing a line in the sand for?
- Would you like to know how partnering with me to create your Ideal Life would look?
- Would you like to talk about the support available to you through working with me?

Handout 8

Compassionate Self-Forgiveness

COMPASSIONATE SELF-FORGIVENESS

"Forgiveness is just another name for freedom."
~ Byron Katie

When we judge ourselves, we forget who we truly are. When we buy into the belief that "I am lazy" or "I am scared" or "I am weak" or whatever the judgment *du jour*, we cut ourselves off from our true nature. We equate who we are with whatever behavior or quality we dislike in the moment. We forget who we are in our fullness, in our essence, in our magnificence.

When we judge others, we are also forgetting who they are. We have our "shoulds" for how they "should" be, we have expectations running, we have some internal "rule" they are violating and they are "wrong" and we are "right." This is all code for "they are not doing X, Y, Z they way I WANT them to. . ." Generally when we are judging others, we are judging ourselves for the very same thing—yet it's too uncomfortable to see this "thing" or this "behavior" in ourselves, so we project it onto the people around us.

We may also have judgments against the world ("life's not fair") or "I'm being punished." Judging as a way of being, and specific judgments, can become so entrenched that we think they are "true facts" instead of seeing them for what they are: misunderstandings.

Self-forgiveness is a process whereby we start to actively identify these judgments and use a process to "delete" them—because they aren't real or "true." We bought into the idea that there is something wrong with us. The part of us that forgot that we are all learning and growing and that mistakes are part of that process—and that there's no such thing as perfection.

It's been said that Self-forgiveness is the cosmic "reset" button. It's a process that helps us clear our lens. It supports us of letting go of judgment, limitation and hurt—so we can see more clearly. As Byron Katie says, "You move totally away from reality when you believe that there is a legitimate reason to suffer." Self-forgiveness is the process of moving away from suffering and wrong-making into greater peace. When greater peace is present, we are more effective in all areas of life and we also experience greater joy and ease in all of our relationships—especially the one with ourself.

This process is NOT about justifying behavior that doesn't serve us or "letting ourselves off the hook." It's about putting down the whip of self-denigration and picking up the balm of Self-love and Self-acceptance so we can make choices from loving and strength, and not in an attempt to be "good enough."

Practicing Self-forgiveness is a lifelong opportunity. Through the process of identifying judgments and systematically forgiving ourselves for the judgments we are running, we can begin to lift the lens of judgment in our lives.

The process and technology of Self-forgiveness is taught as part of the Principles and Practices of Spiritual Psychology at the University of Santa Monica. *

Solo Process

1. Center yourself in your heart (think of what is a source of unconditional loving for you—maybe a pet, a place in nature, a child).
2. Move into acceptance of your feelings, your upset and yourself.
3. Take 100 percent responsibility for the disturbance inside of you.
4. List any judgments you are aware of that relate to others and yourself (e.g., "I am judging my boss as mean and controlling." "I am judging myself as mean and controlling.").
5. Practice Compassionate self-forgiveness for all of the judgments you are aware of. Putting your hand over your heart can assist in accessing the heart.

    I forgive myself for judging my boss **as** wrong.

    I forgive myself for judging myself **as** a bad person.

    I forgive myself for judging my friend **as** mean.

    I forgive myself for judging myself **as** a bad mother/wife/daughter.

I forgive myself for judging my father **as** an uncaring, insensitive father.

I forgive myself for judging XYZ as a loser.

I forgive myself for judging the world as unfair.

I forgive myself for judging God/the Universe/Spirit as not there for me.

I forgive myself for buying into the belief that I'm not enough just as I am.

Note: be willing to get at all the judgments—the most petty, irrational judgments you are holding against yourself and others. Consider the possibility that what you judge in others you also judge in yourself—and it's "easier" to see behaviors and ways of being in others that you judge as wrong than it is to see them and accept them in yourself.

Note also that the languaging is specific. That is, we don't forgive ourselves for judging ourselves "for being mean." We are judging ourselves *as being mean*. "Mean" is not who we truly are.

Another way to practice Self-forgiveness

I forgive myself for buying into the misinterpretation of reality that "XX should" know better.

I forgive myself for buying into the idea that there is a "right" way to live.

I forgive myself for buying into the misinterpretation of reality

>   that my way is the only way.
>   I forgive myself for buying into the misinterpretation of reality that I have to earn my way into worthiness.
>   I forgive myself for buying into the idea that I am not good enough or others are not good enough.

1. Use this process as an opportunity to apply your Loving acceptance and compassion to the places inside that hurt.
2. Ask the wisest part of yourself "what is the Truth?" (e.g., the truth is I am doing the best I know how to do and so is everyone else. The truth is I'm a loving person. The truth is I am courageous).

*For more information about Self-Forgiveness or Spiritual Psychology, check out www.universityofsantamonica.edu or read *Loyalty to your Soul* by Drs. Ron and Mary Hulnick.

Handout 9

Being a Great Professional Coach vs. Wanting to Be Liked

A Key to More Effective Enrollment

BEING A GREAT PROFESSIONAL COACH VS. WANTING TO BE LIKED: A KEY TO MORE EFFECTIVE ENROLLMENT

One of the critical blocks that gets in the way for many coaches is wanting to be liked.

NOTE: There's a difference between being *likeable* (which is important in this profession, as it is in any profession) and WANTING or yearning to be liked, such that your conscious or unconscious desire to be liked prevents or weakens who you are as a professional coach.

You may be thinking, "Well that's not me – I don't want to be liked that much. I'm a strong coach, I know how to do this."

As someone in the profession for over twenty years I sometimes still face the impulse of wanting to be liked and wanting to please (this seems to be true especially for female coaches, who are often raised to be "nice"). It's the social self part of me that we all have (and in different cultures, for example in Italy the social self is HUGE . . . and it's really fun – who doesn't want more vino?).

So how does wanting to be liked/people-pleasing show up in enrollment and get in our way of being a truly GREAT, highly effective coach?

IN ENROLLMENT CONVERSATIONS:

I can't tell you how many debriefs I have had with coaches after they have had what they considered a transformative

enrollment conversation with a prospective client where the person left saying, "I'll think about it."

When we dig deeper into this conversation and slow it down, this is almost always what shows up:

Coach: the prospective client is sharing about the ways in which their spouse is not who they want them to be. They are listing the challenges— "doesn't pay attention to me enough, doesn't want to do things like I want to do them, doesn't do the dishes, doesn't take care of xyz, they don't speak up at work, they aren't working out...."

Me: What did you say then?

Coach: I had them do a big list of everything they didn't like, and then we talked about how they could have a conversation with their spouse.

Me: What were you thinking when they were listing off their complaints—what was going through your mind?

Coach: Just that that they were complaining, that they were behaving like a victim, like their spouse should be exactly as they wanted.

Me: Did you say that at any point?

Coach: No, not really.

Me: What was going on inside of you? (NOTE - THIS IS IMPORTANT HERE) Because those thoughts are EXACTLY your own inner guidance as to what would serve the client . . . you were thinking what this person would benefit from hearing.

Coach: I didn't feel comfortable. I thought it might be too much for the person . . . that they might not like it.

Me: Were you concerned they might not like what you said which is entirely possible . . . or they might not like you?

Coach: Both – and them not being able to handle it.

THIS IS IT!

Many professional coaches have remarkable inner guidance—and they don't listen to it. Especially in the initial enrollment conversation when it's critical, when the relationship is being established and the person can be shown that we are there to serve then—not be liked by them.

IN THE ENROLLMENT CONVERSATION

This is where some of the most powerful and important coaching occurs.

It's where someone has a real experience of being offered a truth—one that no one else may ever have offered to them before.

When I was beginning my coaching practice with Steve Chandler as my coach, when we ran "game film" of my enrollment conversations, he'd often be asking me, "What did you want to say there?"

And I'd respond, "I wanted to say, "Is that an effective strategy, you emailing your boss and talking around the issue?"

He'd say, "Who else is going to say that to this person?"

NOT WITH A SLEDGEHAMMER: THE FINESSE OF PERMISSION and TOLERATING YOUR OWN DISCOMFORT

You may be reading this thinking, "No one will enroll with me if I share what I'm seeing." I offer to you that you are incorrect.

If done properly, with loving finesse and clarity, saying what we see can be the greatest gift we offer someone as a professional coach. It can and often is where they say, "I need to work with this person."

KEY PHRASES

May I offer you something for your consideration?

Do I have permission to share something with you?

May I reflect something I'm seeing to you something that might be uncomfortable to hear?

These phrases are FANTASTIC for setting up an important observation/reflection in a way that both forecasts "this might be important for you" while also allowing a moment of slowing down and creating space before you share something that might be difficult or challenging for someone to hear.

You can never ask for too much permission. I ask for permission all the time with my current clients – because it allows them a moment of reminding themselves that YES, they do want to hear what I am about to say—and they also have the option of saying NO.

Is it uncomfortable? Yes, sometimes.

In the first five years of building my coaching practice this was an edge for me. I could feel the tendency in enrollment conversations to want to be nice, to not want to say things that could make the prospective client uncomfortable.

Part of the process of becoming a coach who says what they see is tolerating our own discomfort and not bowing to the God of being Comfortable (similar to bowing to the God of Wanting to be Liked, only slightly different).

I also saw as I went over conversations with my coach, and really got underneath what was stopping me from saying those things (my own people-pleasing and wanting to be liked) that I wasn't serving in the strongest way possible. That in fact, I was not serving as fully as I could when I left those things unsaid.

The more I was willing to listen to the thoughts I was NOT saying out loud and lean into saying these things (with finesse and permission) it almost always resulted in a transformative moment in the conversation for the prospective client.

It also resulted in a person becoming a client much more often.

PEOPLE WANT TO WORK WITH A COACH WHO'S WILLING TO SAY WHAT THEY SEE

As Steve Chandler says, "Nobody wants an obsequious, shuffling coach."

In addition to this I offer to you, "Nobody wants a people pleasing, golden retriever of a coach who's looking for a best friend."

This profession is one of the few professions where we get paid

to assist someone in seeing their blind spots, professionally and personally.

It's one of the greatest ways we can assist someone in their growth if they aren't already seeing it themselves.

Please don't misunderstand—I want my clients to discover things for themselves, to find their own truths without me "telling" them. When I offer reflections, they are for their consideration and they can disagree.

AND—there are things that I was only willing to see after my coach, in the sanctity of our coaching sessions, reflected them to me. It was too uncomfortable to bring them out in the light of day on my own.

STEPS TO BECOMING A GREAT PROFESSIONAL COACH (VS A COACH WHO'S LEAKING A DESIRE TO BE LIKED)

1. Review your last five enrollment conversations (ideally with your coach). Slow down and look at where you had thoughts that you did not share out loud about the person that might have been of value.

2. Ask yourself why you didn't say something to them. What was in the way? Your own discomfort? Not wanting to "upset" or make the person uncomfortable? A concern that the person "might not like it"? Don't gloss over this—our thoughts matter as professional coaches. What was left unsaid in an enrollment conversation is as important as what was said.

3. Be willing to look at your own hidden people pleasing/wanting to be liked. Look back in your life and look at the decisions you might have made as a child, teenager, or young adult about sacrificing your truth in the name of being liked. Consider how this is influencing you now as a coach.

4. Consider that these decisions are not serving you in this profession. Decide if you are going to begin to practice 5% more of your own truth telling in enrollment conversations and coaching sessions with clients.

5. Take on mastering the art of saying the truth as you see it with loving finesse and permission. Like anything, this is a practice – and it may feel messy or awkward at first!

6. Acknowledge yourself for becoming a better coach by letting go of old behaviors that don't serve you or anyone you meet with.

Sample Coaching Agreement

Sample Coaching Agreement

Coach's Name
Business Name
Contact information

Coaching Agreement for [client's name]

Six month coaching agreement, from: MM/DD/YYYY to MM/DD/YYYY

Coaching fee: XXX

Twelve 90-minute coaching sessions to be scheduled bi-weekly.

Unlimited access to email and spot coaching by phone on an as-needed basis.

Like all things worthwhile, coaching requires a commitment from both the coach and the client. I make a significant commitment to my clients and I ask the same in return. The following agreements will create a strong foundation for our work together.

Agreements:

1. We both agree to be on time for our sessions to honor each other's time.
2. Time is a precious commodity for both of us—when we schedule sessions, we are making an unwavering commitment.

Coaching sessions are high priority, protected real estate on calendars.

3. If a highly unusual circumstance arises and you are unable to make a scheduled session, you agree to give a minimum of 48 hours notice in advance (unless there is a bona fide emergency). Failure to give adequate notice may result in forfeiting your session. The only last-minute cancelations allowed without forfeit are due to a bona fide emergency.
4. Coaching fees are non-refundable. If for some reason I am unable to continue with the work, you can contact my husband XX (xxx-xxx-xxxx) and he will refund fees for unused sessions. If you choose not to continue, any unused fees will be forfeited.
5. You agree to make your coaching time sacred—to make calls from a quiet, private place where you can be present to receive maximum value (e.g., no calls from a cell phone while driving).
6. You agree to come to your coaching sessions with an agenda you'd like to work on, usually 3-4 items—you will send your agenda via email in advance of the session. If there is information you want to convey (e.g., an update), you will convey that via email prior to the session.
7. You agree to take responsibility for getting what you want from the coaching process. If anything we do together doesn't work for you or "feel right," you will bring it to my attention so we can explore other options.
8. You understand that we will communicate in a direct, honest way—giving clear feedback from a constructive and supportive place.

9. You agree to communicate with the same level of transparency and authenticity with me and to ask for support when you need it.
10. We don't ghost each other. If you email me with a coaching request and I respond, you'll let me know you received it, even if you don't have a full response yet. You can count on me to respond to your emails, and if I'm not able to respond instantly you'll know I received it within the same business day.
11. You understand that everything you share will be held in the strictest confidentiality.
12. You agree to be open to receiving feedback and experimenting with new actions, behaviors and strategies to create the results you want.
13. I will respond to email within 48 hours (often sooner) during the business week (Monday through Friday). If you have a more urgent need for feedback from me, indicate "urgent" in the re: line or call me at the number above and leave a message.
14. We will keep all commitments and agreements we make to each other—including "homework." You agree to only make agreements you are committed to keeping.

Recommended Resources

This is by no means a complete list of all the wonderful material out there that can support your personal and professional growth, as well as that of your clients. But these are some of my favorite go-tos.

Books

Arbinger Institute. (2018). *Leadership and self-deception.* Berrett-Koehler Publishers.

Bandison, D. (2017). *Fatherhood is leadership: Your playbook for success, self-leadership, and a richer life.* Maurice Bassett.

Bauman, M. & Freyer-Jones, C. *What if this is the fun part? A book about friendship, coaching, dying, living and using everything for your learning, growth and upliftment.* CFJ Coaching.

Brooks, A. *From strength to strength: Finding success, happiness and deep purpose in the second half of life.* (2022). Portfolio.

Brown, B. (2020). *The gifts of imperfection.* Random House.

- ANY book by Brené Brown

Burg, B. & Mann J.D. (2008). *Go-Giver, The: A Suprising Way of Getting More Than You Expect.* Portfolio.

Chandler, S. (2022). *The Very Best of Steve Chandler*. Maurice Bassett.

- ANY book or audio by Steve Chandler!

Devine, M. (2018). *It's OK that you're NOT OK: Meeting grief and loss in a culture that doesn't understand*. Sounds True.

Ficket, J. & Ficket, L. (2006). *The Collaborative Way: A Story About Engaging the Mind and Spirit of a Company*. Independently published.

Gawande, A. (2017). *Being mortal: Medicine and what matters in the end*. Metropolitan Reprint Edition.

Holden, B. (2011). *Authentic success: Essential lessons and practices from the world's leading coaching program on Success Intelligence*. Hay House Inc.

Hulnick, H. R., & Hulnick, M. R. (2013). *Loyalty to your soul: The heart of spiritual psychology*. Hay House, Inc.

Hulnick, M. R. & Hulnick, H. R. (2017). *Remembering the light within*. Hay House, Inc.

Kline, N. (2015). *More time to think: The power of independent thinking*. Cassell.

Kline, N. (2020). *The promise that changes everything: I won't interrupt you*. Penguin Life.

Leonard, G. (1992). *Mastery*. Plume.

Pressfield, S. (2012). *Turning Pro*. Black Irish Entertainment.

Recommended Resources

Scott, K. (2019). *Radical candor: Be a kick-ass boss without losing your humanity.* St. Martin's Press.

Stanny, B. (2007). *Overcoming underearning: A five-step plan for a richer life.* Collins.

Video & Film

Brown, B. *The Call to Courage.* Netflix. 2019. 76 minutes. (or any other Netflix special by Brené Brown)

Gawande, Atul. (2018). *Want to get great at something? Get a Coach.* YouTube. Retrieved December 6, 2023, from https://www.youtube.com/watch?v=oHDq1PcYkT4

Hill, J. *Stutz.* Netflix. 2022. 96 minutes.

Hooper, T (Director). (2010). *The King's Speech.* Momentum Pictures. 119 minutes.

Sudeikis, J., Lawrence, B., Hunt, B., Kelly, J. creators. *Ted Lasso.* Three Seasons. 2020-2023. Apple TV+.

Websites

The Alchemy Group: thealchemyleaders.com

Devon Bandison / The Gamechanger Experience: devonbandison.com

Megan Devine / Grief Support: refugeingrief.com

Nancy Kline: timetothink.com

Steve Chandler / Coaching Prosperity School: stevechandler.com

University of Santa Monica programs in Spiritual Psychology: universityofsantamonica.com

Acknowledgments

There are a number of people to acknowledge in the writing of this book. First and foremost, I acknowledge the creator of us all (God, Spirit, the Universe, whatever works for you) without whom I wouldn't be here in this lifetime, with these spectacular people.

- My beloved husband John who is the most steadfast person, always rooting me on, making everything better and more fun, and reminding me that all is okay even when it doesn't seem so. Thank you for being there, always, a stand for loving and a stand for goodness. I love you.
- Our amazing daughter Lucinda whose enthusiasm for the things I do is always there. You look at my Instagram stories, you get excited about my book(s), the school, you name it. I love you for who you are and who you are becoming.
- Steve Chandler, without whom I wouldn't be doing the things I'm doing in this profession. Thank you for your way of always saying, "You can do that." When we first met I wasn't even fully aware of the possibility of leaving my full-time job, let alone creating a school for coaches, becoming a real writer and more. Your impact as my coach for over eighteen years of my life is immeasurable. I laugh more because of you, I serve more because of you, and I remember that humility is the way, and that we all can do this and serve in this amazing profession

because of you. Thank you.

- Michelle Bauman, whose friendship catapulted me out of the life I was in, into the life that I had not ever thought imaginable. Your humor, warmth, and clarity about turning pro as coaches made the path real. We did it together, and I still do this with you by my side, in my heart, always there, letting me know how amazing it all is. I love you.
- Drs. Ron and Mary Hulnick, for showing me that all of life can be used for learning, growth and upliftment, and that service is the way, loving is the way, and we can always ask for spiritual assistance. The Principles and Practices of Spiritual Psychology are forever the foundation I use to walk through life. Thank you.
- Nancy Kline, for being the best listener ever, for being willing to share only when I ask, for creating the Thinking Environment and being a leader, a person who shows the way into a greater presence that's available to all of us. Thank you for being a way-shower, a fellow woman who wouldn't take no or anyone else's answer as her answer.
- Chris Nelson, my editor, a great coach, and now my friend, thank you for being willing to read all my words and continue to tell me what works and where I can add more to make it more helpful.
- Nancy O'Leary, thank you for coming back into my world and proofreading the book. I appreciate you and your excellence!
- Amy Hruby, the person who launched the school with me, the first director of the CFJ Coaching Success School, my dearest friend, the person who always wants my books to be on the bestseller list, who champions me and who will go to Target or funerals, whatever is required. Thank YOU, and I love you.

Acknowledgments

- Amber Krzys, you joined me in the launch of the school from day one! You took on enrolling for the school like the champion you are, and you facilitated every class session alongside me as outstanding primary faculty for four years straight. I love you and I thank you.
- To all the faculty past and present at the CFJ Coaching Success School: Amber Krzys, Tarita Preston, Sandy Sullivan, Amber Shirley, Stephen McGhee and Devon Bandison. Thank YOU for your leadership, your excellence, for being willing to use your precious time and share your gifts to serve at the school and be way-showers for coaches and this profession. I am grateful for the work you do and who you are.
- Jonny Roman, the exceptional Director and lead admissions person for the CFJ Coaching Success School, an outstanding coach and guest speaker who leaves the coaches speechless and moved. I am grateful for your partnership, your leadership, and your excellence in all things. Plus, you have a really good laugh.
- To my parents, Hugh and Trudy Freyer, who despite it all, saw me as someone who could do good things and were always proud of me. Thank you for believing in me.

About the Author

Carolyn Freyer-Jones, M.A., has been a leadership and life coach for over eighteen years, assisting corporate executives, business owners, lawyers, salespeople, and more in their growth as leaders and as people, and in creating more fulfilling and successful lives.

She also is the founder and leader of the CFJ Coaching Success School, the only live school for professional coaches dedicated solely to teaching coaches the skills and tools for growing a financially successful coaching business. The school is highly experiential as well as practical—coaches create clients in real time, learning what it truly means to serve and create real financial success through slowed down, meaningful conversations.

Carolyn is also the co-author, with her business partner Michelle Bauman, of *What if This is the Fun Part: A book about Friendship, Coaching, Dying, Living and using Everything for your Learning, Growth and Upliftment.*

She earned a Master's Degree in Spiritual Psychology in 1998 from the University of Santa Monica and considers the Principles and Practices of Spiritual Psychology to be the foundation and springboard for her coaching as well as her personal life. Originally from the Bronx, N.Y., Carolyn lives in Los Angeles with her wonderful, loving husband John and her spectacular daughter Lucinda. She loves to travel, learn, be with people she loves, have fun and drink good coffee—as well as look at Instagram reels way too often.

Also available:
by Carolyn Freyer-Jones & Michelle Bauman

"Once upon a time there were two friends who loved each other very much..."

When Michelle Bauman and Carolyn Freyer-Jones became friends, everything changed: their personal, professional, and *inner* lives. First and foremost *What if This Is the Fun Part?* is the story of that profound, loving friendship, a story told with wit, honesty, insight and grace. It's also a story about professional coaching and personal transformation. About learning and living spiritual principles that deepen and enrich life. And ultimately it's a story about living, loving and dying fully, about embracing *everything*—the good, the bad, the joyful and the devastating—and using it for learning, growth and upliftment.

Best of all, it can be your story too. *What if This Is the Fun Part?* invites you into the realization that your life is yours to create, and you need never stop growing, living, and loving.

"The pages of this book are filled with courageous authenticity and great Heart—true stories that inspire and uplift. They are tender, raw at times, and inspirational. I wholeheartedly recommend this book to anyone called to live a more purpose-driven life filled with Love and meaning. It is both poignant and filled with Spiritual Wisdom that is has been tested in the fiery crucible of lives lived all-in. True gold."

Dr. Mary R. Hulnick, Founding Faculty and Co-Director of the University of Santa Monica

TO BE A PROFESSIONAL COACH IS TO BE OF SERVICE IN THE WORLD.

The CFJ Coaching Success School is the only live school for professional coaches that teaches the skills and tools for growing a financially successful coaching business. The school is known for transformational and practical coaching in what it takes to be a service-centered business owner. Coaches learn to create real success through slowed down, meaningful conversation. This is a school that is committed to seeing professional coaches grow in their ability to be effective enrollers and truly thrive financially as business owners—and as a result, have an even more profound, positive, and meaningful impact in the world.

The moment you arrive at the school we are asking you:

How much money do you want to make while you are in the school?

You will be picking an amount that's at least 50% believable given where you are starting from . . .for some of you that amount might seem "low" and for others the number might be much higher if you have been in this business for a while.

You will be taking action from the moment we begin. You will receive coaching as you go. We won't be letting you sit on the sidelines watching. You will be encouraged to get into action, even if it's uncomfortable or new. This is not a school where we talk about growing your business—this is a school where we DO, where we learn through action, through being on the court.

YOUR COACHING BACKGROUND DOESN'T MATTER . . .

Maybe you are a self-taught coach or you completed a certification program. Maybe your background is Landmark, 3P, Hypnotherapy, Spiritual Psychology, Byron Katie, Integrative Health Nutrition, or another coaching modality—all are welcome. The requirement is that you are called to learn enrollment and that you are willing to become competent at creating consistent income and no longer live in lack and frustration, making this profession or yourself WRONG.

The CFJ Coaching Success School consists of:

- Live Classes
- Report Tracking
- Facebook Group
- Group Calls
- Peer Support
- Private Coaching
- Bonus Sessions

WHAT WILL HAPPEN IN LIVE CLASS SESSIONS

Class time will be dynamic, fun, and engaging. Participants will work solo, in small groups, and in the large group. Learning will take place through coaching demonstrations, presentations, small group processes, large group exercises and intimate reflection.

THIS SCHOOL IS FOR YOU IF:

- You love coaching and are already serving people.
- You are called to grow your business and experience greater financial ease and prosperity.
- You haven't quite cracked the code on creating a strong income in coaching - it's up and down and you ride waves of panic or relief depending on your income flow.
- You have hit a plateau in your earnings and have not been able to move past it.
- You are willing to experiment with new approaches and ways of being in service to your growth and the growth of your business.
- You are willing to be challenged, encouraged, and coached into playing a bigger game.
- You are willing to drop limiting beliefs and stories about your

ability to create an even stronger practice and/or ideas/thoughts around "what it takes to be a successful coach."

- You are open to new ways of seeing your business and knowing that the thought, "Where are clients? How do I get clients?" is temporary and that there's a process and system you can learn and use for the rest of your life.

- You have created a solid practice, yet you see opportunities to be more effective and would like to be coached and strengthened in going to your next level in your business.

- You are called to be part of a dynamic community of like-minded and like-hearted professional coaches who are committed to having successful businesses.

To learn more:

www.carolynfreyerjones.com/cfj-information-enrollment

Made in the USA
Las Vegas, NV
25 May 2024

90320933R10243